OFFICE SPACES
1000 INSPIRATIONAL IDEAS

LINKS

Edition 2013

Author: Carles Broto
Graphic design & production: Cuboctaedro
Collaborator: Oriol Vallès
Text: Contributed by the architects, edited by Naomi Ferguson

Jonqueres, 10, 1-5
08003 Barcelona, Spain
Tel.: +34-93-301-21-99
info@linksbooks.net
www.linksbooks.net

OFFICE SPACES
1000 INSPIRATIONAL IDEAS

LINKS

Introduction

The work environment, as a space for professional and interpersonal exchange, has undergone dramatic changes in recent years. The continuing swift pace of developments in communication technology, bringing with it new ways of handling information, has greatly contributed to these changes. Gone are the bulky filing cabinets and desks of yesteryear; the work surface has been reduced to the size of a computer, while home working and videoconferencing facilitate collaborations with colleagues outside of the office who may be down the street or on the other side of the world.

At the same time, the environmental sustainability of projects is ever more closely monitored, making the investigation of energy-saving measures, renewable energy and low-carbon materials an integral part of the design process.

The aesthetic demands of an office project include representing the company's corporate identity, which must be translated into the spatial qualities, color and ambiance of the interior and define the image of the whole building. The modern office also requires versatility and dynamism – it must be flexible enough to quickly adapt to changing working styles, as well as being an attractive, comfortable and motivating space, and should encourage interpersonal communication among employees, while diffusing outdated hierarchical barriers.

These complex design issues, together with others such as accessibility, acoustics, lighting and construction, are explored in a 20-page in-depth guidelines chapter that opens this volume.

The rest of the book presents a selection of inspirational built examples organized in ten thematic chapters. The highly practical structure of the book makes the wealth of ideas it contains instantly accessible to the reader, whether they are looking for ideas for façades, plan layouts, collective working spaces, building services, or materials.

DESIGN OF THE BUILDING

Organizational diagram of a large manufacturing company

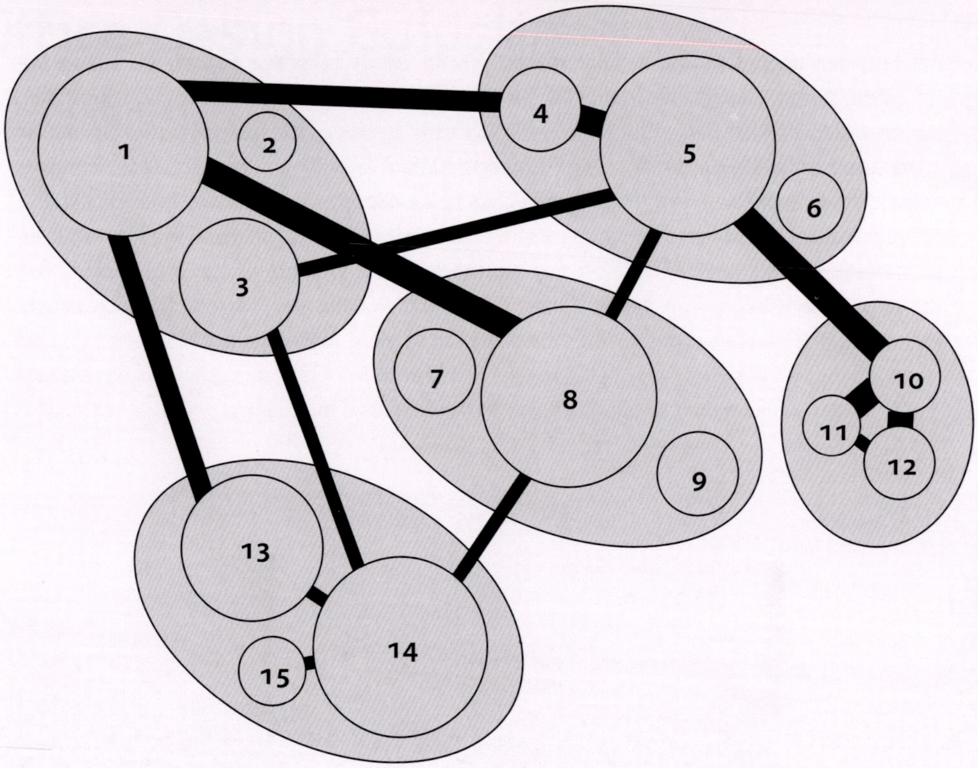

1. Financial planning
2. Internal control
3. Financial department
4. Engineers
5. Product control
6. Acquisitions
7. Infrastructure planning
8. Production information
9. Manufacturing engineers
10. Billing control
11. Job scheduling dept.
12. Personnel
13. Mechanical and electrical services
14. Manufacturing
15. Factory

Layouts for office buildings

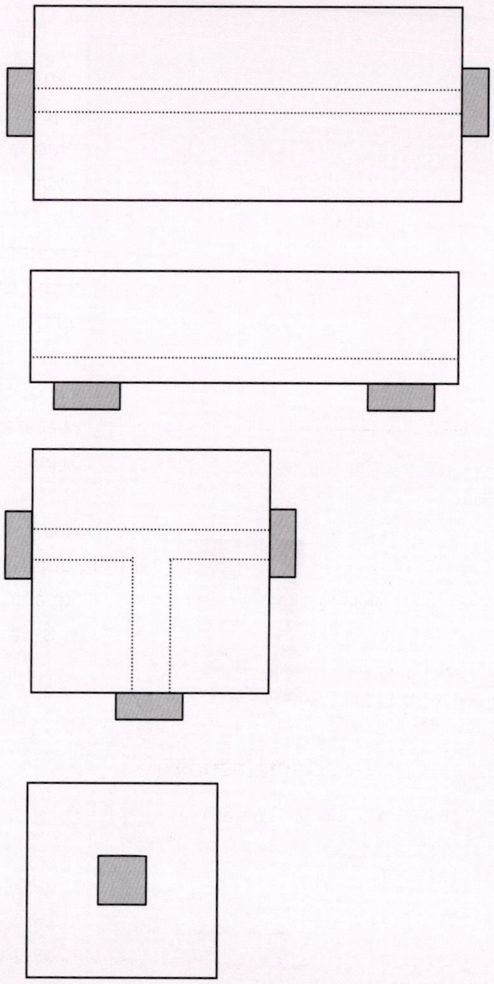

The optimal dimensions for an office building are dictated by the location and the incidence of natural light. Generally, a good width is accepted to be 5 to 7.5 meters and a height 2 to 2.5 times the width. The depth of the space should ideally be less than 15 meters to guarantee effective passive ventilation, while depths less than 13 meters are incompatible with open-plan or mixed office layouts. Internal atria are often incorporated with the objective of ensuring the incidence of natural light to the center of the building but are incompatible with certain office layouts.

Both the depth of the building and the modulation of the façades should be adapted to the office model, from the traditional modular office to mixed models of the "business club" model for flexible working systems.

While steel structure are well suited to office buildings with rectangular floor planes or of very large area, concrete structures are efficacious in square plan buildings and with relatively small areas. The rational integration of all building elements is essential, from exterior walls to structural elements, ceilings, floors, partition walls etc. The positioning of windows and vertical load-bearing elements are the most critical factors since they determine the size and position of the partitions. It is preferable that the column spacing is as wide as possible.

It is also preferable that the elevators, stairs and washrooms are concentrated in a single point, in the center of the building, although a large central area and one or two smaller areas in the perimeter of the floor is a viable alternative. The position of these elements strongly conditions the use of the building and its subdivision in different spaces. Placing the stairs, elevators and washrooms in the center of the plan enables a single floor to be divided between different companies although it also limits the conversion of the floor into a single open-plan space.

OFFICE SPACES
1000 INSPIRATIONAL IDEAS

LINKS

Spatial typologies and working modes

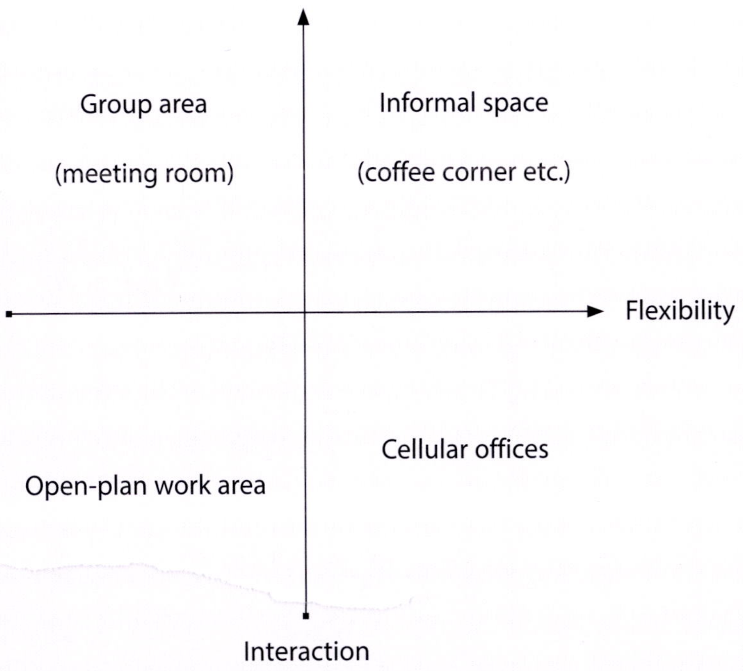

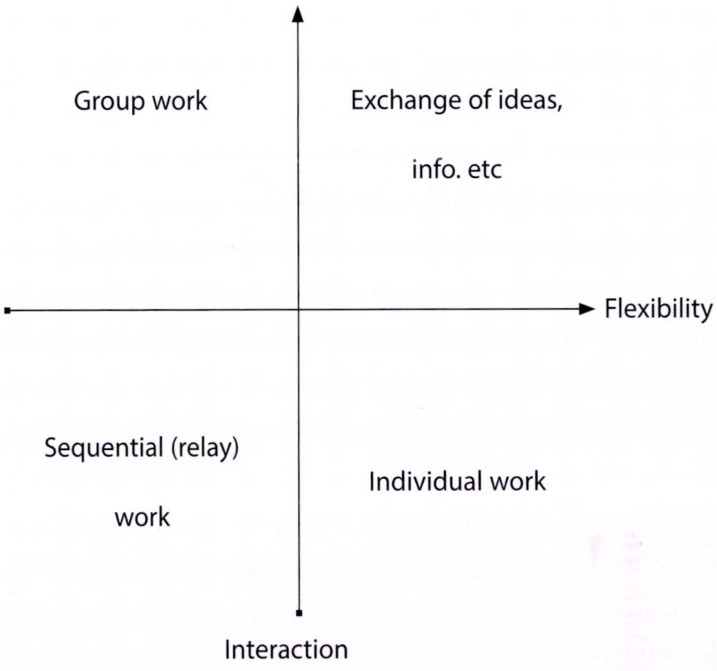

A principle consideration in designing office spaces is the intention to create a building with a long life in a rapidly changing context. As such, the first and most important point is that they need to be **flexible spaces** that can be easily adapted to the demographic, functional, hierarchical and technological changes in companies.

The second fundamental aspect is **communication**, above all informal communication. Although there are no clearly defined spaces for this type of communication, since by the nature of the spontaneity of the interaction they are not designable, they can be consciously cultivated through a successful spatial distribution. The way of connecting individual workspaces and distributing circulation flows influences communication processes and the exchange of information. It should also be taken into account that new ICT infrastructure and knowledge management allow information and data to flow between people without the need for physical proximity.

The most common classification is still that of the **cellular office layout** (where individual workspaces are physically segregated); **open-plan** (with the minimum vertical barriers and organized in work groups); **combined** (a mixed solution containing both open and closed spaces) and the so-called **landscape office**, a sort of business club, without walls, with a free and creative spatial distribution, that combines areas for work, interchange, meetings and relaxation.

LAYOUT OF THE SPACES

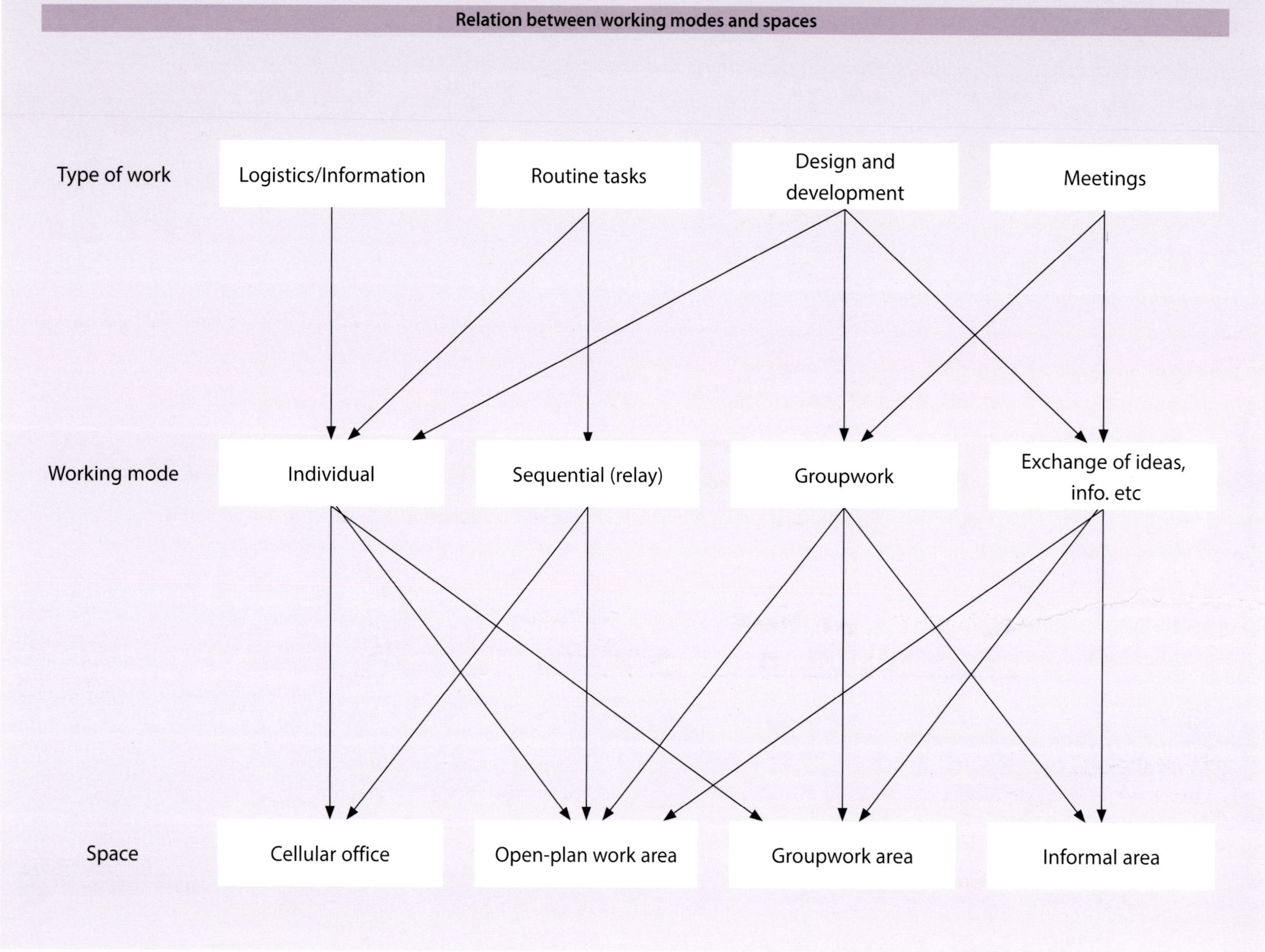

However the spaces are distributed, the ideal proportion of each function, in relation with the net surface area of the office to be the following:

- 50 % for individual workstations arranged in work groups or not.
- 20 % for support spaces for individual work, such as archives, photocopying and printing areas, areas for group work, storage spaces etc.
- 20 % for collective areas for working and relaxing such as meeting or conference rooms, kitchens and washrooms.
- Up to 10 % of the space will not enter into the calculation of usable space, according to the configuration of the building or as consequence of the distribution of the work groups.

An acceptable ratio is around 80 % of the total floor area occupied by work spaces (excluding stairs, elevators and washrooms). Within this 80 % no more than 15 % should be occupied by primary circulation spaces (the routes that connect the principal entrances with the different departments).

Optimal workstation design

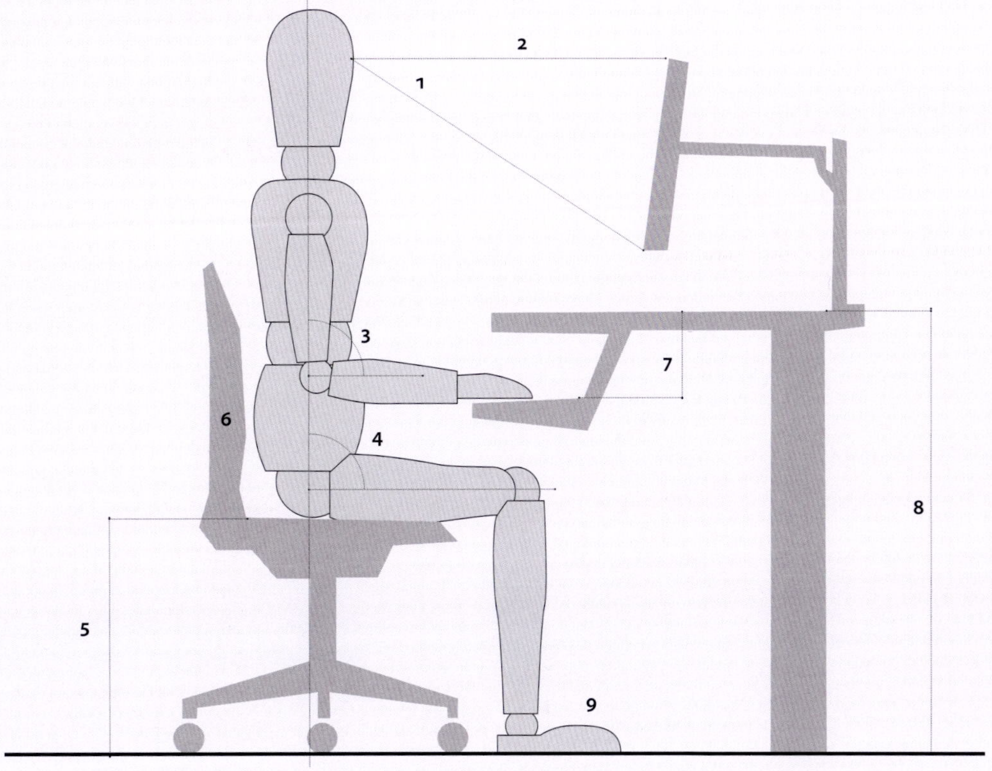

1. Angle of vision for screen: 20°
2. Upper edge of screen at eye level or lower. Distance from eye at arm's length (approx. 42-50 cm (17"-20"))
3. Forearm horizontal or lower (90°-110°)
4. Thighs horizontal or lower (90°-110°)
5. Adjustable seat height (average 42-50 cm (17"-20"))
6. Chair back adjustable in height and tilt, provides firm lower back support
7. Keyboard at 5-10 cm (2" - 4") lower than table surface.
8. Table surface at 65-75 cm (26" - 30") height
9. Feet must rest horizontally on floor or foot rest with ample space under table

THE WORKSTATION

The **individual workstation**, essentially comprised of a table, a chair and the necessary circulation space, is the **basic module** of office design and serves as much for conventional office plans as for more interactive working spaces. The delimitation of the workstation is key to communication at the heart of the company, since it is determinant in the creation of work "neighborhoods" and a team ethos.

The area occupied by one person is calculated at 9 sqm (100 sqft), of which a significant proportion is occupied by the work table and the rest by secondary space, including circulation. The surface area per employee invariably includes a part of the common spaces, such as meeting rooms, and lounges.

The area of the workstation itself ranges from 2.5 sqm to 6 sqm (27 - 65 sqft) per person. The average occupation of offices of 60 sqm (650 sqft) and above is 6 sqm (65 sqft) per person or 7 sqm (75 sqft) in the case of cellular office layouts.

Furniture for an office reception area

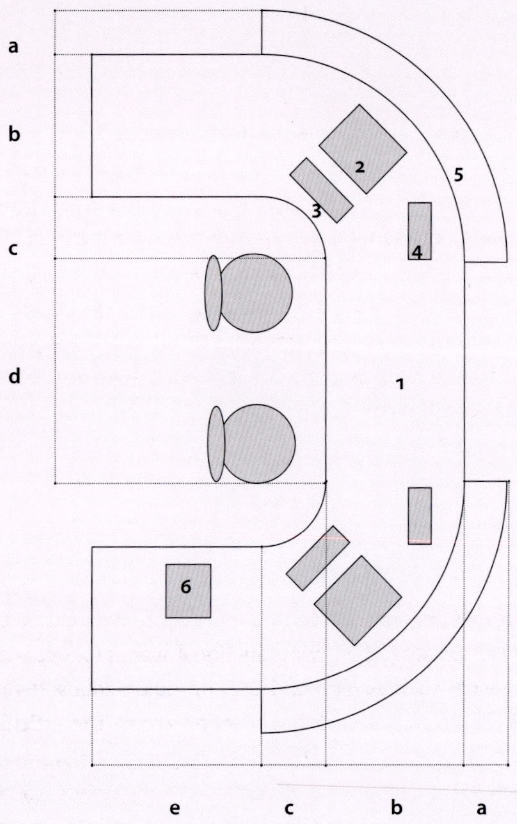

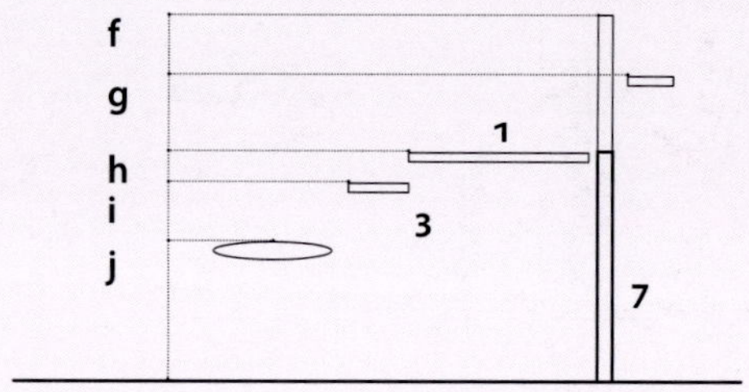

1. Desk
2. Computer screen
3. Keyboard
4. Printer
5. Reception counter
6. Security screen
7. Non-transparent backboard to desk (hides receptionists' feet and computer cables)

a. Counter for visitors: 200 - 250 mm (8" - 10")
b. Table: 600 - 750 mm (2' - 2 1/2')
c. Radius 300 - 400 mm (1' - 1' 4")
d. Desk width: 900 - 1100 mm (3' - 3' 7")
e. Length of side of desk: 700 - 900 mm (2' 4" - 3')
f. Screen height off floor: 1000 - 1200 mm (3' 3" - 4')
g. Counter height: 1000 - 1050 mm (3' 3" - 3' 5")
h. Desk height: 700 - 750 mm (2' 4" - 2 1/2')
i. Keyboard height: 580 - 700 cm (1' 11" - 2' 4")
j. Seat height: 350 - 500 mm (1' 2" - 1' 8")

RECEPTION AND ENTRANCE SPACES

The reception area has become the heart of many companies, the space where the corporate image and brand identity are most intensely expressed. These areas can also accelerate or slow down the flow of employees and forment informal exchanges. They are spaces where square footage is not economized, but rather they are designed as places in which employees can pause and establish contact between one another. A recent tendency is for the concentration of functions in the reception area that go beyond their traditional remit of welcoming and directing visitors. It is an ideal place for establishing relationships, giving rise to the location of small meeting rooms off the reception space for use not only by visitors but also by internal staff.

The entrances can be located in the center of the building, off-center or in a line. Office buildings with off-center entrances often have linear floor plans (well suited to individual, autonomous working) or in a comb formation (ideal for organizations with large groups or departments). Extensions between the wings in the latter case can generate communication spaces between departments.

Centralized entrances are typical of buildings with a circular distribution or a star-shaped distribution that radiates from a central communal circulation space.

Office spaces

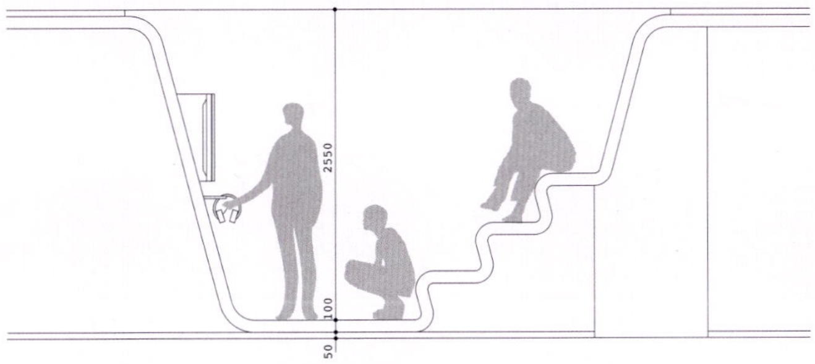

Conversation space

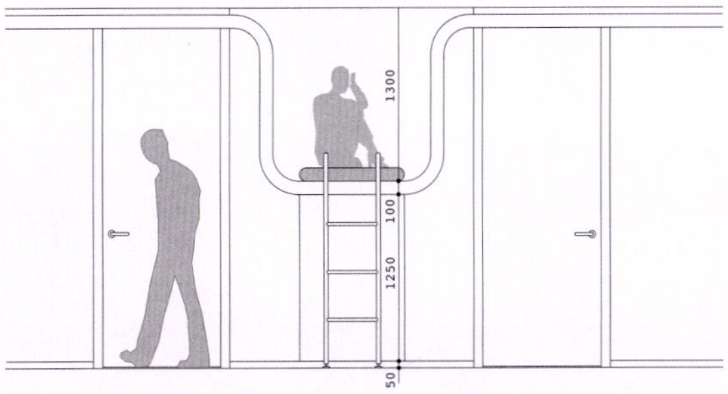

Rest area

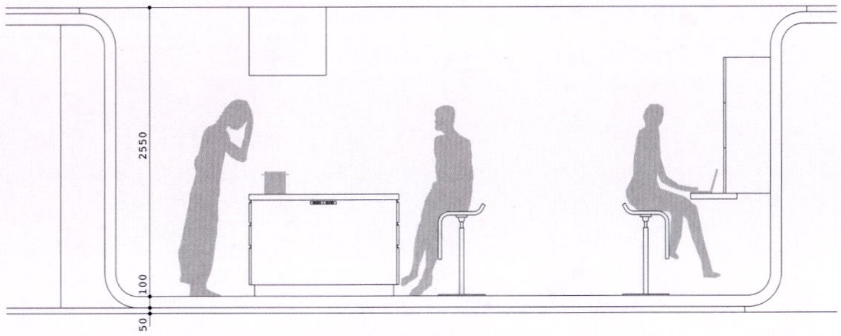

Kitchen area

REST AND RELAXATION AREAS

The new work culture gives great importance to areas for rest and relaxation within the workplace. They may contain vending machines, small kitchens and coffee-making facilities in an attractive environment, the visibility of which will attract users. It is positive for the furniture and the décor to mark the difference of this space form the rest of the building, to create an atmosphere that Is completely different form that of the work areas. Special attention should be given to the selection of the furniture and the design of the lighting and acoustics for these spaces, and they should be well ventilated.

In some office buildings, the cafeteria has acquired an essential role as an area for relaxation and is designed not only as a food zone, but also as a space for informal meetings and even individual work.

Another essential space is the staff kitchen or a place where staff can heat food brought from home and do some simple food preparation. This space should be well ventilated and have hardwearing surfaces, appropriate furniture and a series of equipment that will make It a useful area.

MEETING ROOMS

It is becoming more common for different companies that share the same building to use the same meeting rooms. This strategy has a double advantage: it saves space and reduces costs. Open meeting spaces that occupy less room and combine an area for group work with a lounge space are also becoming common. Small closed meeting rooms, from four people, are generally the most useful for meetings that do not involve audiovisual presentations, while **meeting "islands"** (furnished with sofas, coffee tables and stools) and used by all staff for informal and formal communication are a modern alternative to the traditional meeting room with a central table.

COLLECTIVE WORK SPACES

Complementary modules or additional computer stations complement the basic work stations. They are specialized or monofunctional spaces for occasional use, and may provide services such as high-end CAD or multimedia software or be places with special characteristics such as reflection zones. The articulation of meeting spaces and communal areas facilitates exchange between different work groups, so such spaces should be placed in strategic points, for example, alongside principal circulation spaces where they are accessible to everyone. They should be semi-public in character while offering the possibility for more private discussion.

RESTROOMS

This is a key space in an office building, since its location is usually predetermined. The restrooms form part of a group of facilities that, like the stairs and elevators, have an important influence on the distribution of the office, since all users of the building must have easy access and be practically equidistant from these spaces.

The minimum dimensions of an accessible toilet are 2 x 1.5 meters. Doors should also open outwards and, in the case of them opening inwards, sufficient space should be allowed for the door leaf and for the user to open and shut it. Adapting a toilet for wheelchair users requires the toilet and hand basin to be changed, a wider door to be fitted and the installation of security handrails on walls with a sufficient loading capacity.

Special attention should be given critical aspects such as anti-slip floor surfaces; the installation of buttons, faucets and handles within reaching distance of a wheelchair user and control of the water temperature. Electronic faucets which detect the presence of a hand beneath them, are gradually replacing timer faucets, for their convenience, hygiene (the user does not touch the device) and their greater water consumption efficiency.

CIRCULATION

Types of stairs

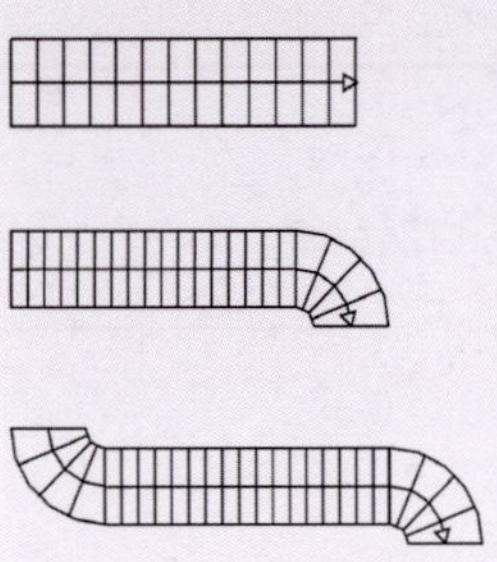

Stairs with one flight

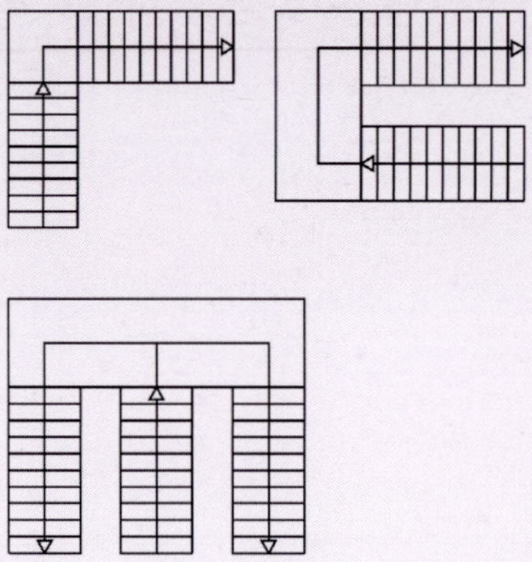

Stairs with several flights

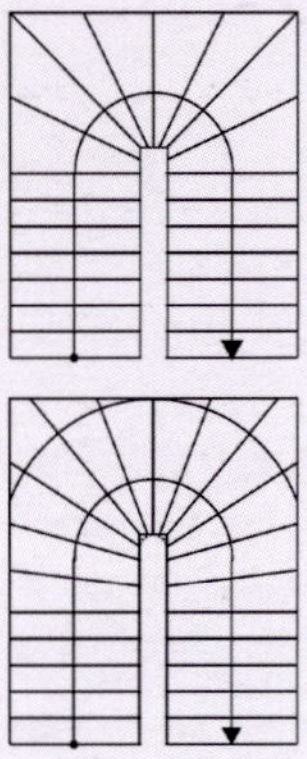

Winding stairs

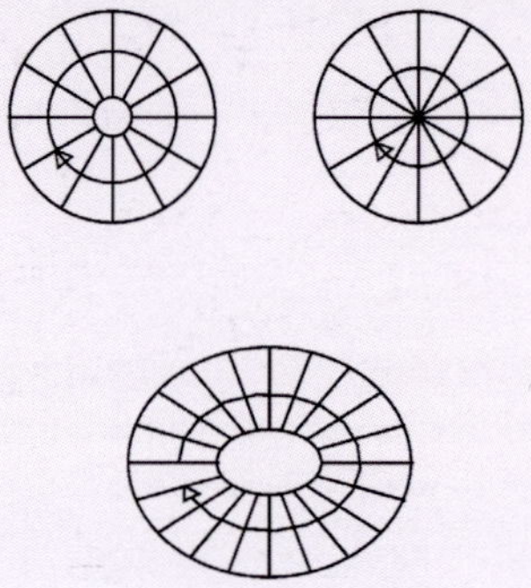

Curved stairs

Stair width

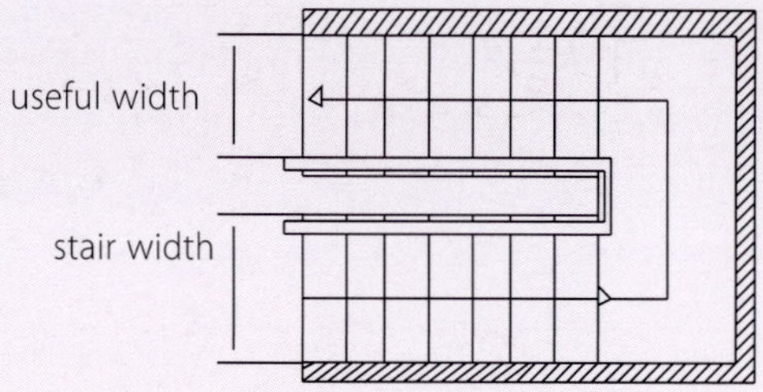

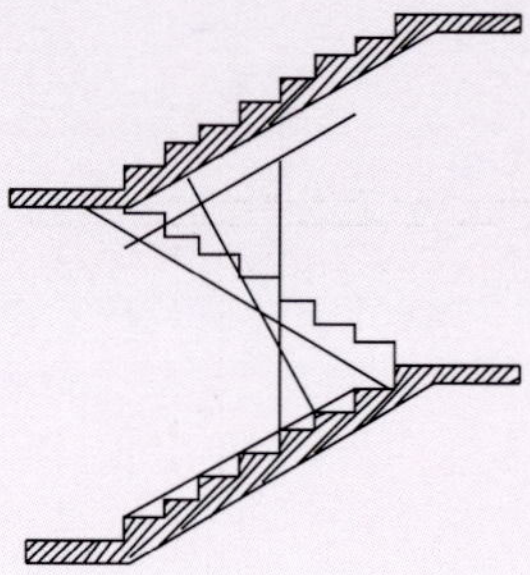

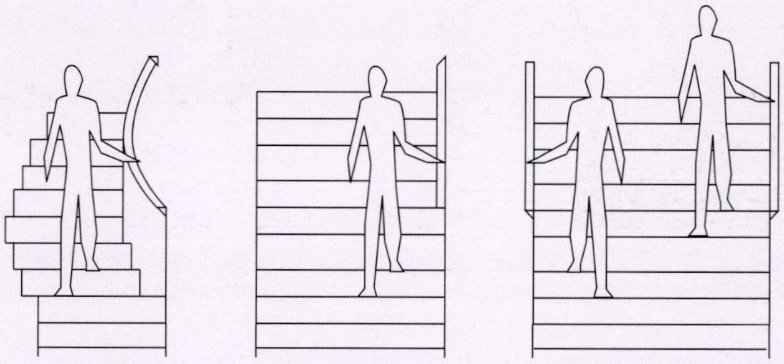

2.13 feet

3.28 feet (>2.46 feet)

1. 4.26 feet (>3.61 feet) 30 m (>1.10 m)

Primary circulation spaces are those that define the most important routes in the building, connecting the principal spaces in the building with the different departments; and secondary circulation spaces that connect the individual workspaces. The way in which people move through the building affects how they interact and relate to each other.

Although staircases can resolve the circulation of large volumes of people, they are inefficient in terms of the area they occupy and their cost. This means that they are often placed at strategic points in office buildings, to facilitate the movement of certain large groups or to connect the first floor and the ground floor.

Elevators should be able to move at least 15% of the workforce in a period of 5 minutes, with a maximum waiting time of 30 seconds. For buildings of more than 10,000 sqm (108,000 sqft) a separate service elevator should be installed.

In offices distributed over various floors, the vertical circulation between each floor is realized via stairs and elevators. The latter are indispensable as they enable wheelchair users and other reduced-mobility users to navigate the building. As in the case of corridors and doors, the dimensions of a wheelchair should be considered when choosing the elevator model.

Staircases are elements that mark the design of a space. They are fixed elements that determine the distribution of the offices. There are many different designs of staircase: straight stairs, those that change direction between flights, compensated stairs and curved stairs.

The form and style of a staircase is also determined by the construction materials chosen: stone or concrete will give a more monumental appearance, while glass or plastic can be used to achieve more minimalist designs.

The width of a staircase is defined by its limits, but it is often reduced at the sides by a banister or string. The useful width of a staircase is thus defined as the span between the two handrails or between the handrail and the wall.

The width of stairs is also determined by the number of persons who must circulate in both directions, by the time in which a building must be evacuated and by the importance of the building in which they are located. According to the number of persons that use the stairs, they are classified as follows:

- For 1 person (Winding stair or narrow straight stair)	2.13 feet (minimum 1.15)
- For 1 person	3.28 feet (minimum 2.46)
- For 2 persons	4.26 feet (minimum 3.61)
- For 3 persons	6.23 feet (minimum 5.90)

Doors and switches

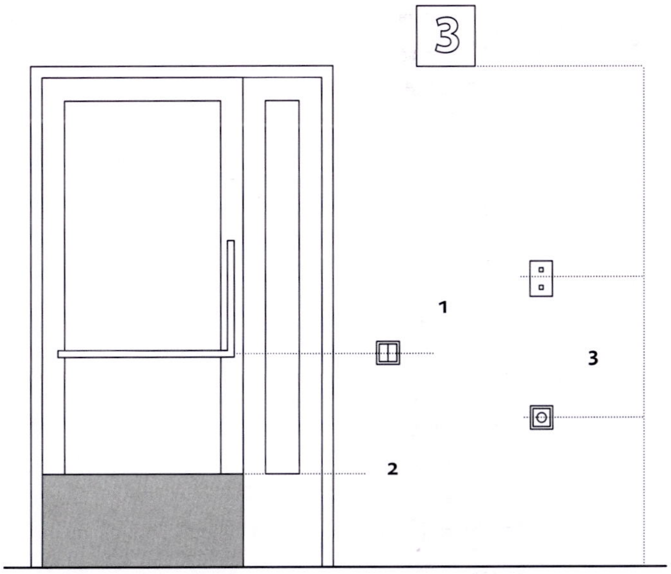

1. Height 900-1000 mm (3' - 3' 3"). Handles and switches should be aligned at this height.
2. 400 mm (1' 4") high protection panel in doors.
3. Maximum and minimum heights for control elements: 600 mm (2'); 1200 mm (4').

Minimum space requirements for hinged doors

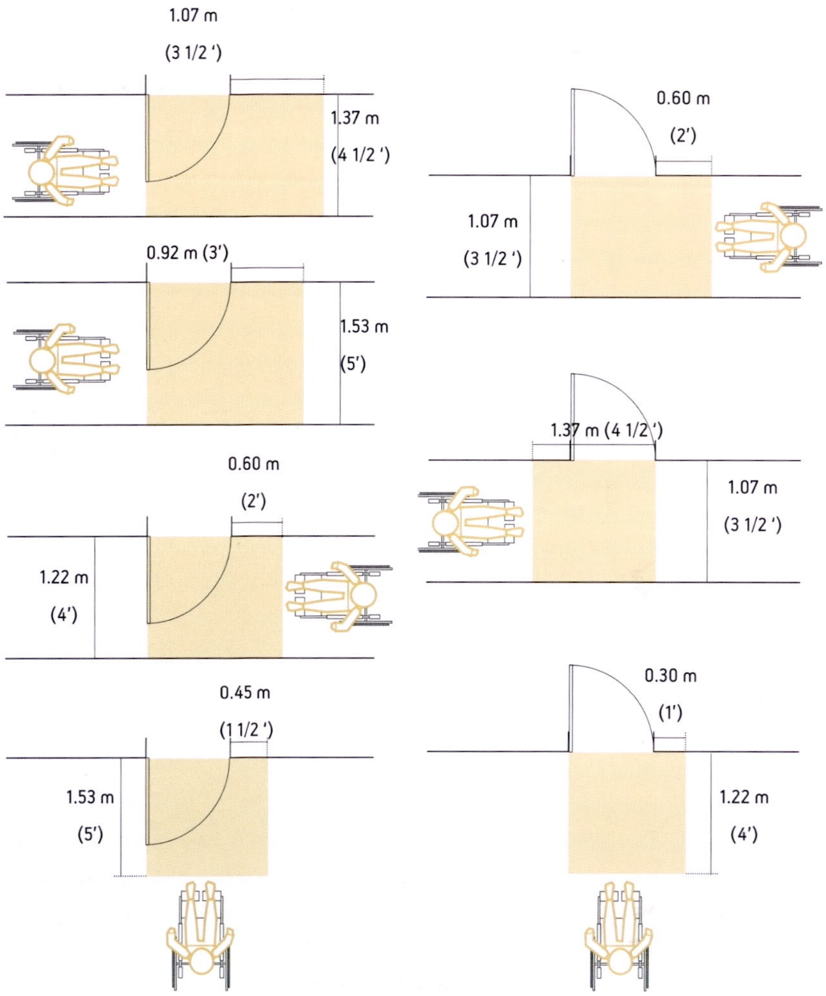

All public buildings should be fitted with control panels and signage designed for users with reduced mobility and installed within the standard reach of a wheelchair user: up to 1220 mm (4') from the finished floor level for depths of up to 510 mm (20") , and 1120 mm (3'8") from the F.F.L. for depths of up to 635 mm (25") when the device is accessed from the front. When the wheelchair user can access the device laterally their reach is from 380 mm (15") to 1370 mm (4-1/2') above the F.F.L.

All control panels should fulfil three conditions: they should be installed at an accessible height, easy to use (they should be easy to hold, non-slip and require minimal force in their manipulation), while information should be easy to read and comprehend (large lettering and clear communication). Electronic controls can resolve many accessibility barriers presented by elements such as windows, blinds and doors.

Stairlifts are a space-efficient alternative to ramps for small changes of level. Incorporating either a seat or a platform for the wheelchair user, **stairlifts** can cover large distances and even be fitted in staircases with various flights and changes in direction. They are an ideal solution for improving the accesibility of existing buildings, although the building regulations prohibit their installation on stairs in emergency evacuation routes.

The main entrance should serve both able-bodied and reduced-mobility users. The most practical door type are two-leaf automatic sliding doors with detectors that ensure that they will only shut once the user has passed right through the doorway. Rotating and pivoting doors are not recommendable and any door that requires the user to open it physically should be avoided.

ACCESIBILITY

Dimensions of the human body

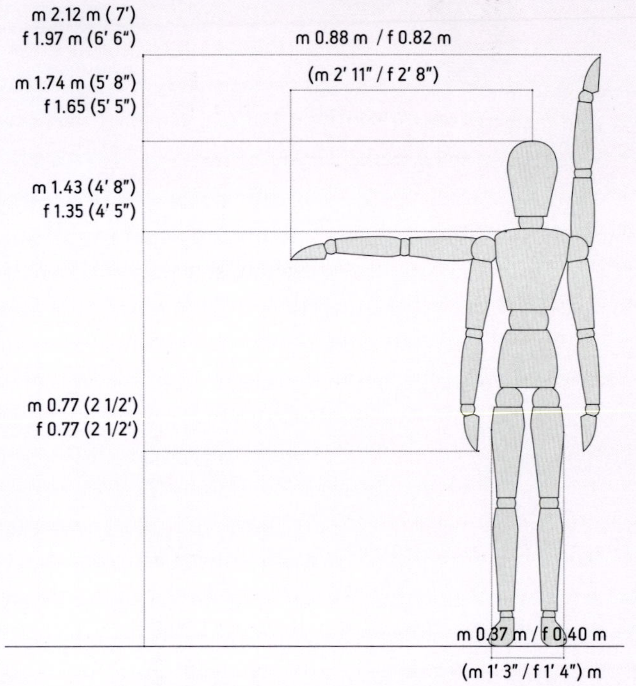

Wheelchair dimensions

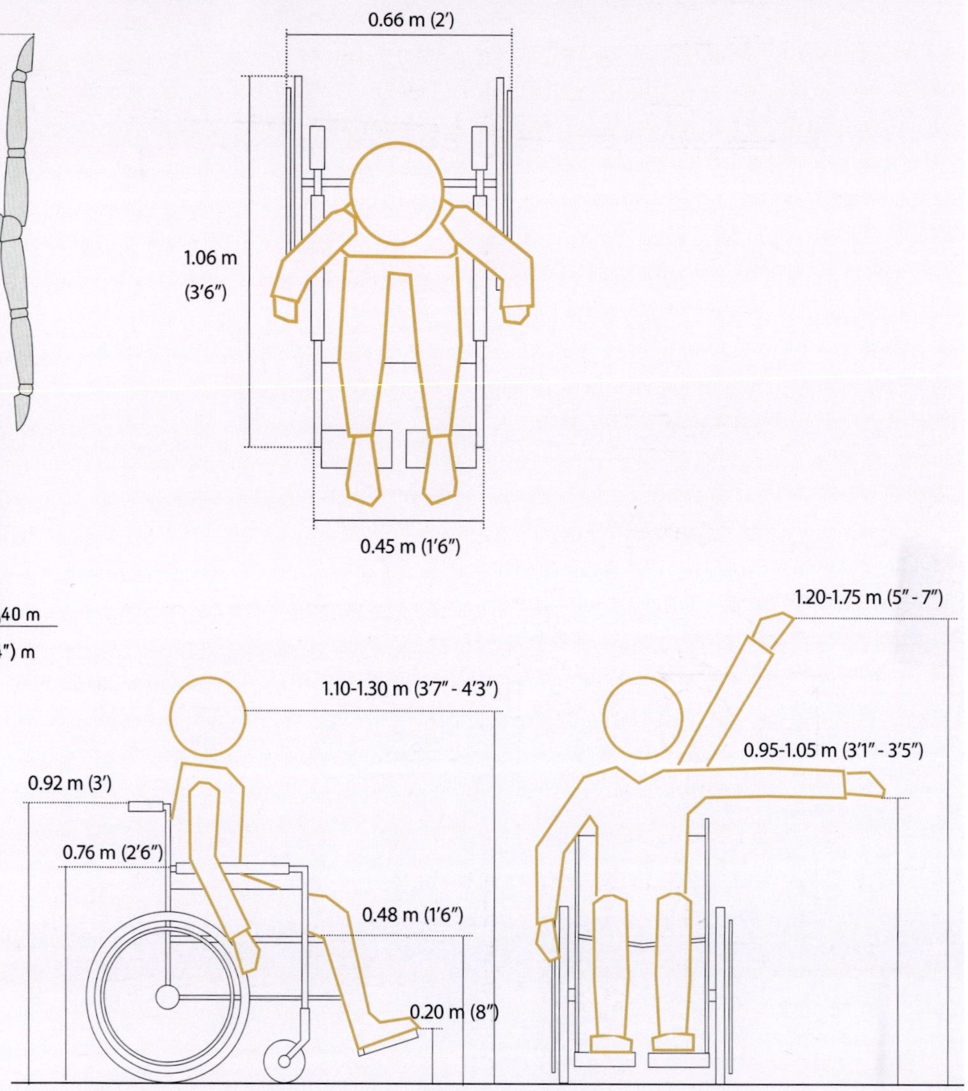

Although there are many types and degrees of disability, the minimum requirement for a public building is adaptation to the needs of a user in a wheelchair since this condition requires certain adaptations of the built environment that are assumed to make the building more functional for those with other types and degrees of disability.

There are essentially three components to consider in a project for improving the accessibility of an existing building: increasing the width of doors and circulation spaces; inserting additional elevators and ramps to reduce circulation distances and ensure access to all levels can be achieved without using stairs; the use of appropriate mechanical apparatus and new technologies to increase comfort.

Based on the dimensions of a standard wheelchair, its turning circle and the standard reach of a wheelchair user, the building regulations for accessibility define dimensions for room widths, doorways, corridors, the height of switches, taps, telephones, and control panels. People with reduced mobility need more space than other people. While the minimum area for an individual workstation is around 4 sqm (43 sqft), a wheelchair user will need around 5 or 6 sqm (54 - 65 sqft).

A wheelchair user needs a minimum unobstructed width of 915 mm (3ft 2 in) when moving forwards in a straight line, and a circle with a diameter of 1525 mm (5 ft) to turn the chair. In general, 1.3 meters (4 ft 3 in) has been established as the standard width of corridors.

Changes in the floor level of more than 13 mm (5 in) should be accompanied by a ramp, while level changes between 6 and 13 mm (2 and 5 in) should be resolved without a step, by connecting the two floor heights with a continuous sloping plane no steeper than 45 °. Ramps should be straight, with a gradient no greater than 7 % and a length of less than 6 meters (20 ft).

Ramp designs

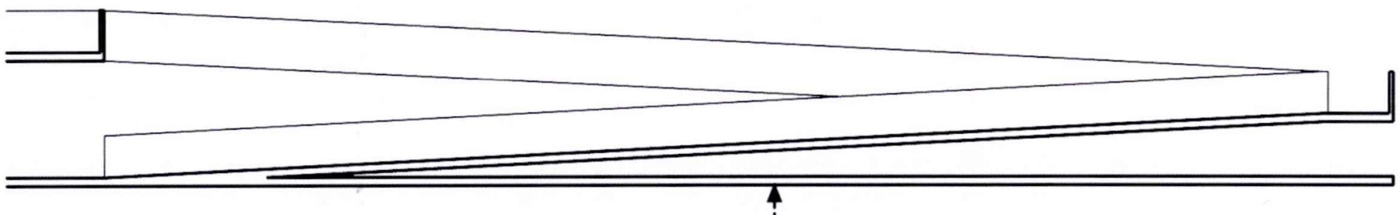

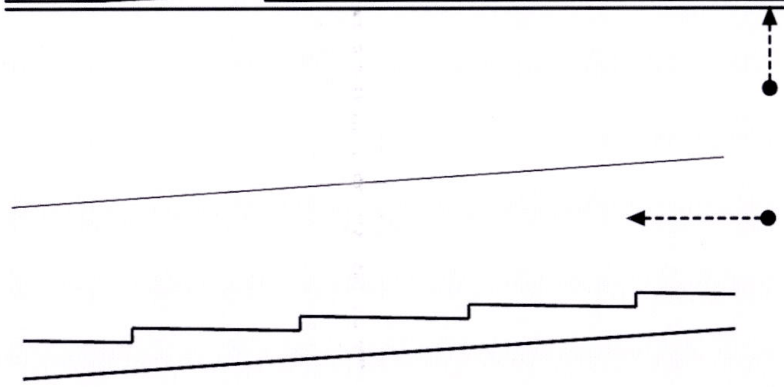

Access ramp:
A ramp that leads from one floor to another, and may or may not connect with the exterior.

Stepped ramp:
A sequence of ramps connected by low steps.

Banisters and handrails

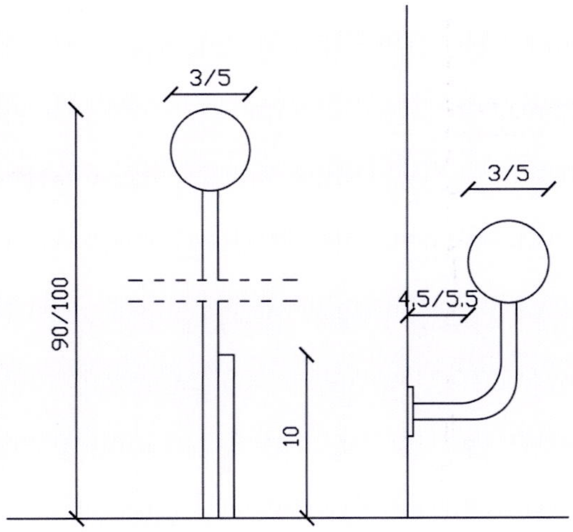

Height differences in entrances from the exterior

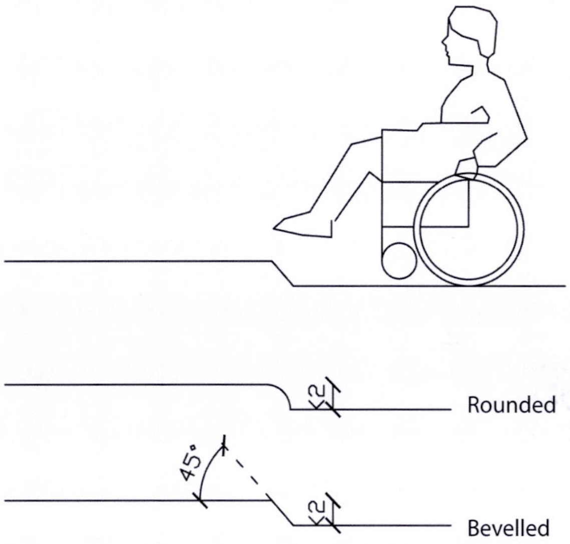

The unobstructed width of the ramp must be greater than or equal to 1.2 m (4 ft) and it must be equipped with a handrail that accompanies the its full length and continues beyond its beginning and end, which are considered critical points. Ramps that are especially wide should be fitted with a double central handrail.

A ramp, defined as an inclined plane that connects two levels at different heights, is the element that allows uneven ground to become accessible to all. The design of a ramp is a basic element for accessibility, but the way it is implemented is also important and regular maintenance is required to ensure that the element does not deteriorate. A ramp should be protected as much as possible from environmental agents and lit at night.

Details of brick or blockwork partition walls

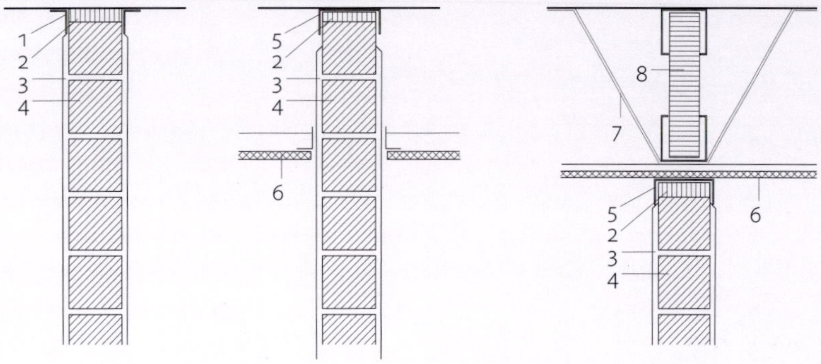

1. Steel angle
2. Rockwool
3. Plaster
4. Brick / blockwork
5. Steel U-section
6. False ceiling
7. Suspension elements
8. Insulation

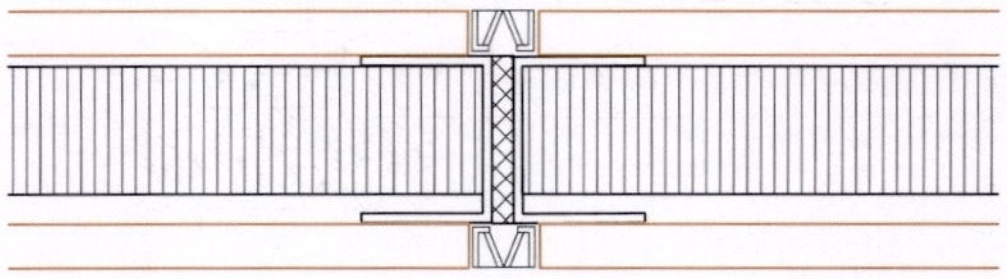

Expansion joint

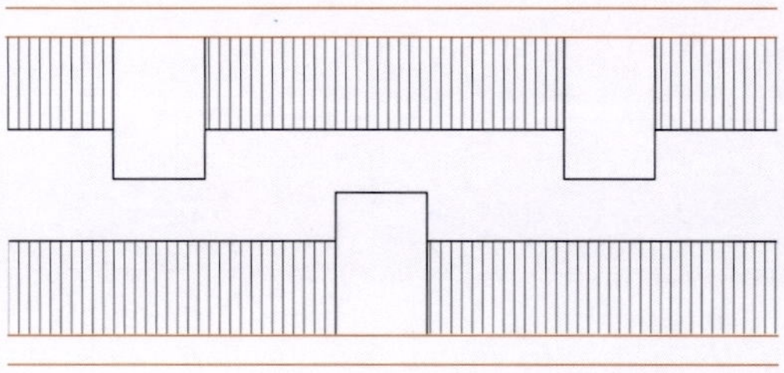

Double leaf partition for greater acoustic insulation

Armstrong suspended ceiling systems

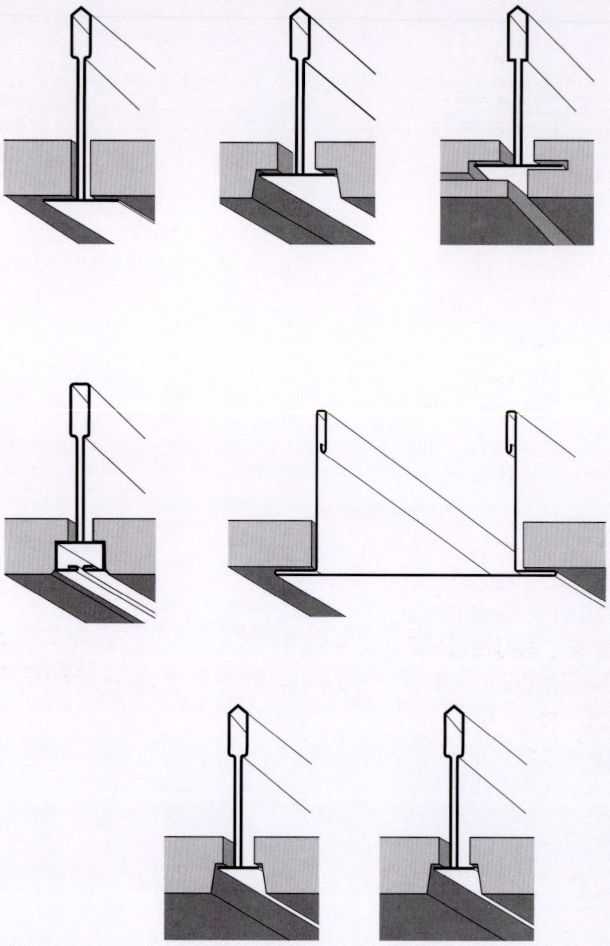

PARTITIONS

Limits between different areas can be marked by different elements - with freestanding partitions or walls - or simply left implicit in the distribution of the furniture. Partitions can be **fixed or movable**, the latter being particularly relevant for auditoriums or conference rooms. The function if the partition is as much to attenuate noise as it is to create visual privacy. Movable partitions can be quickly and easily installed and removed, and there are models available that are designed with high acoustic specifications. They are however more expensive than fixed partitions, have a shorter lifespan and are less effective as fire barriers and acoustic barriers than plasterboard, ceramic or brick partitions.

CEILINGS

False, or suspended, ceilings reduce the height of the space by around 140 mm when they are used to house lighting fittings, smoke detectors, cabling and sprinklers. Acoustic panels fixed on lightweight metallic substructures are the most common solution. They are available in a wide range of sizes and finishes and with a great variety of fixing systems. Cabling and fittings installed within the ceiling void should be easily accessible.

Types of flooring

1. Ceramic tiles
2. Tiling mortar
3. Concrete slab
4. Waterproof barrier (2 layers)
5. Insulation
6. Fill strip
7. Elastic sealant
8. Skirting board
9. Parquet
10. OSB board
11. Cellulose panel
12. Mineral board
13. Anti-capillary layer
14. Composite timber board
15. Wooden board
16. Timber joist
17. Reinforced concrete
18. Glass bricks
19. Support
20. Elastic seal
21. Expansion joint

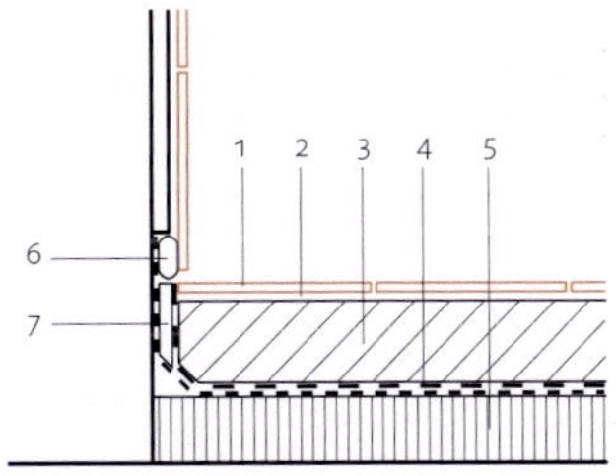

Ceramic tiles on concrete slab

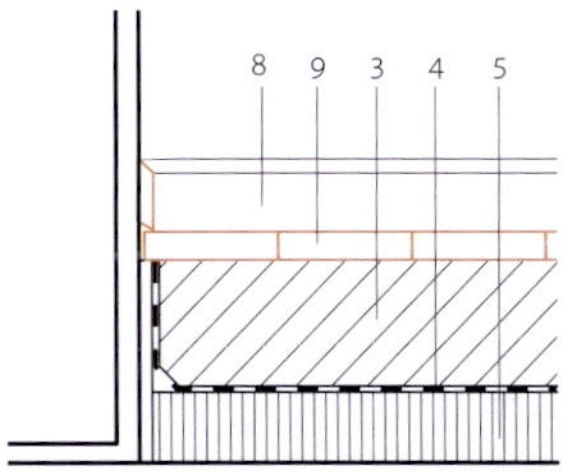

Wooden parquet on concrete slab

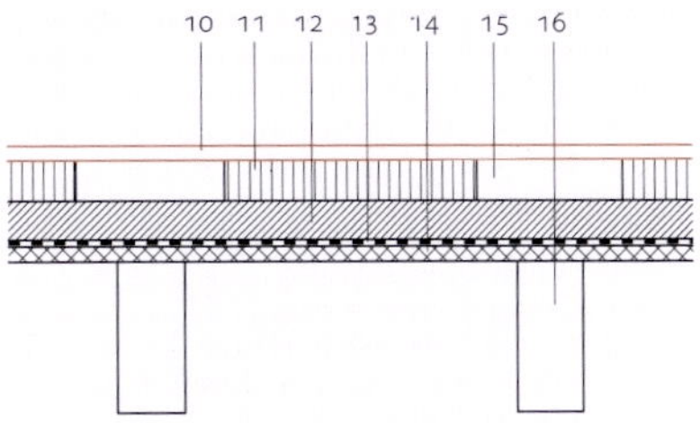

OSB on timber joists

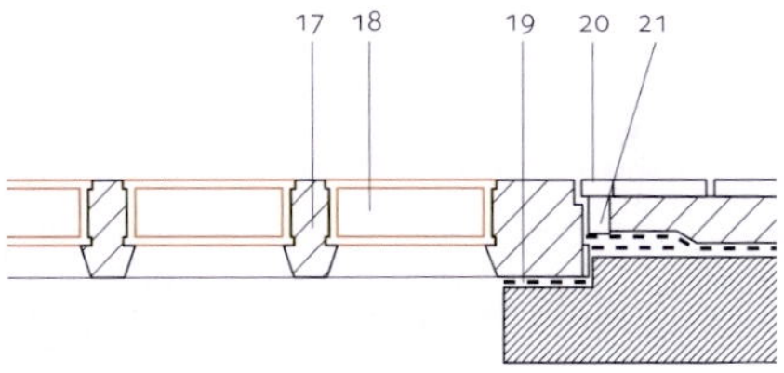

Glass brick floor (max. dimensions 3.50 x 1.60 m)

FLOORING

The ideal floor to ceiling height is 2.6 to 3 meters (8-1/2' - 10'), so when specifying the installation of **technical floors**, the finished floor level should be taken into account. Technical floors are generally installed at a height of 150 mm (6") above the floor slab, although they can be as high as 200 or 250 mm (8" - 10") in special cases and can even be 450 mm (18") high if they contain ventilation ducts and air-conditioning conduits. These flooring solutions, that are invariably very difficult to install in historic buildings, should be defined according to a series of considerations, such as the strength of the floor structure and the correct distribution of supports so that the loading will not become uneven if the applied loads increase or are redistributed. The under floor area should be easy to access for maintenance and replacement of cabling and other elements. Vertical fire barriers should be installed in the under floor area to prevent the propagation of fire.

The choice of **flooring material** will depend on various factors: not only its appearance and the company's corporate image, but also the cost, health and safety, durability, and the ease of maintenance and installation. There is a wide range of options, from ceramic tiles to carpet, laminated flooring or parquet, linoleum and vinyl or even metallic floors.

Light color and temperature for various spaces

	Skywhite	Cool daylight		Daylight	Cool white		White	Warm white	Extra warm white
color name:	**Skywhite**	**Cool daylight**		**Daylight**	**Cool white**		**White**	**Warm white**	**Extra warm white**
color code:	880	865	965	954	840	940	835	830	835
color temperature:	8000 K	6500 K	6500 K	5400 K	4000 K	4000 K	3500 K	3000 K	3500 K
Offices, corridors	⊠				⊠		⊠	⊠	
Meeting rooms	⊠						⊠	⊠	⊠
Electrical industry		⊠			⊠				
Textile industry		⊠	⊠	⊠					
Woodworking industry		⊠	⊠	⊠	⊠				
Graphics industry, laboratories		⊠	⊠	⊠	⊠				
Color matching			⊠	⊠		⊠			
Warehouses, transport depots					⊠				

Typical luminance values (cd/m²)

The Sun	1 650 000 000
Incandescent lamp	7 000 000
Fluorescent lamp	8 000
Full moon	2 500

Typical illuminance values (lx)

Sunny day	80 000
Overcast day	5 000
Table lamp	300
Ceiling lamp	100
Full moon	0,1

Conversions for units of temperature

	into Fahrenheit	into Celsius	into Kelvin
from Fahrenheit	F	(ºF - 32) / 1,8	(ºF - 32) × 5/9 + 273,15
from Celsius	(ºC × 1,8) + 32	C	ºC + 273,15
from Kelvin	(K - 273,15) × 9/5 + 32	K - 273,15	K

The internal environment of the workplace affects how people work. It has been demonstrated that in uncomfortable temperature or lighting conditions productivity is reduced, while noise reduces concentration levels. The current trend is towards healthier, more cost efficient and more environmentally sustainable working environments.

Psychologists have also shown that being able to control the **comfort** conditions of their immediate environment (for example being able to open the windows) gives workers a positive perception of their work station.

The **ventilation** is one of the most critical aspects in the design of an office, since users invariably value natural ventilation through windows above any mechanical system, however efficient or healthy it may be.

Floor depths of less than 15 meters (50') are optimal for natural ventilation, but buildings narrower than 13 meters (43') become difficult to distribute with open-plan offices in combination with enclosed work spaces. The ideal solution is to use a combination of ventilation systems that can accommodate spaces with specific demands such as restrooms, photocopying rooms, laboratories or kitchens. It would be unacceptable for odors from a staff kitchen to spread into work areas.

LIGHTING AND NOISE

Lamp types

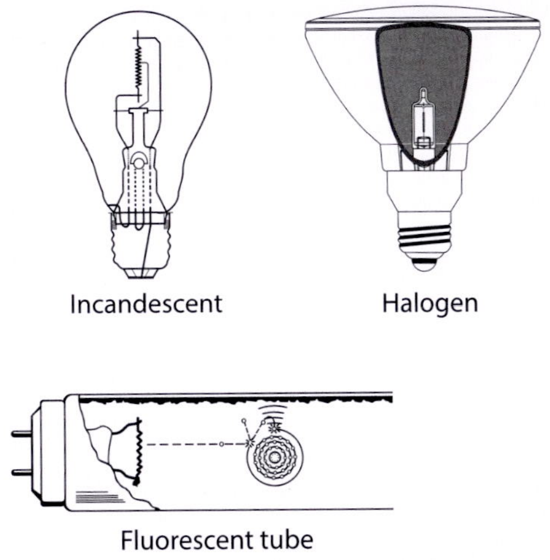

Recommended illuminance levels for offices (lx)

work surfaces	500
drawing desks	1 000
open plan offices	1 000

LIGHTING

Lighting is another critical aspect as it directly affects comfort and productivity. The current belief is that visual contact with the exterior is essential for effective working: this is why the façades of office buildings are extensively glazed and workstations are placed close to windows.

The amount of light needed to realize a given task varies from person to person, and especially in function of age: people over sixty need lighting levels with an intensity four times greater than that required by under-twenties, for example.

Natural light is always preferable for workspaces. Daylighting levels depend on the building design and principally on the floor to ceiling height that will determine how far it enters the building. It is considered that spaces lit from only one side should be no deeper than 2.5 times the floor to ceiling height. A distance of up to 7.5 meters (25′) is generally acceptable in sunny climates.

Natural light contributes considerably to the **energy efficiency** of the building when daylight levels at the workstations reaches 500 lux and the artificial lighting can be turned off. It is important to remember, however, that the lighting level does not depend only on incident light but also on the reflected light. On very bright days the intensity of the natural light may cause internal lighting conditions with excessive contrast, in which case artificial lighting will need to be used. The possibility of regulating the natural light at their workstation and the intensity and orientation of artificial light is one of the characteristics that users value most highly. Natural light can be controlled and modified using blinds fitted on the eastern, southern and western façades of the building.

Human hearing

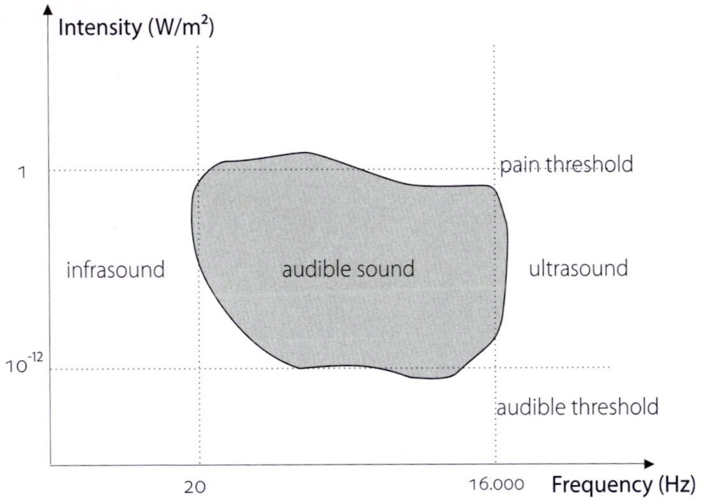

Airborne noise (a) impact noise (b)

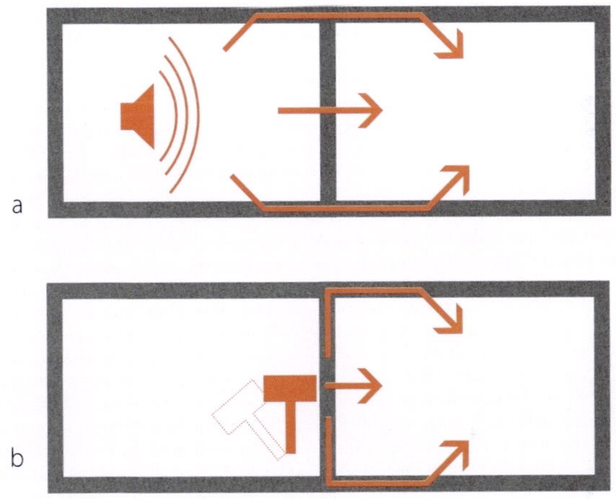

NOISE

Noise is the last key design issue and one of the most conflictive in open office spaces: achieving **acoustic privacy** contradicts the visual openness of the space. Walls and partitions are the most effective devices for reducing noise levels, blocking its propagation and absorbing, masking or diffusing sound. There are various suspended ceiling or flooring solutions that are designed to absorb or diffuse airborne sound and impact noise.

Protection against external noise can be improved by installing a double façade, the outer skin acting as an acoustic panel. The effectiveness of this solution depends largely on the size and position of windows and ventilation openings.

The void between the two leaves of the façade can also be used to attenuate sound by fitting it with acousticallly absorbent surfaces. This strategy can achieve an improvement of 3 to 6 decibels in the acoustic insulation of a façade with a window area of 10 % of the total surface area.

ENERGY EFFICIENCY ON THE FAÇADE

Façades. Designing to reduce heating and lighting energy loads.

External factors

External ambient temperature
Air movement
External relative humidity
Solar radiation
Ambient noise
Precipitation

→

Control systems

Façade - Roof
Heating and air-conditioning systems
Artificial lighting

←

User needs

Internal temperature
Air quality
Internal relative humidity
Lighting
Absence of noise

Points in the façade vulnerable to damp

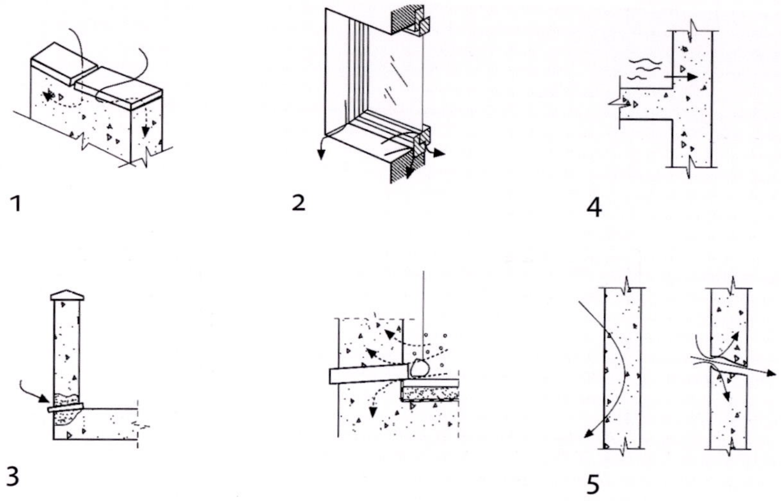

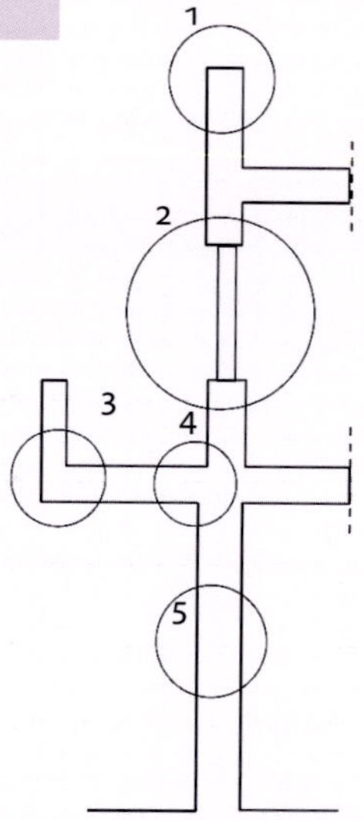

In all types of buildings, particularly in office buildings, the façade has evolved from a structural function to a non load-bearing, simple function of enclosure. The envelopes are **lightweight**, thin and multi-layer; and fulfil with greater or lesser efficiency the functions of insulation, water-proofing and air tightness. The façade design determines the natural illumination of the interior, The façade design is key to controlling the daylighting conditions of the interior, managing the solar gains and the natural ventilation to ensure a good air quality and the elimination of excess heat through convection.

The contemporary tendency is for energy consumption and the use of passive strategies to form a key consideration from the earliest stages of the design of the building. The form the building and the façade impact directly on the building's climatic relationship with the surroundings through two principle factors: the surface area – the larger the surface area, the greater the capacity for energy exchange between the interior and exterior.

The independization of the structure from the façade enclosure represents a definitive advance in the process of the increasing autonomy of the façade.

The most universal façade solution in office buildings is the glazed curtain wall. Realized with industrially manufactured components, it is designed to resist wind loads and its own self-weight which is transmitted to the structure of the building through the fixings. This element has to resolve a complex series of problems: the dimensional limits of the glazing lites, the transmission of forces to the building structure, differential movement between the building structure and the curtain wall, etc.

Wind pressure can cause the glazing to flex and even break. This can be controlled by giving the panels sufficient points of support with appropriate spans. The most effective solution is to support the glazing panels on bars that distribute the wind loads and self-weight along their length and are fixed to the floor plates. A continuous façade can be achieved by placing the building envelope outside the plane of the building structure supported on its own substructure such that it is not interrupted by the floor plates. This solution has the advantages of eliminating thermal bridges and reducing the vulnerability to damp.

Passive ventilation draw through a façade

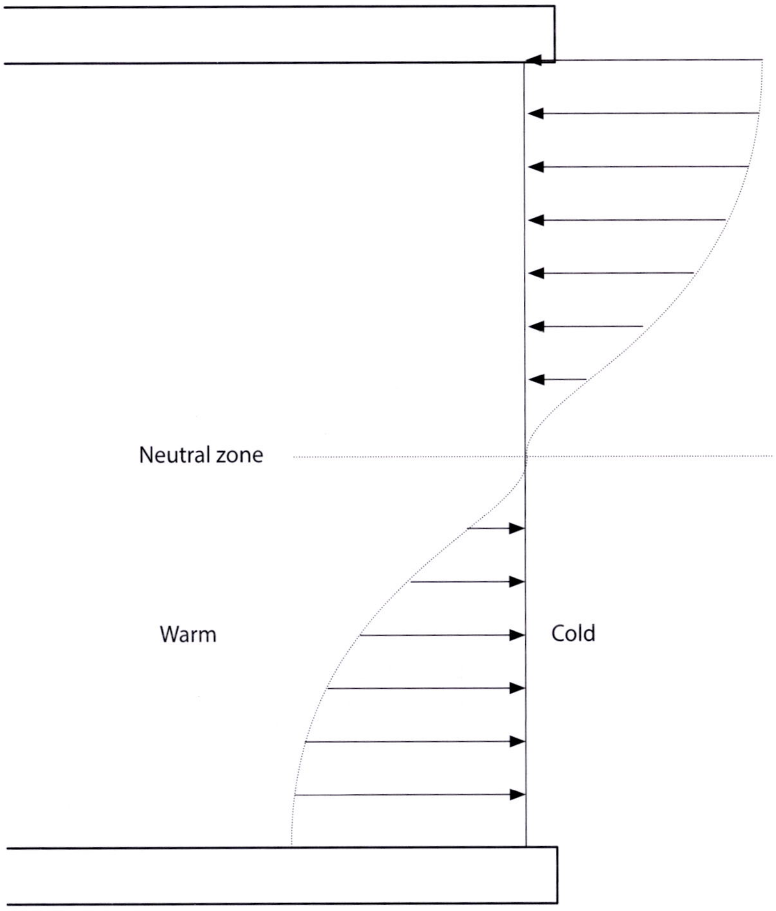

Passive solar heating principles

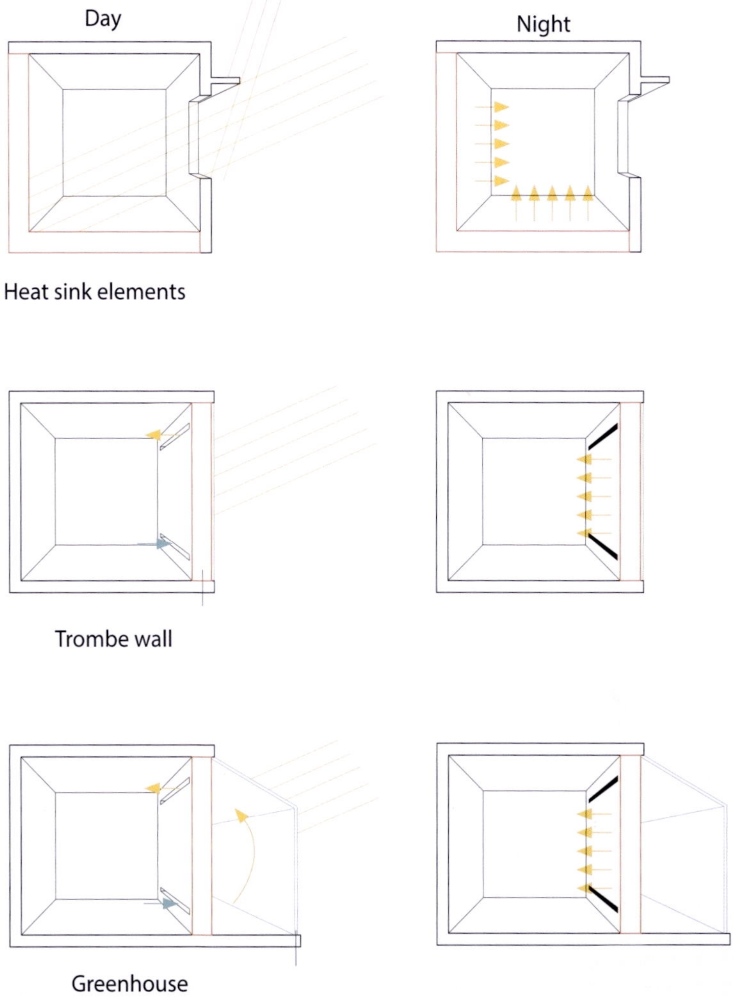

Another problem is the **thermal expansion** of the building envelope: if the panels and substructure of the façade are independent between floors, the dimensional changes will be minimal, but if the curtain wall is continuous is will need expansion joints.

The solutions to the waterproofing and drainage of the façade as well as its impermeability to water vapor are in the design of the joints of the curtain-walling system: whether those of the frame, between the glazing and the frame or between glazing panels directly. The common design options are elastic sealants, overlapping elements, joint covering elements or the "open joint".

Condensation can occur not only on the surface of the glazing but also on the framing elements. These latter should be thermally broken if they are in contact with exterior and interior air, while the use of low-emissivity glass reduces the energy lost through the glazing. Moisture that has condensed on the inside of the façade or that has filtered through should have means of draining through drainage channels incorporated in the framing elements.

The energy gains and losses through the glazing will be affected by the design of units and the glass, options including the incorporation of translucent insulation, double or triple glazing and the use of special glasses with high reflectivity, low emissivity etc.

A factor that can prove problematic in the use of glazed curtain walls is controlling solar gains, since the greenhouse effect means that the façade allows energy into the building which then cannot radiate back out.

Façade solutions using metal panels are also common in office buildings, the most common being of aluminum and galvanized steel although stainless steel, copper and zinc are also common materials. New materials include plastic panels, used especially in cases with very tight loading constraints and high strength and rigidity demands.

HEAT

Passive solar control elements

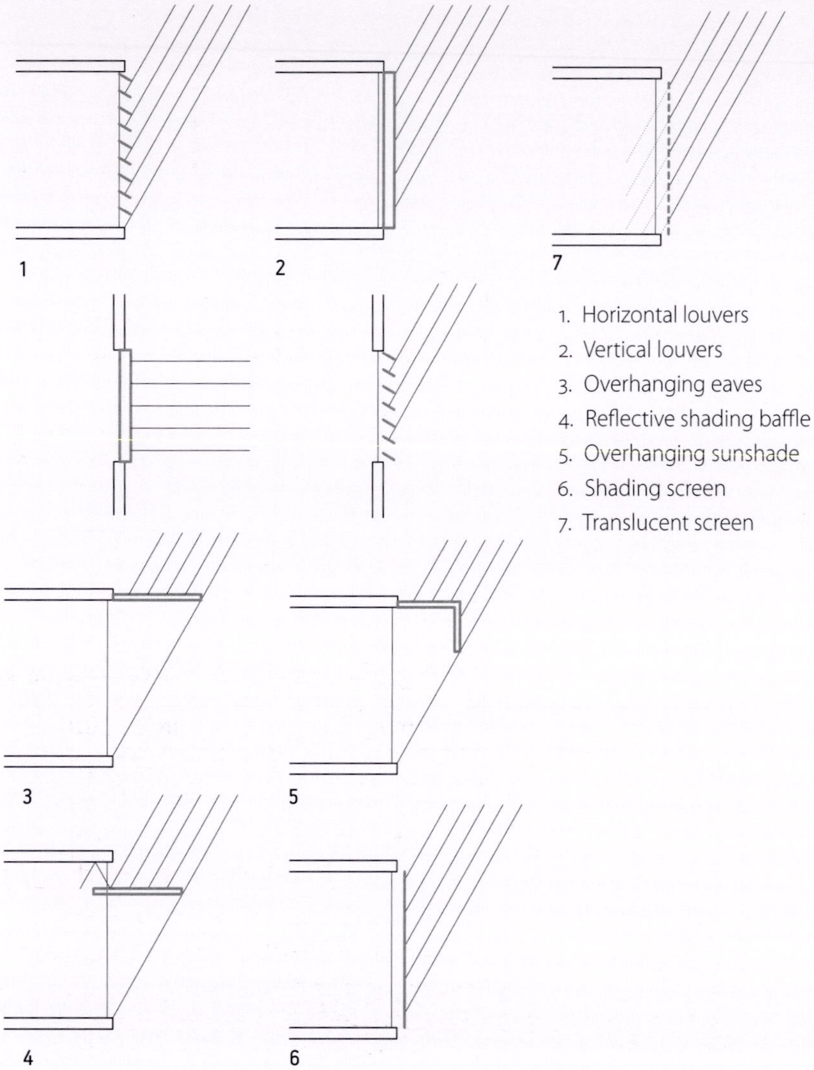

Heat transmission

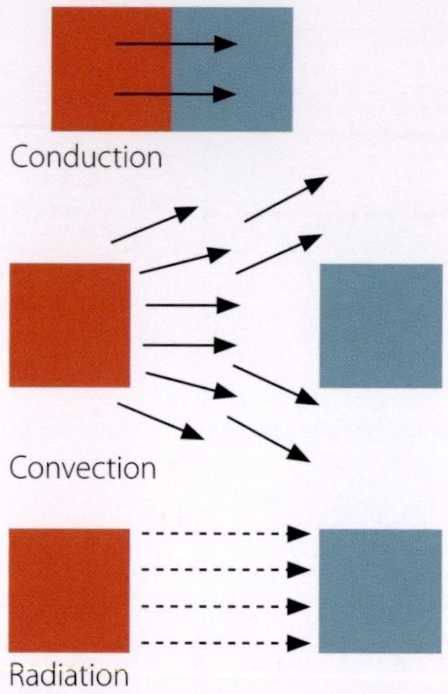

Heat pump

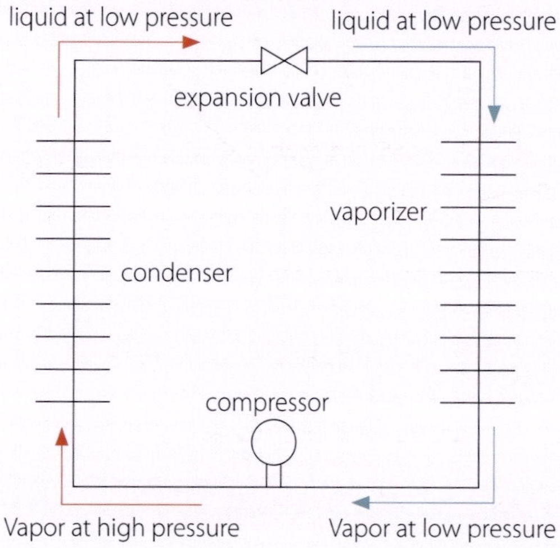

The regulation of the internal temperature of an office building should be understood holistically, from the thermal insulation to the heating and air-conditioning systems, while always bearing in mind the use of renewable energies.

Adapting the internal conditions of the building to the local climatic and microclimatic conditions should be a fundamental parameter in the design of the building. Multi-layered façades can offer important advantages, enabling nighttime cooling and reducing pressure fluctuations even when windows are open. Double-layered façades with box windows are an interesting option for renovation projects, allowing the climatic performance of an existing façade to be improved at the same time as giving the façade a whole new appearance.

The universally accepted ideal temperature is 21 ºC (70ºF) in the summer (up to maximum of 24 ºC (75 ºF)) and 22 ºC (72 ºF) in the winter, with a fresh air intake of 8-12 liters per person per second. Large low temperature radiant surfaces are taking over from convection radiators since they operate at lower temperatures (around 30ºC (86ºF)) and are more energy efficient. Large surfaces are needed to transmit the heat, favoring systems in which the heat source is integrated into the fabric of building, typically in the floor, walls or ceiling.

Mechanical air renovation systems, (supplying 30-50 m³/h (1060-1870 cu.ft)) mean that heat is not lost through open windows, and heat can be recovered from the exhaust air with high efficiency heat-exchangers. The specific requirements of areas such as restrooms, kitchens, laboratories or photocopying rooms should be taken into account in the design of the air systems.

Evacuation routes

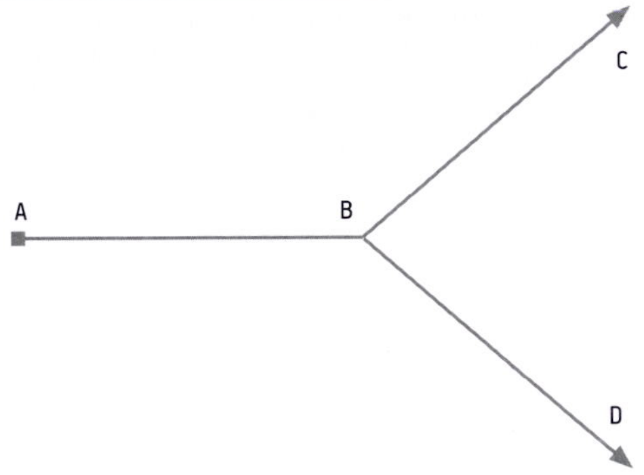

If the escape route starts at point D and separates in two at point E, angle FEG must be greater than or equal to 45º + 2.5º for each additional meter between D and E. (In the previous case in which the routes separate at the starting point, the equivalent distance DE was 0.)

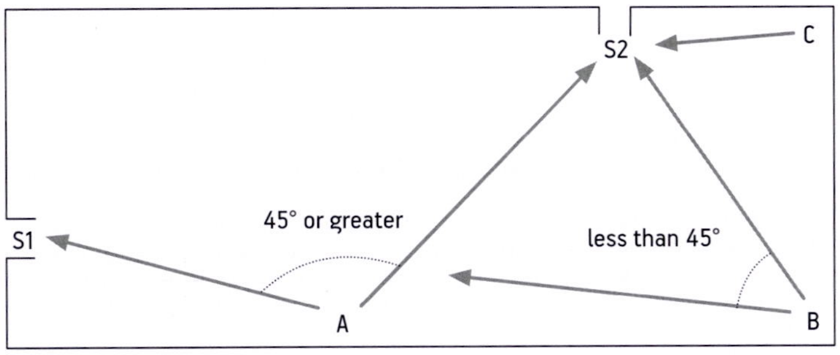

Point A has two alternative routes because angle S1-A-S2 is 45º or more. Point B hasn't got two alternative routes because angle S1-B-S2 is less than 45º. Point C also has only one evacuation route.

Positioning of protected stair cores and emergency exits

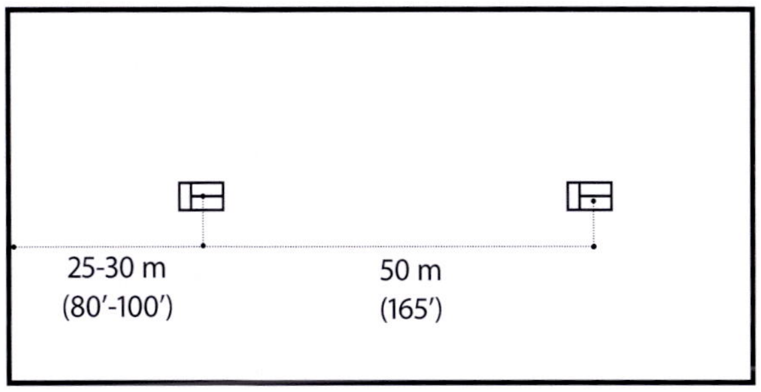

Multistory building with stair cores in the center of the floor plates

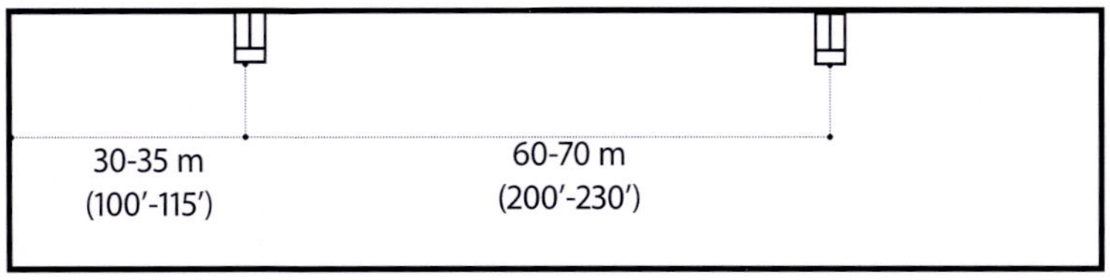

Multistory building with stair cores giving onto a façade

Evacuation routes distances

	One escape route		Two escape routes	
	(m)	(ft)	(m)	(ft)
Offices	18	60′	45	150′
Assembly halls				
a. with fixed seating	15	50′	32[b]	100′
b. without fixed seating	18	60′	45[c]	150′
Storage	18	60′		

a: The evacuation distances for industrial buildings depend on the danger level. In this case a "normal" danger level is assumed.
b: This can be up to 15 meters in one direction.
c: This can be up to 18 meters in one direction.

The building regulations relating to fire safety mark the maximum volume of each fire compartment. This volume can be increased if automatic smoke extraction or sprinkler systems are to be installed and by relocating key elements such as the stairs. The minimum width for evacuation routes is also stipulated along with other criteria, including adequate signage to make the routes easily identifiable by all users of the building.

Plan

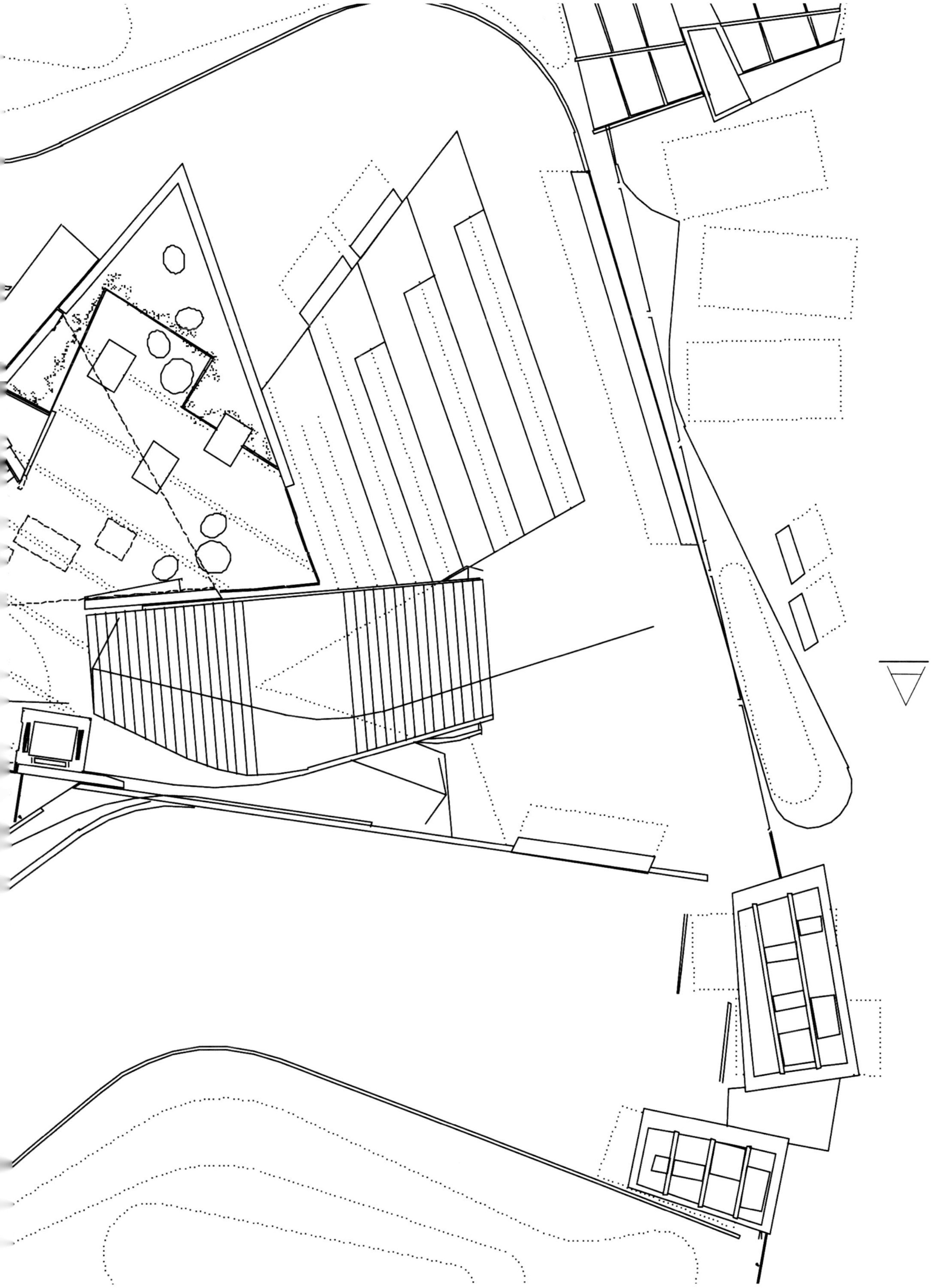

↓ → The Moving Picture Company •
Patrick Tighe Architecture

The Moving Picture Company is a UK-based visual effects post production company, a forerunner in the visual effects and animation fields for the feature film, advertising, music and television industries. The company is highly regarded for its work in the field of color manipulation in film. With this in mind, the project explores the notion of light as it relates to color. The forms and patterns employed in the design have been generated through analyses and three-dimensional modelling of light patterns. Frames from the resultant animation sequence have been selected and layered to organize spatial qualities and movement through the office environment. An organic, sinuous spine weaves its way through the suite. An appendaged soffit grows from the serpentine walls and serves as an armature for cable trays, mechanical and electrical systems.

1. Lobby
2. Kitchen
3. Common area
4. Terrace
5. Office
6. Project room
7. Conference room
8. Open office
9. Edit room
10. Tape op roo
11. Scan
12. Film / tape
13. Machine room
14. Grading room
15. Aluminum laser-cut panels

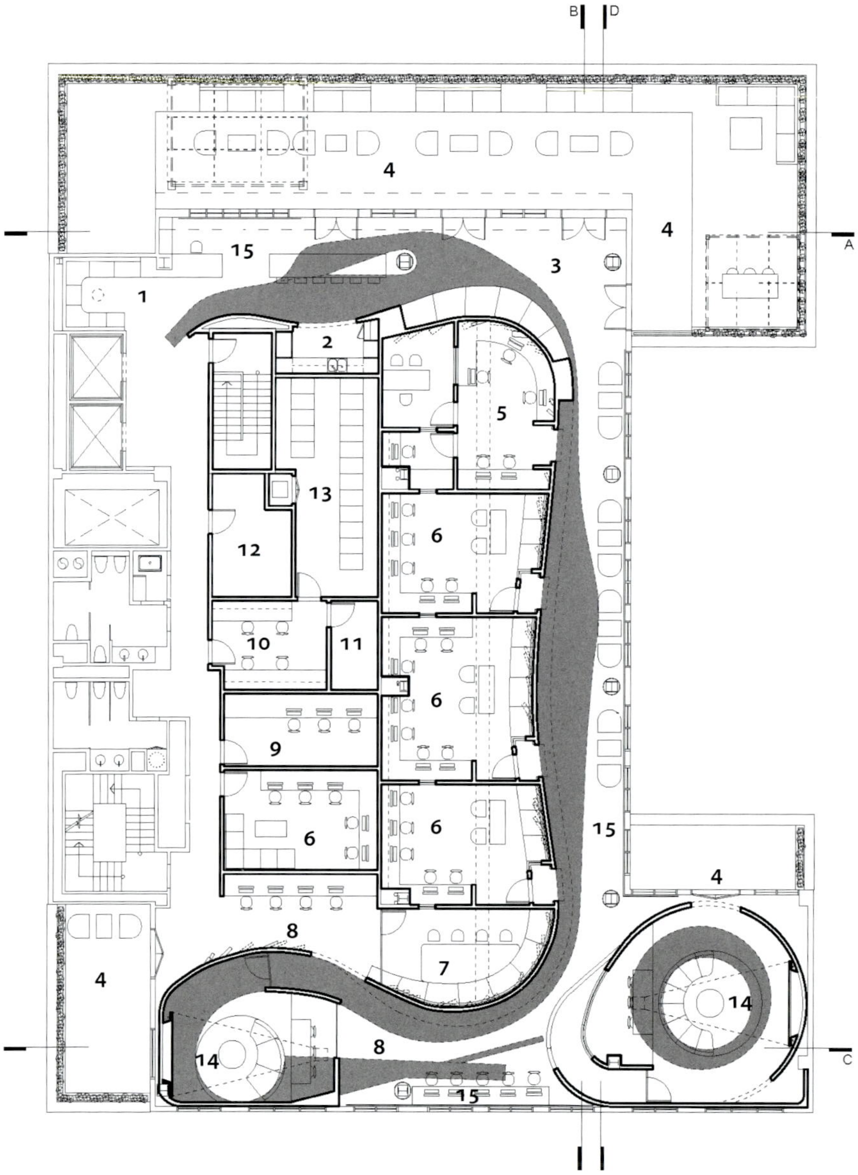

↓ → **WongDoody** • Shubin + Donaldson Architects

The Los Angeles office of WongDoody is the adaptive reuse of a former warehouse. While the shell of the building was mainly left unchanged, the interior construction partitioned the space to accommodate the company's needs. The space is organized into three wings: a public wing flanked by two private work wings. All four of the public meeting/war rooms—the cork room, green room, black room, and silver room—are in the center of the space, marked by rectangular enclosures of different materials. The private work wings include the creative zone, interactive zone, communications, administrative, and account executives areas.

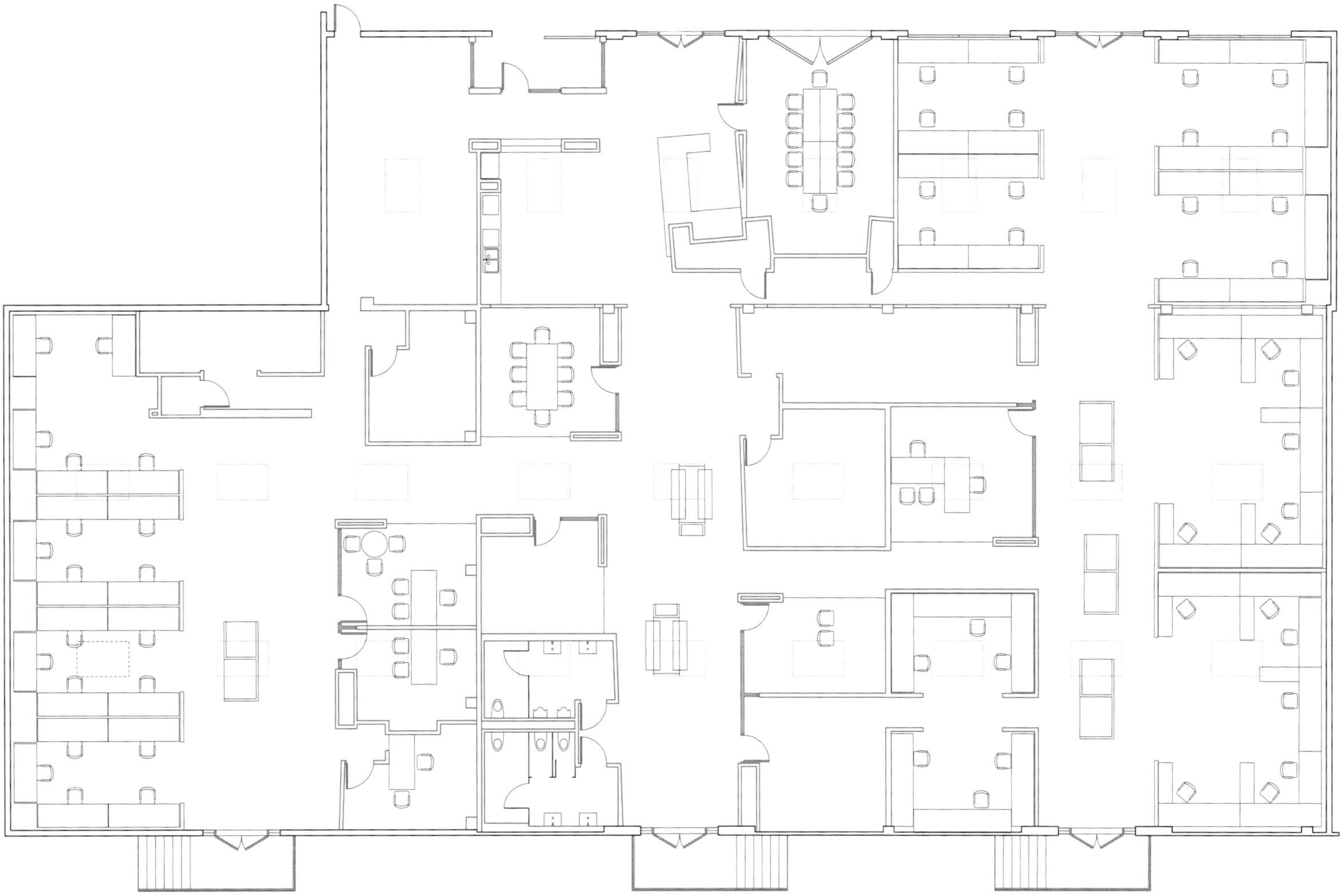

PLAN

↓ → Raiffeisenbank Zürich • NAU + DGJ

Raiffeisen's flagship branch on Zurich's Kreuzplatz dissolves traditional barriers between customer and employee, creating a new type of "open bank," a space of encounter. Elegantly flowing walls blend the different areas of the bank into one smooth continuum, spanning from the customer reception at the front, to employee workstations oriented to the courtyard. The plan carefully controls views to create different grades of privacy and to maximize daylight throughout. The walls themselves act as a membrane mediating between the open public spaces and intimately scaled conference rooms.

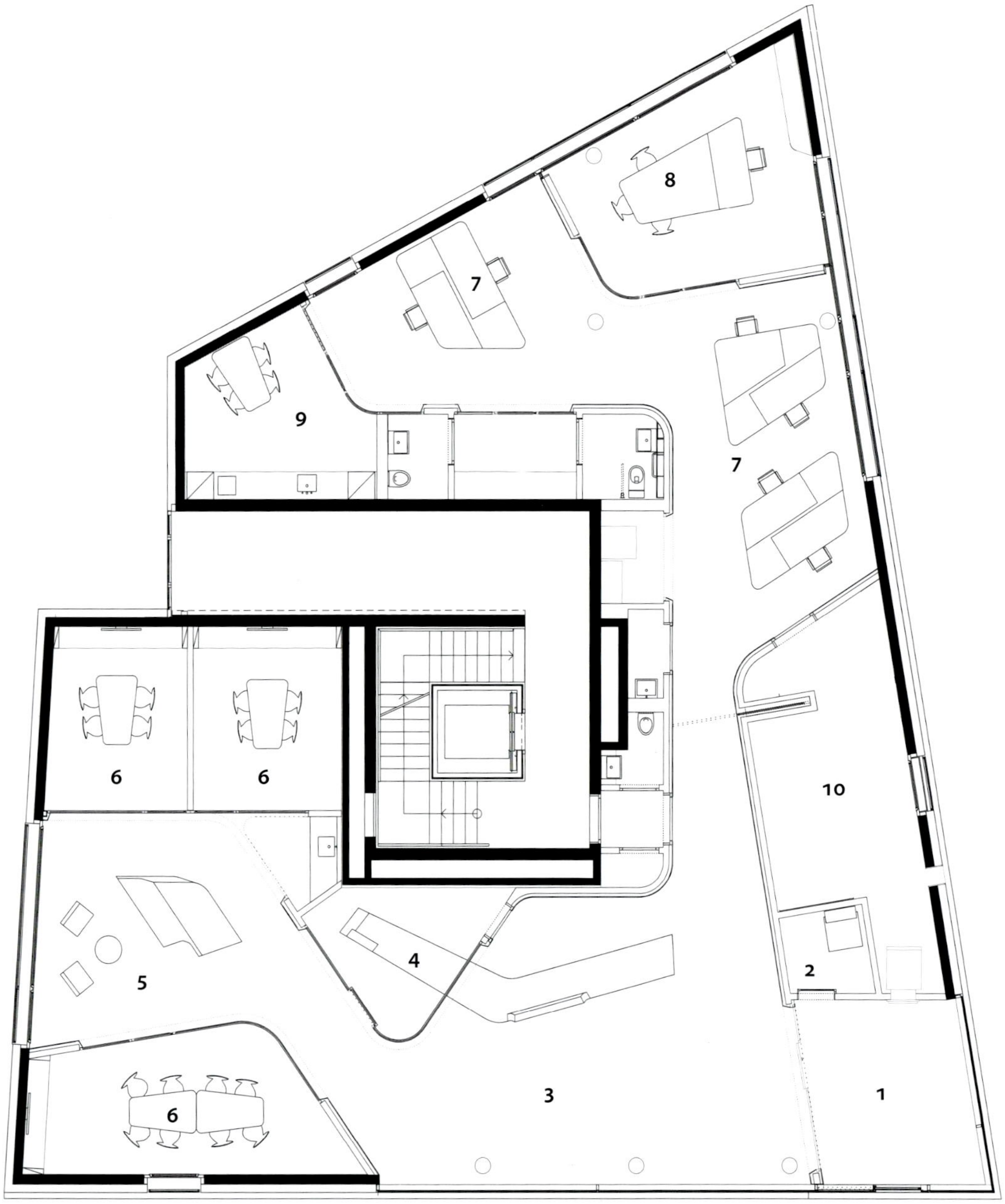

1. Entrance/ATM
2. Safety deposit access
3. Lobby/reception
4. Cash desk
5. Lounge/info-table
6. Meeting room
7. Offices
8. Head office
9. Break room
10. Secure zone

↓ → Forward Media Group Publishing House
• za bor architects

In addition to several popular and well-recognized magazines such as 'Hello', Forward Media Group publishes the largest and the most popular magazines on interior design in Russia.
The project was clearly going to be fairly complex from the outset – the premises comprised a huge loft of 4200 sqm with a narrow, elongated plan, located in the mansard level of a new business center. The situation was further complicated by the particularities of the program – the need for open plan editorial offices as well as commercial and retail departments, separate offices for directors and editors-in-chief with a conference corner, conference rooms, an archive with a library, storage rooms etc. All of these facilities were placed along the corridor which runs the length of the space. Open plan workstations have been concentrated on one side, and cabinets located on the other side of the corridor.

Corridor
Service rooms
Work spaces
Editors-in-chief and heads of department offices
Conference rooms

PLAN

↓ → Nendo • Meguro Office

The firm wanted the usual spaces and functions -meeting space, management, workspace and storage- to be separated from one another while at the same time maintaining a sense of connection between them. To achieve this effect, the architects divided the space with walls that seem to sag and flop like a piece of cloth held up between two hands. The various spaces are thus enclosed to a greater extent than they would be by the usual office dividers, but less so than by actual walls.

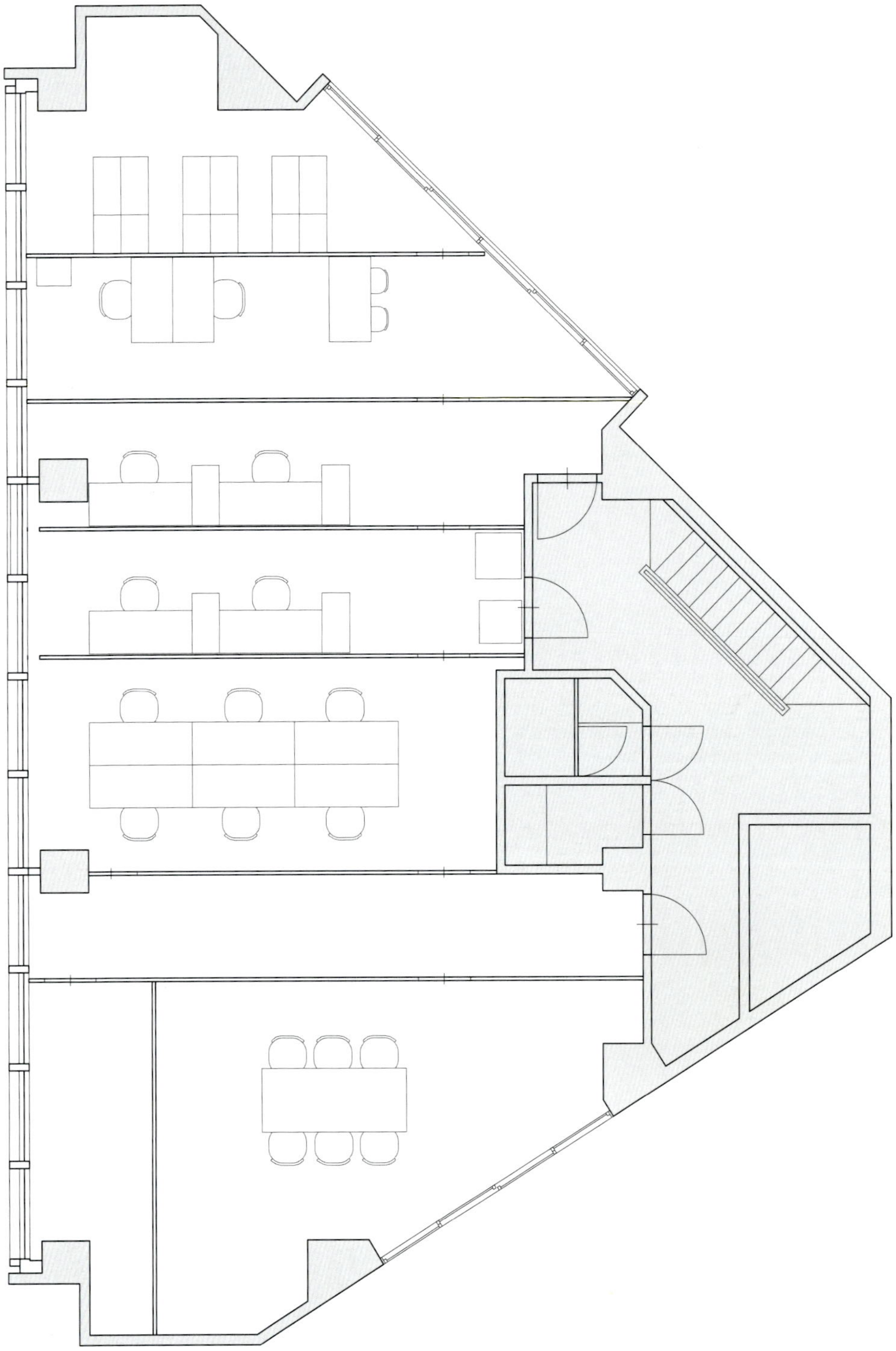

↓ → **Studio Spec** • Facet Studio

Three functions, two characters, one irregular office space: this demanding project cleverly integrates three separate programs – a graphic design studio, a graphic design school and a beauty consultation room – by creating spaces within the main space through the installation of two opposed wooden boxes.

1. Entry
2. Reception
3. Beauty consultant office
4. Graphic design studio
5. Server room
6. Kitchen
7. Class room 2
8. Work room
9. Class room 1

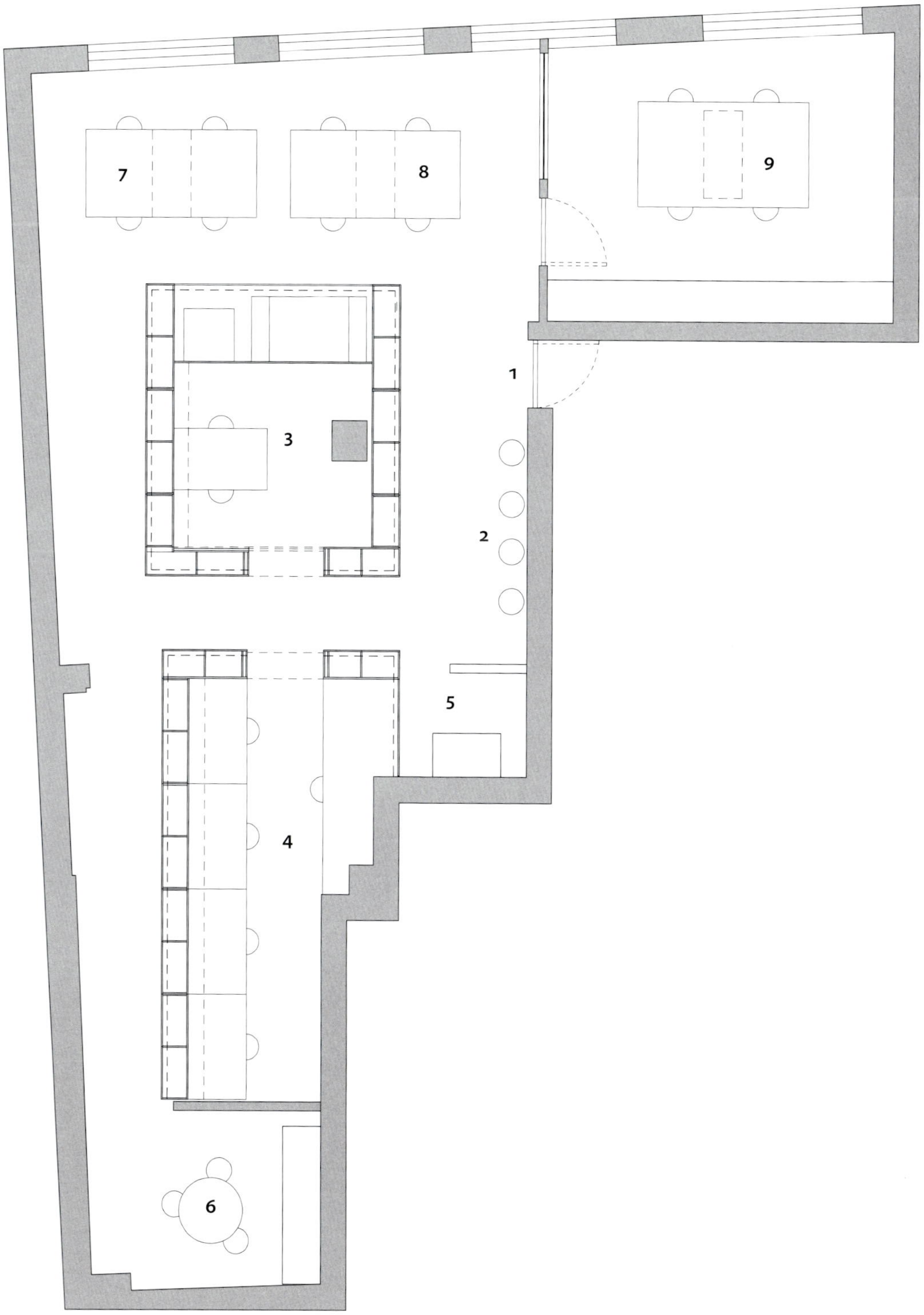

↓ → **Thin Office** • Studio SKLIM

The program brief was for an office space shared by two companies, an IT company and a multi-media setup. Located in a refurbished post-war building in Singapore's CBD outskirts, the space was long and narrow with split levels, offering the possibility of a raised space. Throughout the long and narrow office, the ceiling and wall conditions were left unaltered as much as possible, along with the existing light fixtures. The designed space was to reflect the ethos of the companies: flexibility, technology and creativity. The office space was loosely organised into eight clusters, namely: the Boss Boxes, Long Work Top, Discussion Table, Welcome Mat, Sanitary & Storage, Recharging Point, Twist Platform and Multi-media Corner. Each of these clusters was arranged around an open plan configuration, with the exception of Sanitary & Storage, to allow a multifarious overlap of working trajectories.

1. Multimedia corner
2. Twist platform
3. Recharging point
4. Welcome mat
5. Sanitary and storage
6. Long worktop
7. Discussion table
8. Boss boxes

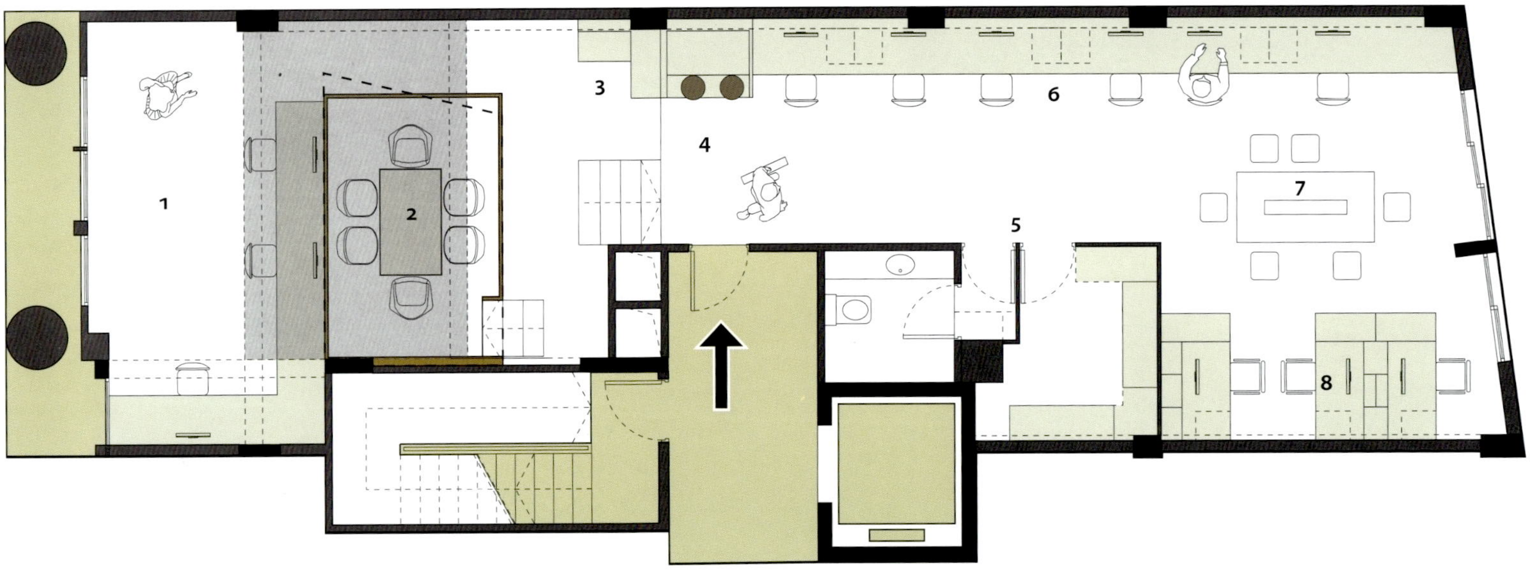

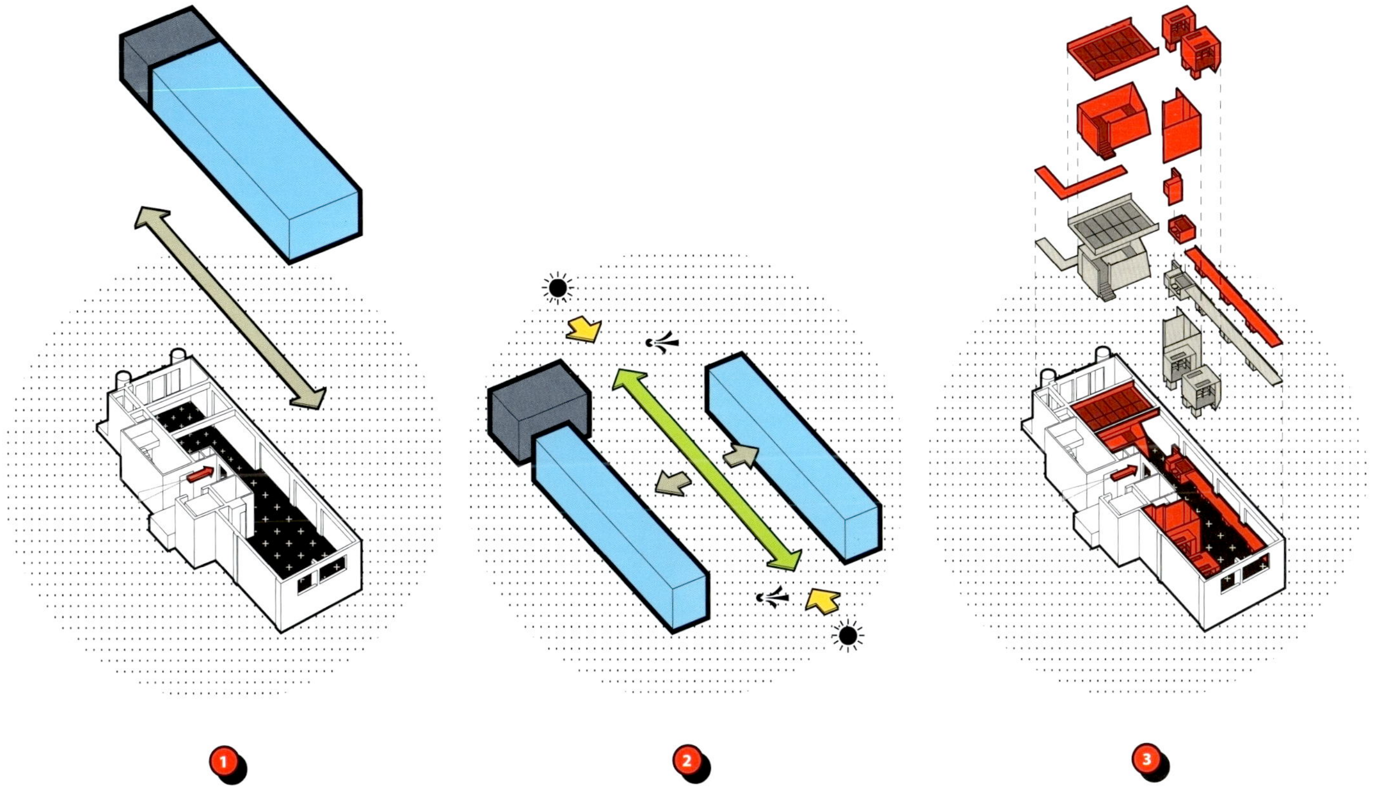
1
2
3

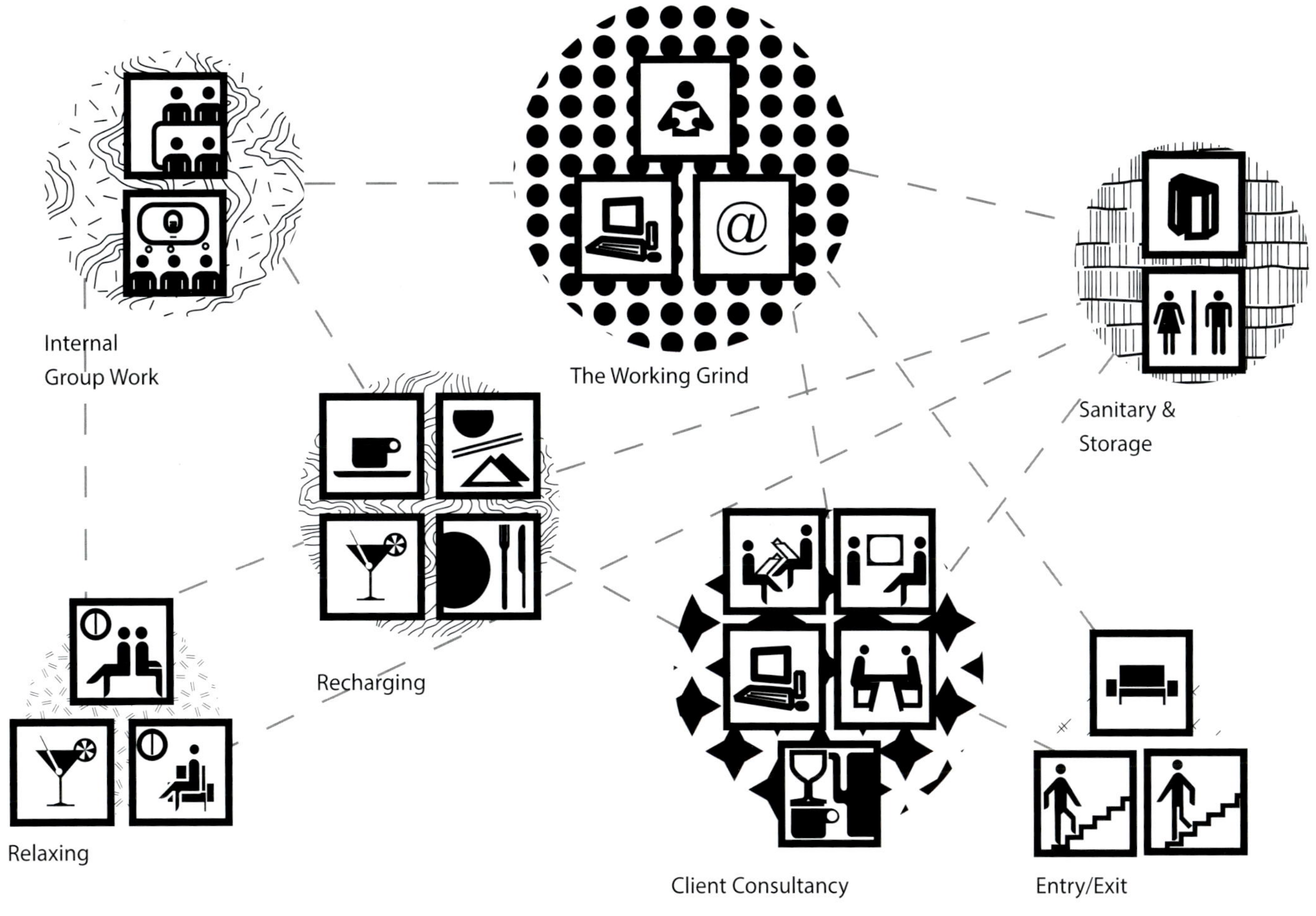
Internal
Group Work
The Working Grind
Sanitary &
Storage
Recharging
Relaxing
Client Consultancy
Entry/Exit

↓ → **Saegeling Medizintechnik** • GPAC

Based on the existing small scale building structures in the vicinity, the studio of GPAC designed an elegantly curved two-story building structure that despite is deliberately unique form fits harmoniously into the existing urban fabric. Two functional areas divide the building. To the south, the reception area or public space welcomes visitors and leads them through a two-storey lobby that doubles as an events space. Adjoining the area on the ground floor is a meeting room for clients, while a gallery is located on the upper floor. The internal functions are situated on the building's north side. Here, individual office space as well as a copy room and a generous open office area are integrated into the design.

1. Break room
2. Kitchen
3. Storage
4. Open office area
5. Customer area
6. Restroom
7. Wardrobe
8. Reception
9. Lobby
10. Entrance
11. Head of business
12. Accounting
13. Conference room
14. Gallery

Ground floor

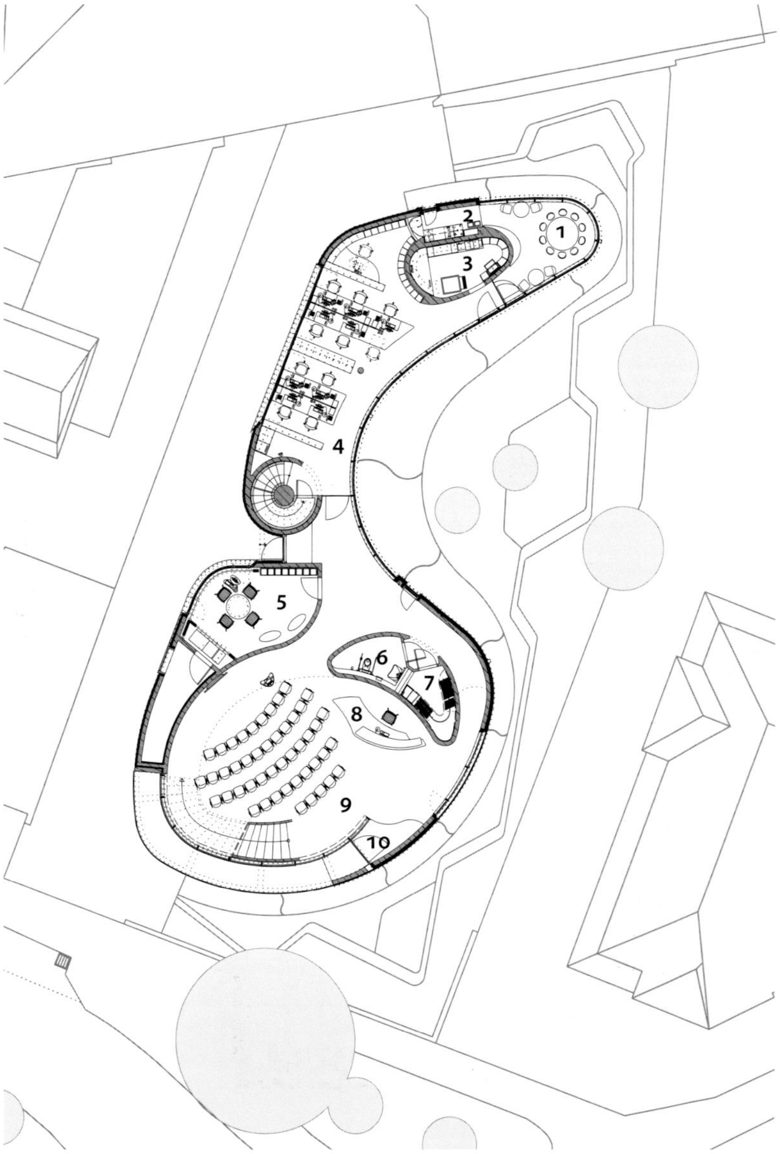

First floor

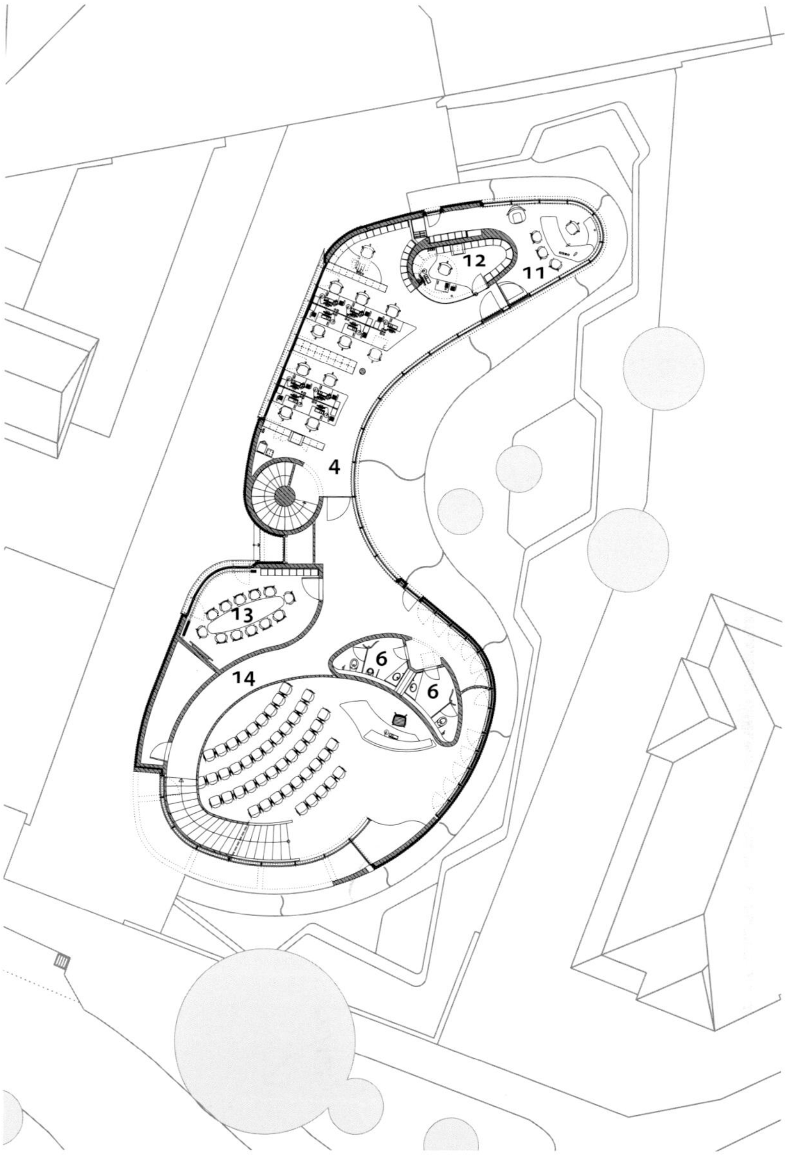

↓ → **Oktavilla** • Elding Oscarson

This design bureau for magazines and websites is housed in an old textile factory in the center of Stockholm. The client loved the bare, tall and bright spaces, but the building needed to be fully reformed to house the business. There was a mezzanine in the space, with a windowless meeting room underneath and a country style kitchen sprawling along the walls, all arranged in an L-shaped space. The client liked the uninterrupted row of windows, which he wanted to retain. But the program required a bigger meeting room with windows, an atelier table for informal meetings and more workstations, along with an entrance lobby and a small kitchen with a dining table. Dividing the space with a wall created a large and bright meeting room, as well as a clean rectangular room for the rest of the program. This large space is softly divided with a box containing service functions and a kitchen. By compressing the contents of the box and positioning it carefully, the program effortlessly falls into place without breaking the impression of a single large room.

Before

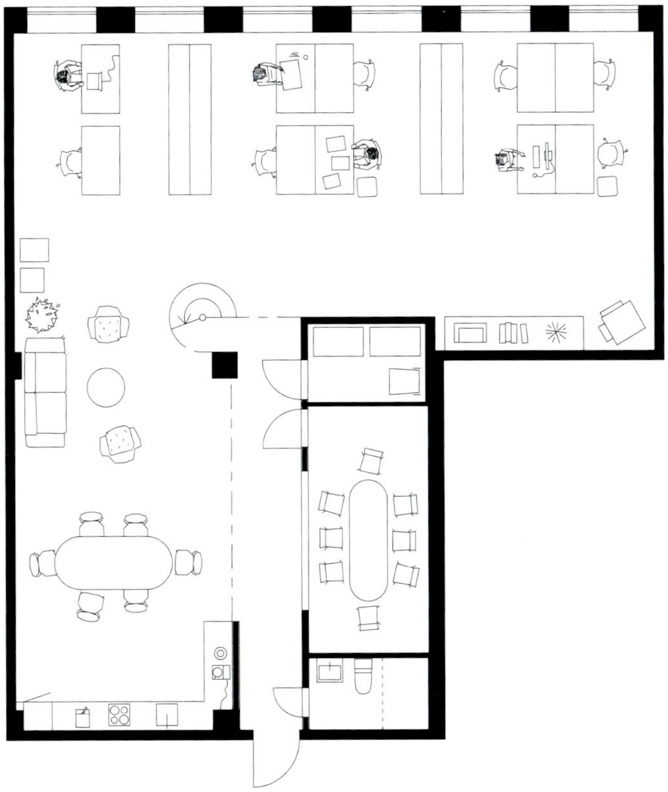

After

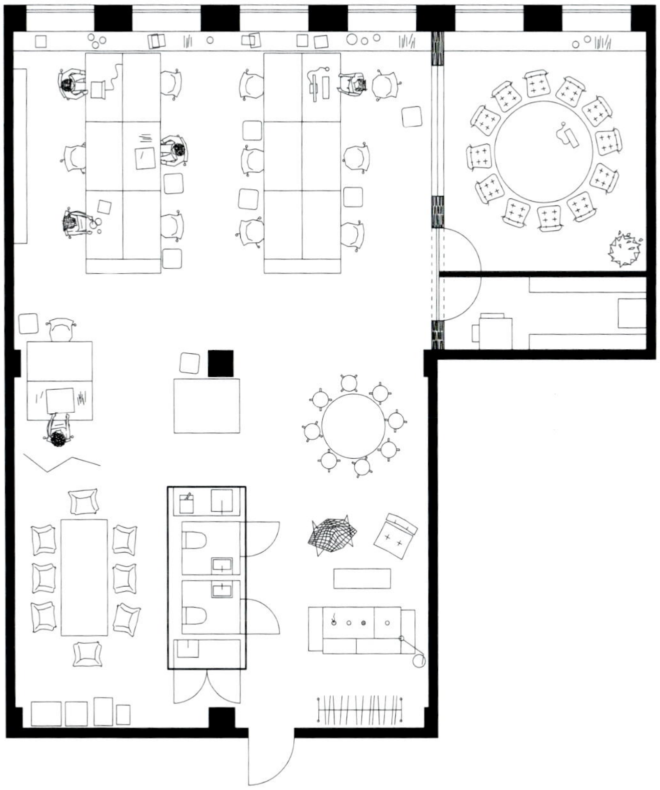

↓ → **Cargo** • Group 8

The offices are housed within a former industrial warehouse, close to the center of the city, and have been designed to take full advantage of the building's 8,395 sqft (780 sqm) of floor space and 30 ft (9 m) high ceilings.

The white and luminous warehouse space contains a hidden treasure: 16 recycled shipping containers, all of which have traveled thousands of miles around the globe. On a practical level, the use of containers represents a gain of 2,150 sqft (200 sqm), and makes excellent use of the ceiling height. Each container embodies a collective form or a work-related situation: meeting rooms, cafeteria, lounge zone, bathrooms and showers, etc.

The other half of the scheme is in opposition with the containers' structured zone: an open space enlightened by natural light that pours in through the glass-roof. This informal meeting space gathers all the employees together, thereby generating a strong sense of synergy in the workplace.

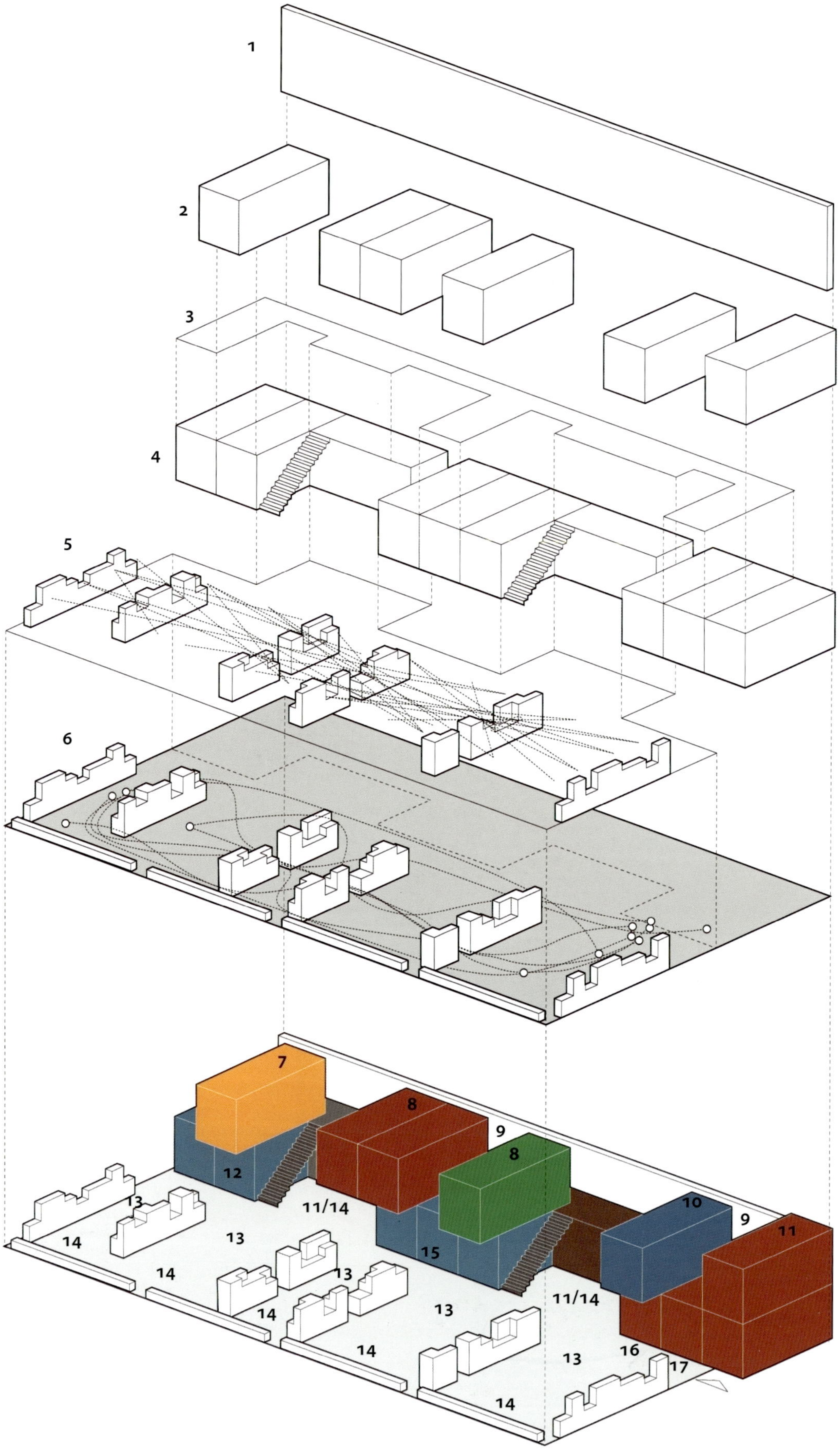

1. Storage
2. Containers 01
3. Informal interstice
4. Containers 00
5. Visual interactions
6. Physical connections
7. Brainstorm
8. Meet
9. Informal space
10. Eat
11. Relax
12. Model workshop
13. Teamwork
14. Informal meet
15. Videoconference
16. Info
17. Wait

↓ → **Ynno Workplace** • Sprikk

Since their consultants spend more time at their client's place of work than in their own office, YNNO asked for a workplace that functions as a home base rather than a conventional office. A working environment was created that suits the nature of the consultant's way of working in which communication and networking play a vital role. The floor plan is kept entirely open with the exception of two acoustically separated glass volumes. In this open plan, organically shaped birchwood structures were placed that form partitions, niches, storage spaces and bookshelves. The wood structures contain a number of ergonomic workplaces that embrace daylight and offer a view to the outside.

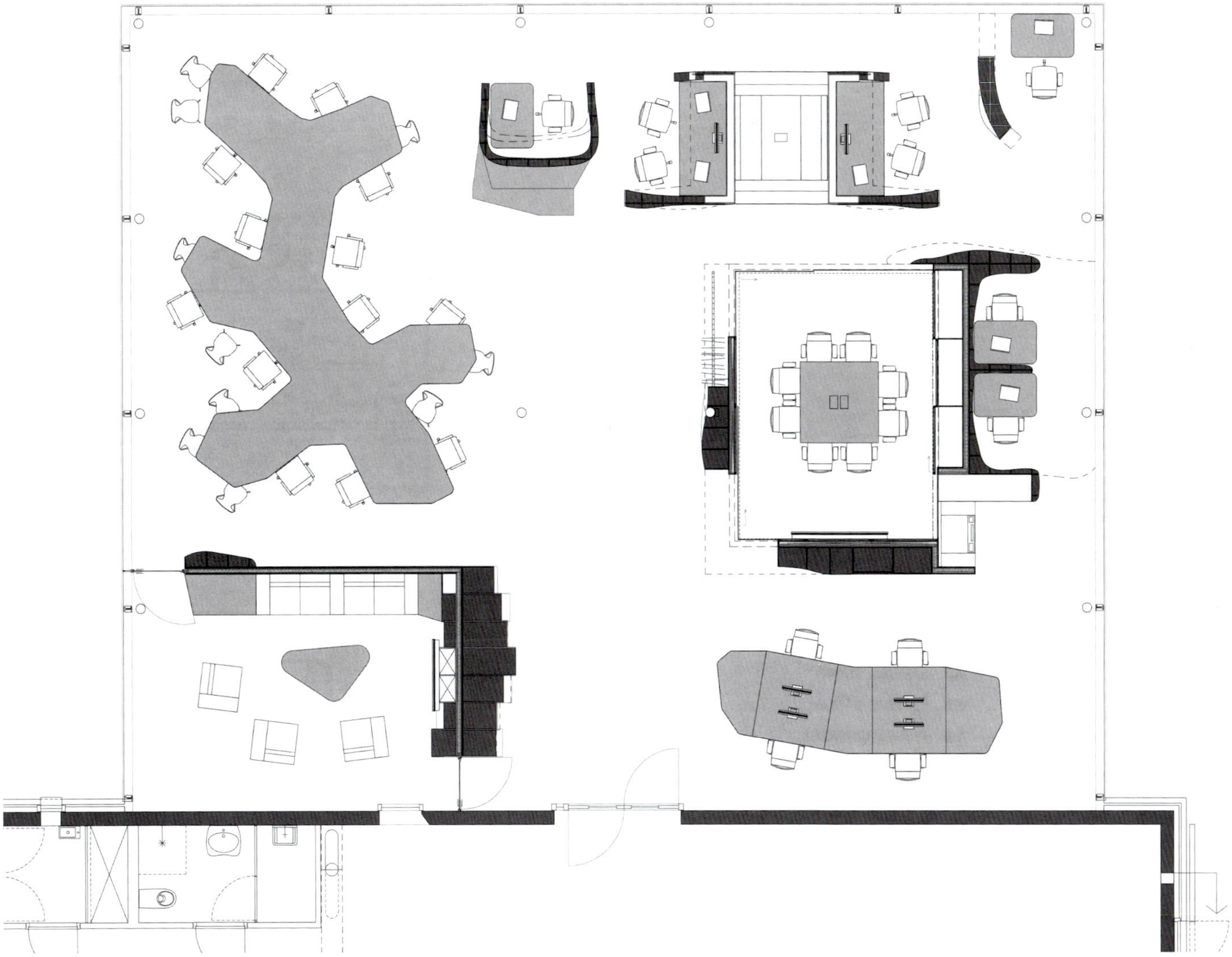

↓ → Z58 • Kengo Kuma & Associates

Zhongtai is one of the best known lighting design companies in China headed by Mr. Kepei Cheng, who commissioned Japanese architect, Kengo Kuma, to design a multipurpose building that integrated offices, a studio for lighting designers, and lodgings for overseas guests. The intention was to offer a "gentle and relaxed" response to the high speed and fast pace of Shanghai. The construction, which uses the pre existing three-story structure, can be seen as three filters that connect the building with the city: the huge atrium, the green-louver façade and the glass boxes on the top floor.

1. Fangyu Road
2. Main entranve
3. Reception
4. Pool/atrium
5. Elevator
6. Shop/showroom
7. Bar
8. Cafe
9. Sales lounge
10. Office/sales
11. Staff entrance
12. Zongtai office
13. Storage
14. Bath/staff
15. Void/atrium
16. EV bridge
17. Design room
18. Private office
19. Meeting room
20. Coat
21. Pantry
22. Pool
23. Guest room
24. Water lounge
25. Lounge/library
26. Bath
27. Sauna
28. Fitness
29. Kitchen

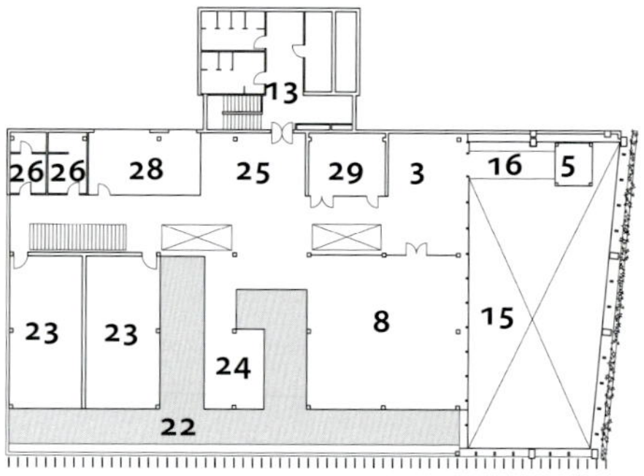

Third floor

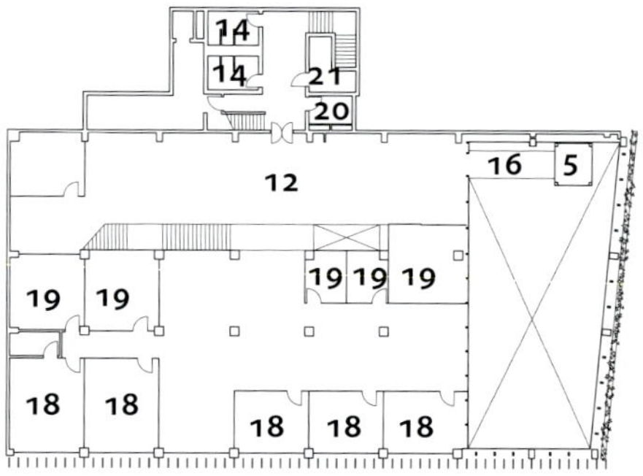

Second floor

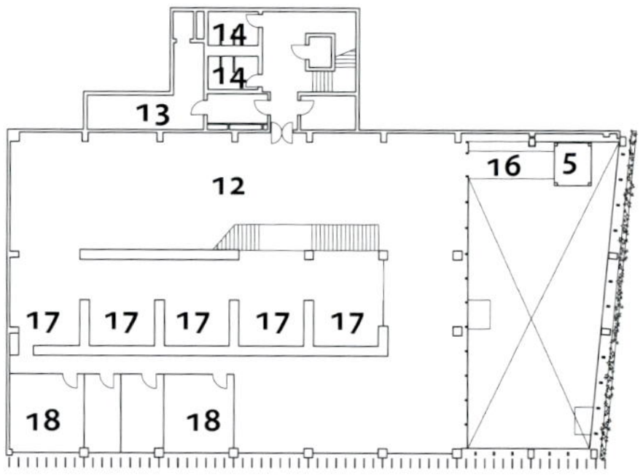

First floor

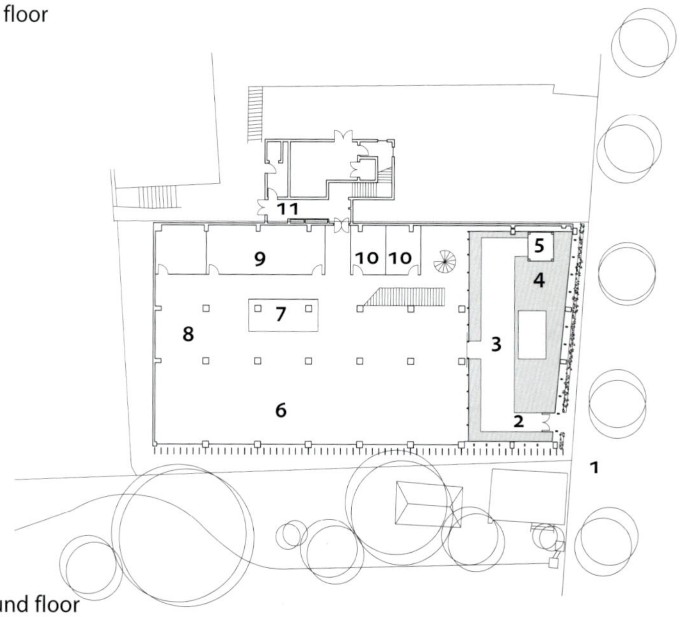

Ground floor

↓ → Pack Line Headquarters • Lea Katz architecturearchitects

The design premise for the headquarters demanded flexibility in its spatial organization, since the activities held within it change on a regular basis.
The total area of the original space was not quite enough to accommodate Pack Line's requirements, so 180 sqm (2000 sqft) of loading bay were added as well as an entrance area, 40 sqm (430 sqft) of connection space between the two buildings and a gallery space inside the shed. All the redundant walls and beams were removed and reorganized to accommodate the company's production process.

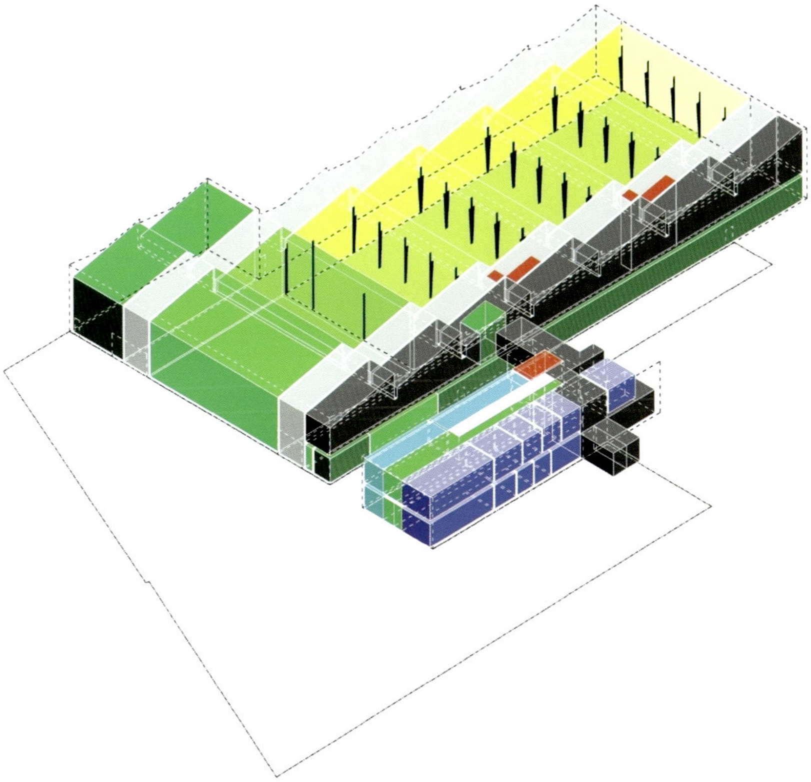

- Production storage
- Production offices
- Assembly area
- Production circulation
- Vertical circulation
- Open plan offices
- Private offices
- Public circulation
- Office service area
- Water area

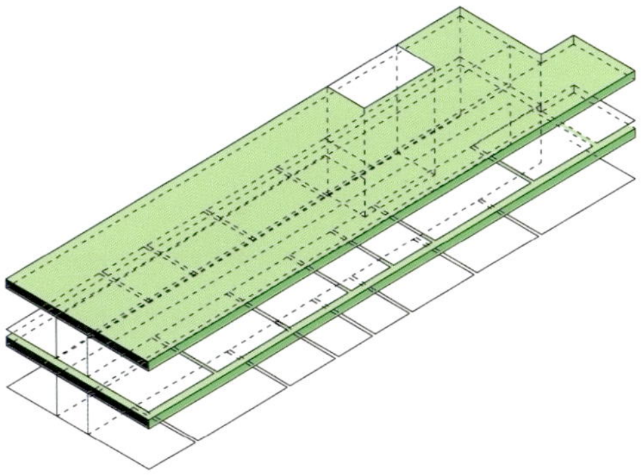

Original state, where the services occupy the 50 cm of the ceiling height

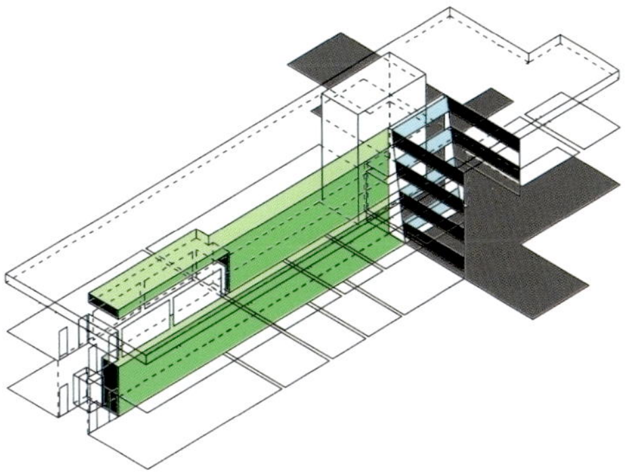

Concentrating the services in the central spine

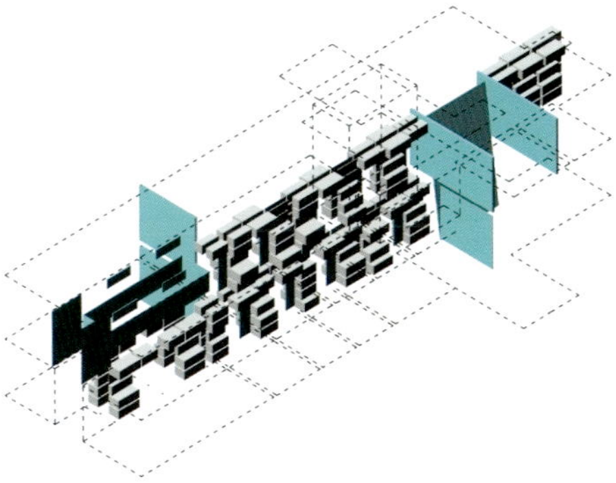

The final geometry and organization of the service wall

↓ → **Prayer Rahs** • SUE Architekten

Two notaries joined forces and founded a new office in Vienna with the desire to bring a fresh and contemporary feel to their workplace. The plan for the office was honed in numerous meetings with the clients, the goal being a workplace that not only creates a communicative climate, but also enables concentrated and uninterrupted work. The result is a layering of the office structure that maximises the potential of the location: at first a friendly entrance area to receive clients, followed by a general office and working area to provide an intimate and concentrated, while still relaxed, communicative atmosphere. The focus in the central working area is on communication between staff. Stretched storage furniture separates the working area from the hall and communication zone. On one side there are generous cubicles and a meeting room, on the other side of the hall are seating niches, space for photocopiers and a common working area that is shaped by storage furniture. Small windows from the hall allow glimpses into the working areas. The other side of the hall leads to further individual offices.

↓ → TBWA \ HAKUHODO • Klein Dytham architecture

TBWA is a global advertising agency that joined forces with Hakuhodo, one of Japan's largest advertising firms, to establish a Tokyo-based joint venture. The design of TBWA \ Hakuhodo's Tokyo HQ was the result of a three-way collaboration between the two agencies and the Tokyo-based firm of architecture and design KDa.

The search throughout Tokyo for a new space led to a disused bowling alley in a large, eight-storey amusement complex in downtown Tokyo, which was still in daily use. A golf driving-range and another bowling alley were operating on the upper and lower floors, but a whole floor in the middle of the building was being used as a warehouse. When the existing ceiling was removed the bowling alley became a double-height space, and the 2 m (6.5 ft) beams that span the full width of the floor were revealed. As a column-free space, the bowling alley allowed complete freedom in laying out the office. The powerful rhythm of the beams suggested arranging the desks and circulation zones in a pattern that re-established the original dynamic of the bowling lanes. The wide-open space, however, inspired KDa to imagine the office as a park, so they filled it with fun "landscape" elements. The park combines both real and fake greenery – living plants and green shag-pile carpet.

Scattered across the floor are a series of shelters that serve as meeting rooms, project rooms, and director's offices. The shelters subtly divide the space occupied by the office's 340 staff into intimate neighborhoods connected by narrow lanes.

PLAN

↓ → **The Power House** • Cannon Design

After standing vacant for nearly 30 years, the St. Louis Municipal Power House building in downtown St. Louis opened as the new regional offices of Cannon Design in September 2008. Although the building's exterior shell and original steel structure were fundamentally sound, reuse for a large architecture and engineering practice required a creative spatial solution that exploited the building's massive volume. Two new floor plates have been inserted inside the tall volume, thereby creating two extra floors and ample collaborative meeting space and workspaces for approximately 120 employees. The floor plates are separated from the external walls on two sides to preserve the full height of the arched windows on the north and east elevations, generating a partially full height gallery and exhibition space on the ground floor for use by the firm and the larger community. An elevator shaft, kitchenettes on each floor and two staircases have been inserted against the back wall in the northwest and southwest corners of the building. A model shop and materials library plus a boardroom have been excavated in the basement. On the roof, an oblong structure originally used to store coal conveyor equipment now houses another boardroom and staff lunchroom.

Ground floor

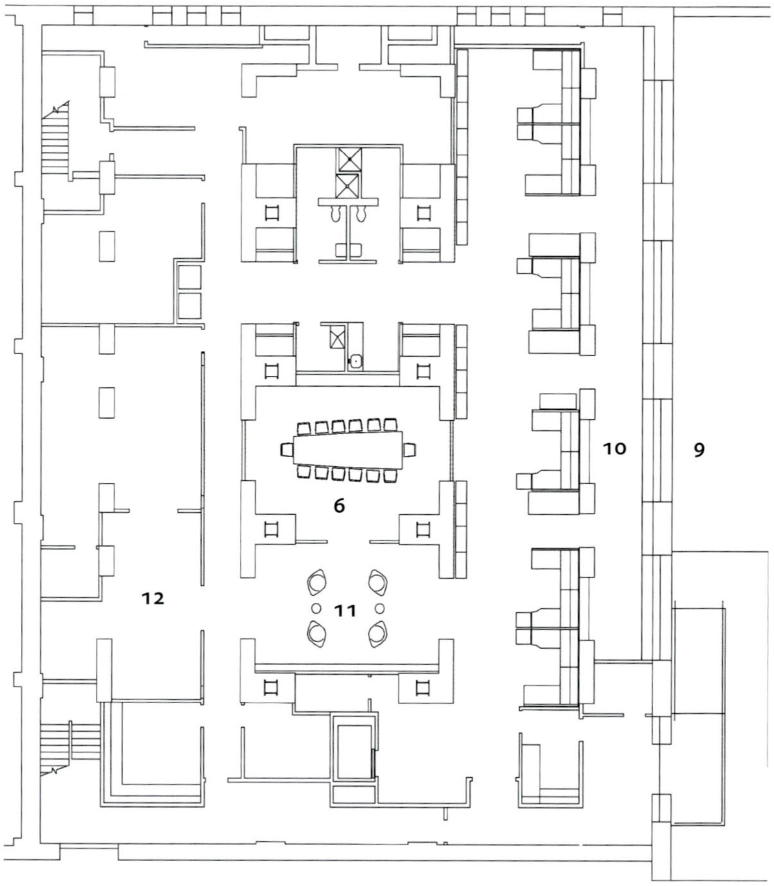

First floor

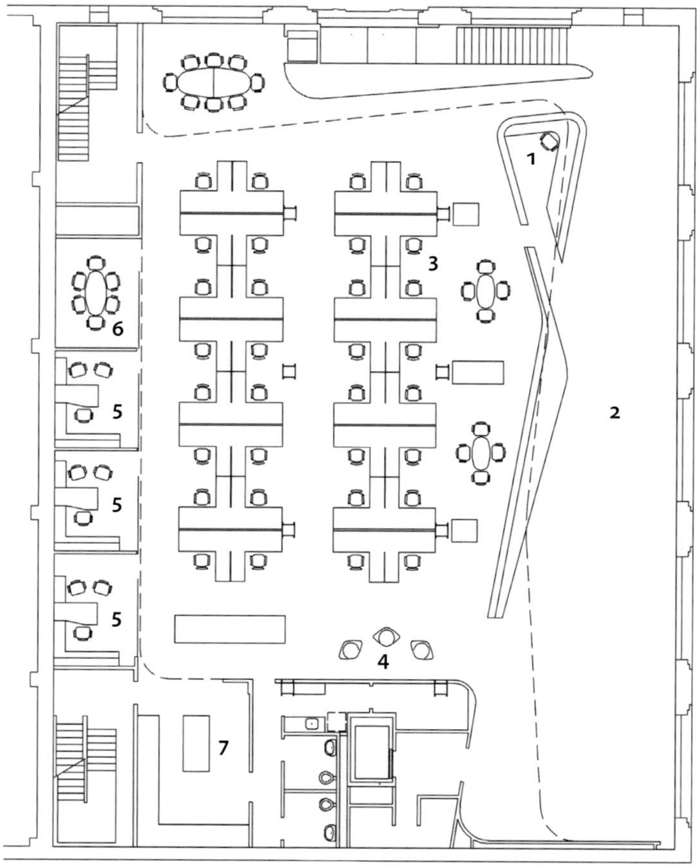

1. Reception
2. Gallery
3. Open office
4. Open team space
5. Crit space
6. Office
7. Conference
8. Open to gallery below
9. Garden
10. Materials library
11. Design library
12. Model shop

Second floor

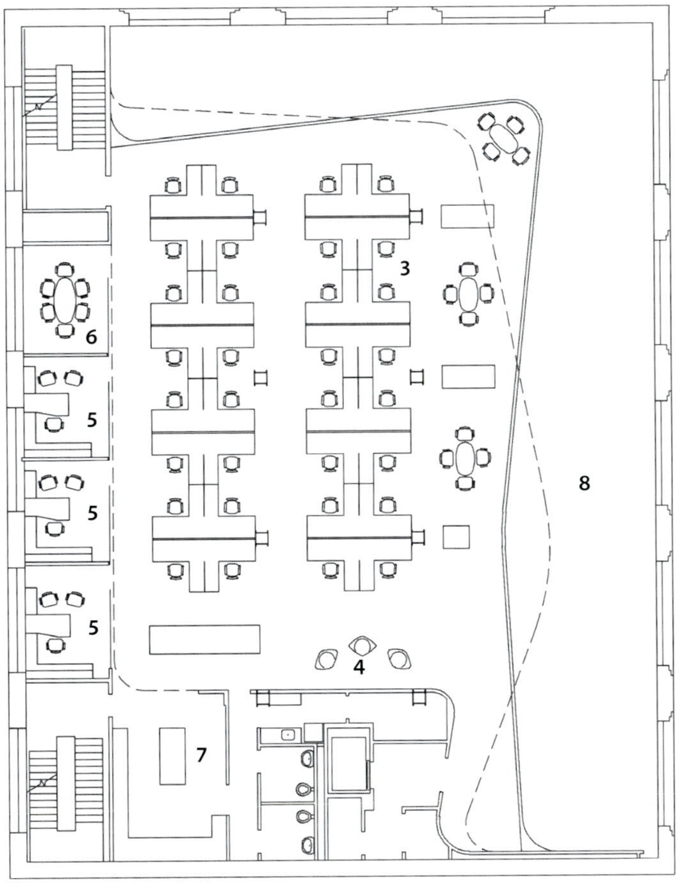

Third floor

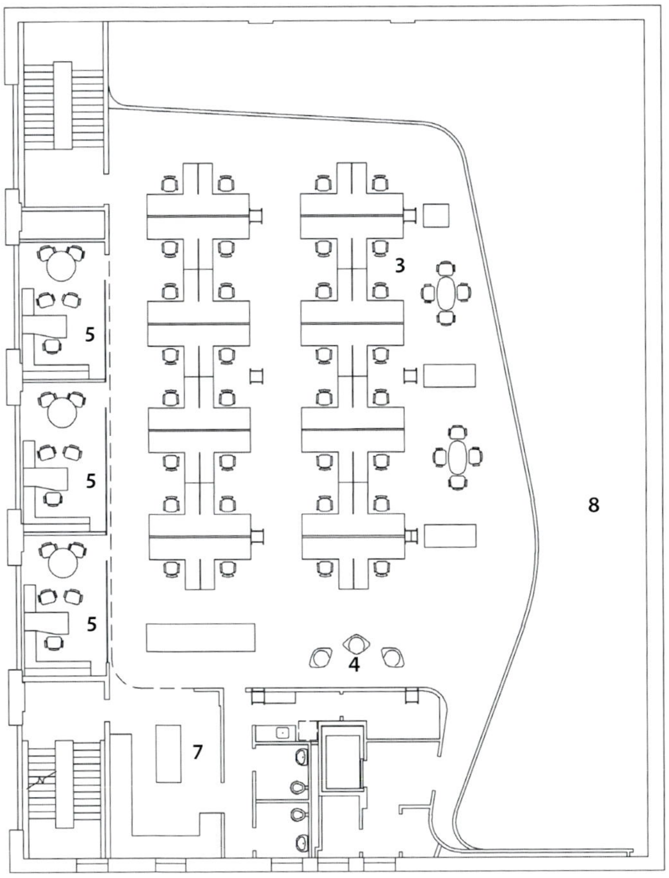

↓ → United Business Media • Gensler

The angular floor plate presented challenges in plan. The designers decided to use the odd geometry to UBM's benefit – workstations are placed in the more regular, rectilinear areas of the plan, while meeting rooms and collaborative spaces take advantage of the plan's triangular oddities. The designers met the challenge of achieving a 75 sqft (7 sqm) per person metric by providing a completely open office environment that is complemented by gathering, amenity and meeting spaces.

1. Meeting garden
2. Conversation pit
3. Town hall
4. Storage
5. Reception
6. Elevator lobby
7. Chat box
8. Phone room
9. Copier alcove
10. Eat
11. Informal teaming area
12. Pantry
13. Support area

↓ → **Nije Gritenije** • FLATarchitects

The Nije Gritenije foundation is a Rabobank initiative to stimulate local and regional entrepreneurship. The foundation asked Amsterdam based FLATarchitects to design twenty workstations and a conference room on the ninth and tenth floors of the brand new Rabobank building. Four of the workstations were to be used by the permanent staff of the foundation while the remaining sixteen were to accomodate a continuously changing group of start-up entrepreneurs and artists. FLATarchitects devised a simple interior design which could be customized and completed by the users so that they could adapt their space to their specific needs. In this way temporary users are able to appropriate their place of work in a relatively short period of time. Also, the interior is designed to encourage innovation and discussion among users and visitors. The stairs to the ninth floor end in an entrance space configured by four irregularly shaped objects. Together they form a 'porous wall', filtering views of and sounds from the workspace beyond. From the entrance space the stairs lead on to the conference and presentation room on the tenth floor.

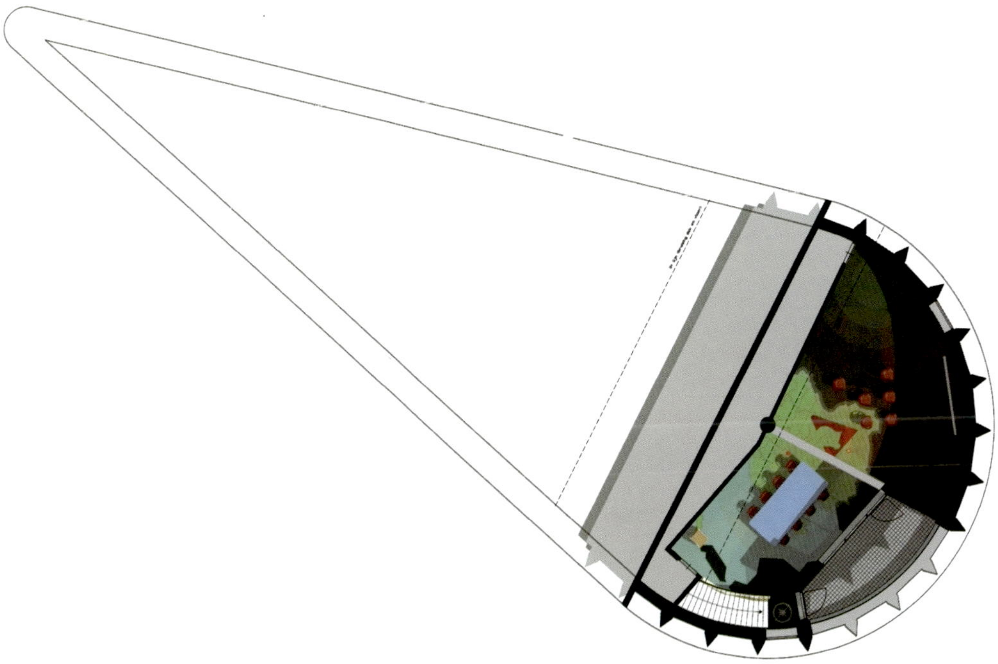

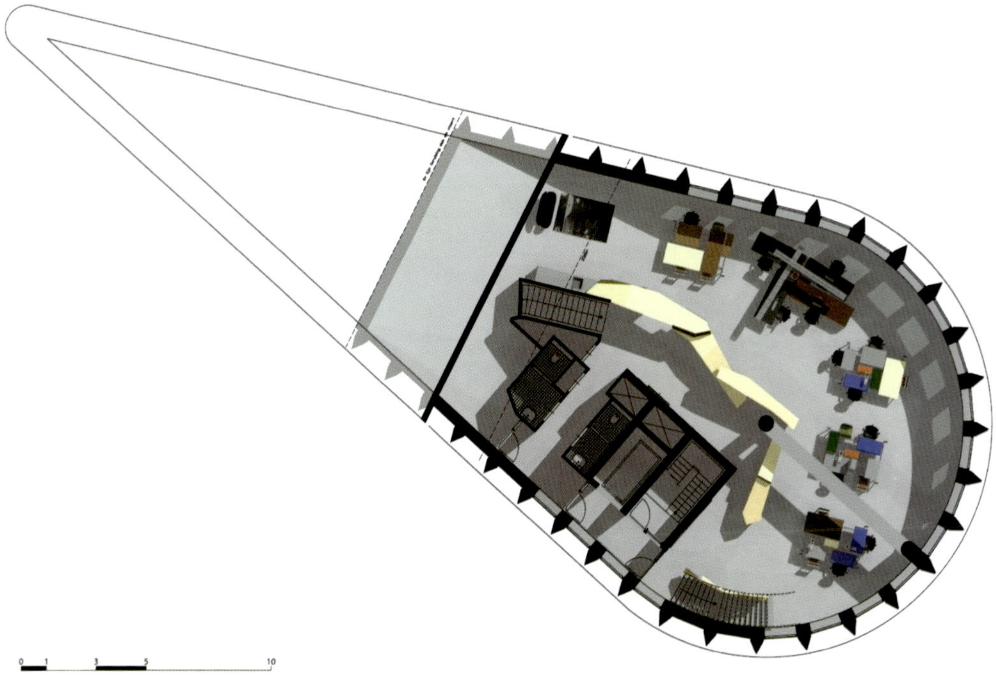

↓ → Toolbox • Caterina Tiazzoldi

From a functional point of view, the project consists of the creation of an open space with 44 individual workstations combined with other services and activities. The goal has been to keep the modular concrete structure unaltered. The main span of the building has been divided lengthwise by a series of 'filter volumes' used as technical spaces for storing lockers and equipment. On one side there is the co-working space, on the other side the corridors and the functional 'box' containing shared facilities such as meeting rooms, print rooms, informal meeting spaces, mailboxes, a patio and a kitchen.

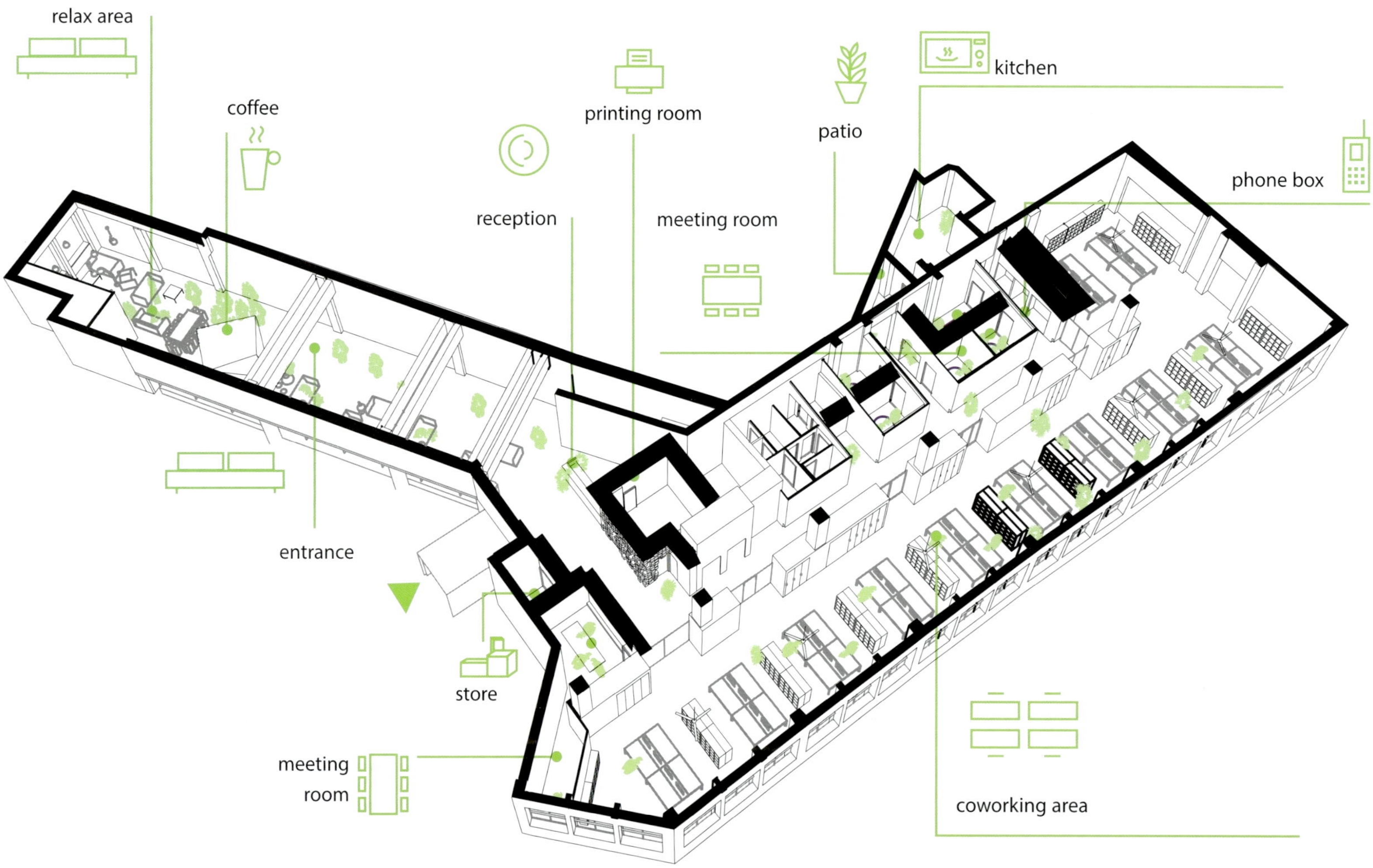

↓ → **Yuras** • Sinato

New rooms were constructed in the middle of the floor plan for this office without touching or modifying in any way the existing floor, walls or ceiling including the lights and the air conditioners. The new rooms were required to be closed, intimate spaces because of the purposes they would serve. The upper part of the partitions that separates the rooms was therefore bent so that the section form of each room might taper off as it rises. Openings in these walls allow natural light to enter the interior and offer a connection with the surrounding office space, avoiding any sense of claustrophobia. The bending form of these new offices, which is designed to affect the inside of the rooms, also has a direct consequence on the form as seen from the exterior. An outward appearance similar to a connection of gabled cabins or a mountain range appears by placing the aforementioned section form side by side. In addition, this symbolic mountain range mass is arranged diagonally and becomes a thick partition which divides the site into work space and common space.

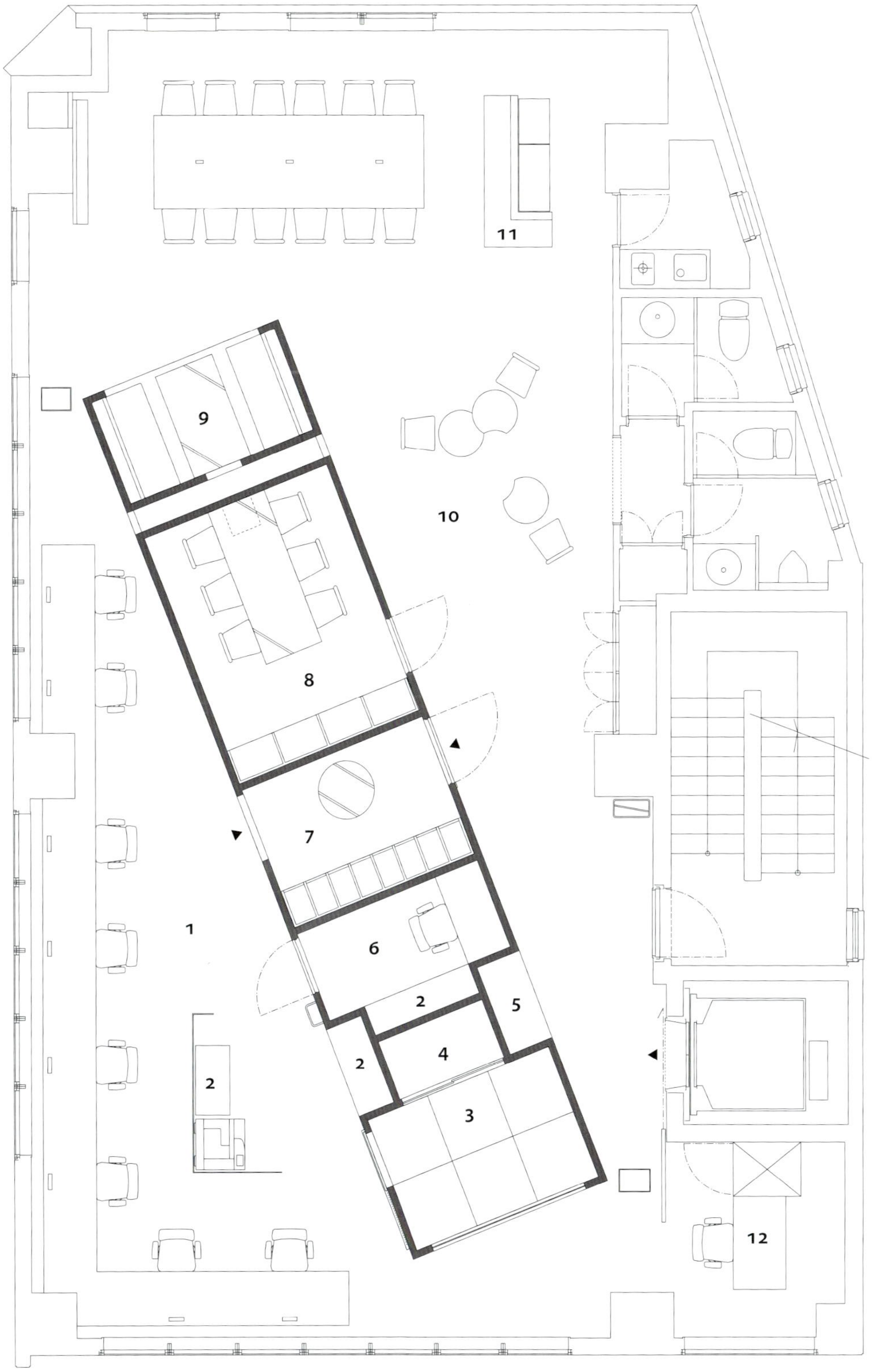

1. Work space
2. Shelf
3. Meditation room
4. Storage
5. Reception counter
6. Concentrated work room
7. Hall
8. Meeting space
9. Sofa
10. Common space
11. Counter
12. Server room

RA-DA architects decided to approach the design from a practical and minimal perspective. The Bugaboo "strollers" are characterized by a simple no-fuss form and an intentional use of color. It was decided to use the work-area as a backdrop to the product so that the strollers would be the primary elements activating the space. This was achieved by keeping the layout simple and making most of the space white: white floors, white desks, white light fixtures, mimicking a photographer's product backdrop. The strollers are set on platforms that bookend each row of desks, for easy viewing and reference. Rather than separating the departments, the desks were organized around internally-lit, partial height walls so that employees would have some sense of privacy, but also be able to have visual access throughout the entire office and communicate readily with other departments.

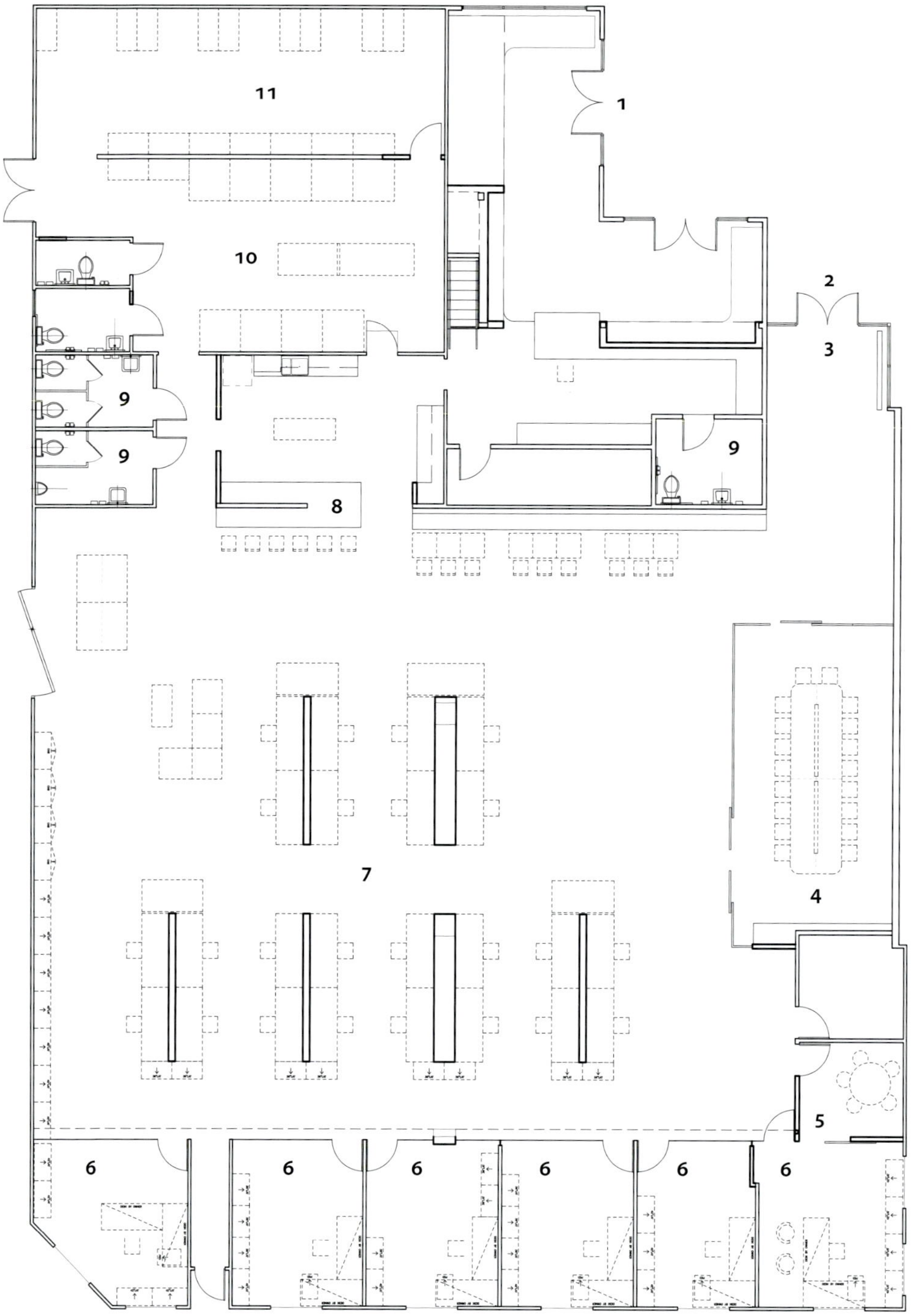

1. Entrance - retail / showroom
2. Entrance - office/workspace
3. Lobby and reception
4. Conference room
5. Small meeting room
6. Office
7. Main workspace
8. Café / bar
9. Restroom
10. Outlet center
11. Storage
12. Showroom
13. Stairs

PLAN

↓ → Forum 3, Novartis •
Diener & Diener Architekten

In total there are five floors of open office landscape for approximately 400 employees. On the north and south sides, walkable loggias were integrated into the façade, while to the west, a winter garden that contains many exotic plants rises up four stories. The entirety of one of the building's façades overhangs the area that provides the main access to the building.

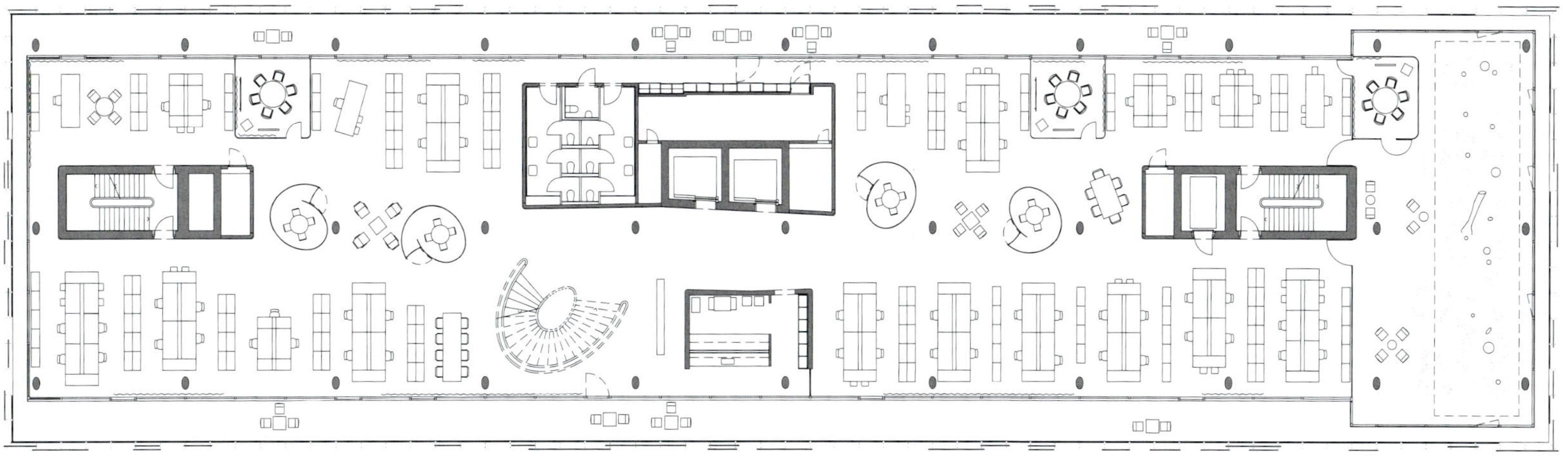

First floor

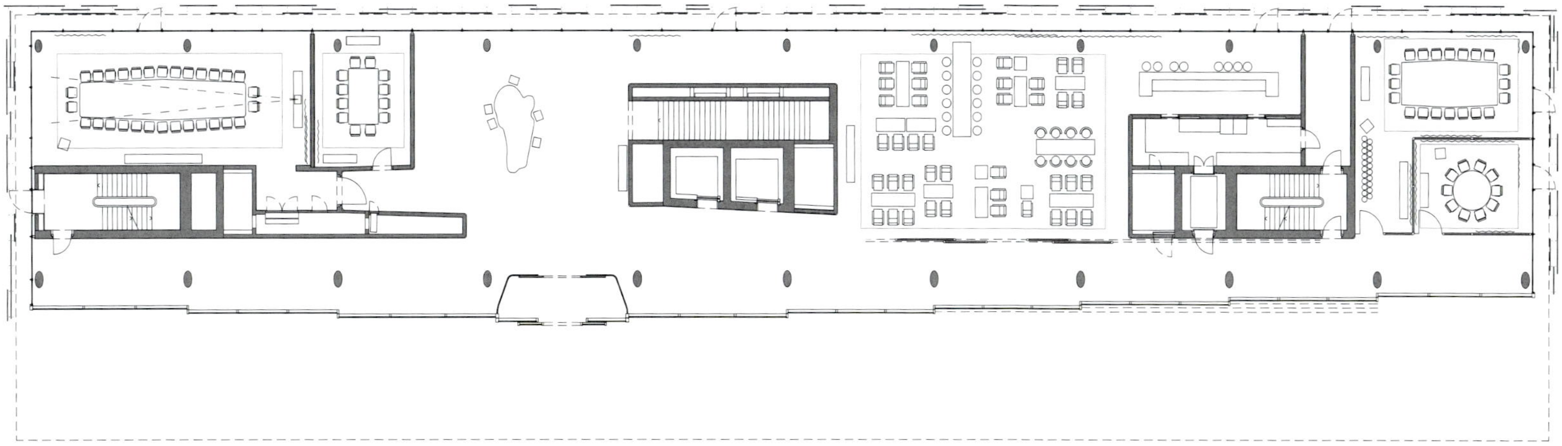

Ground floor

↓ → Media House • Bates Smart Architects

Entering the building, the café lies to the left and The Age Gallery to the right. A 100-seat auditorium allows for both public and internal meetings, live presentations and debates.
The workplace has been designed with an open plan layout to favor teamwork. The workspace design ensures a high degree of equity, with all work points separated from the windows – nobody 'owns' the windows. Workflows formed the basis for the design solution including the unique arrangement of the News Desk of the future, where the design reflects the deadline-focused critical information flows within the news team. Desks arranged in concentric circles focus on a central meeting table from where the management of the news can be orchestrated.

1. Piazza lawn
2. Outdoor seating
3. Waiting area
4. Café and servery
5. Reception
6. Lift lobby
7. Security
8. Auditorium
9. Mail room
10. Store
11. Facility management
12. Kitchen
13. Entry
14. The Age Gallery
15. Training room
16. Photographic studio
17. Quiet room
18. Open plan work area
19. News desk
20. Multimedia studio

Ground floor

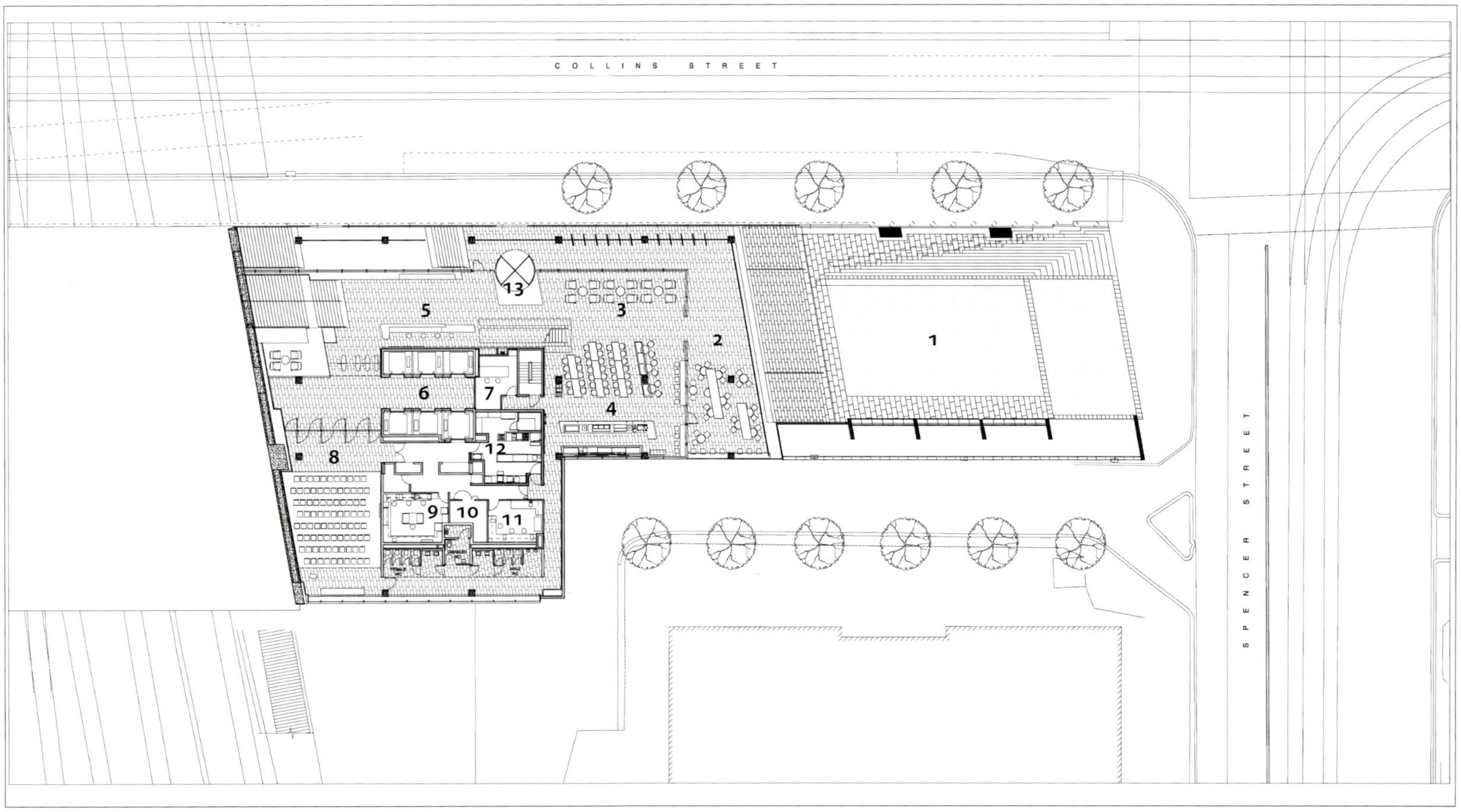

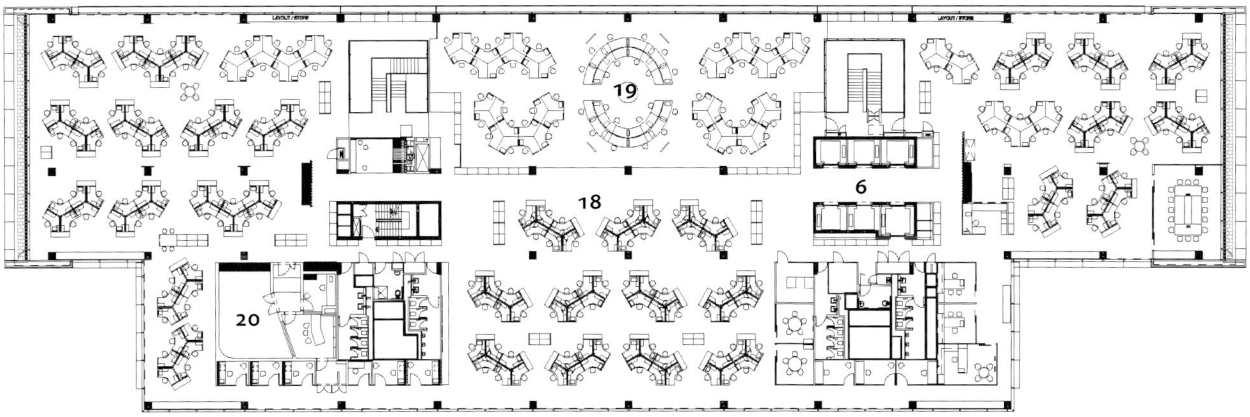

Second floor

First floor

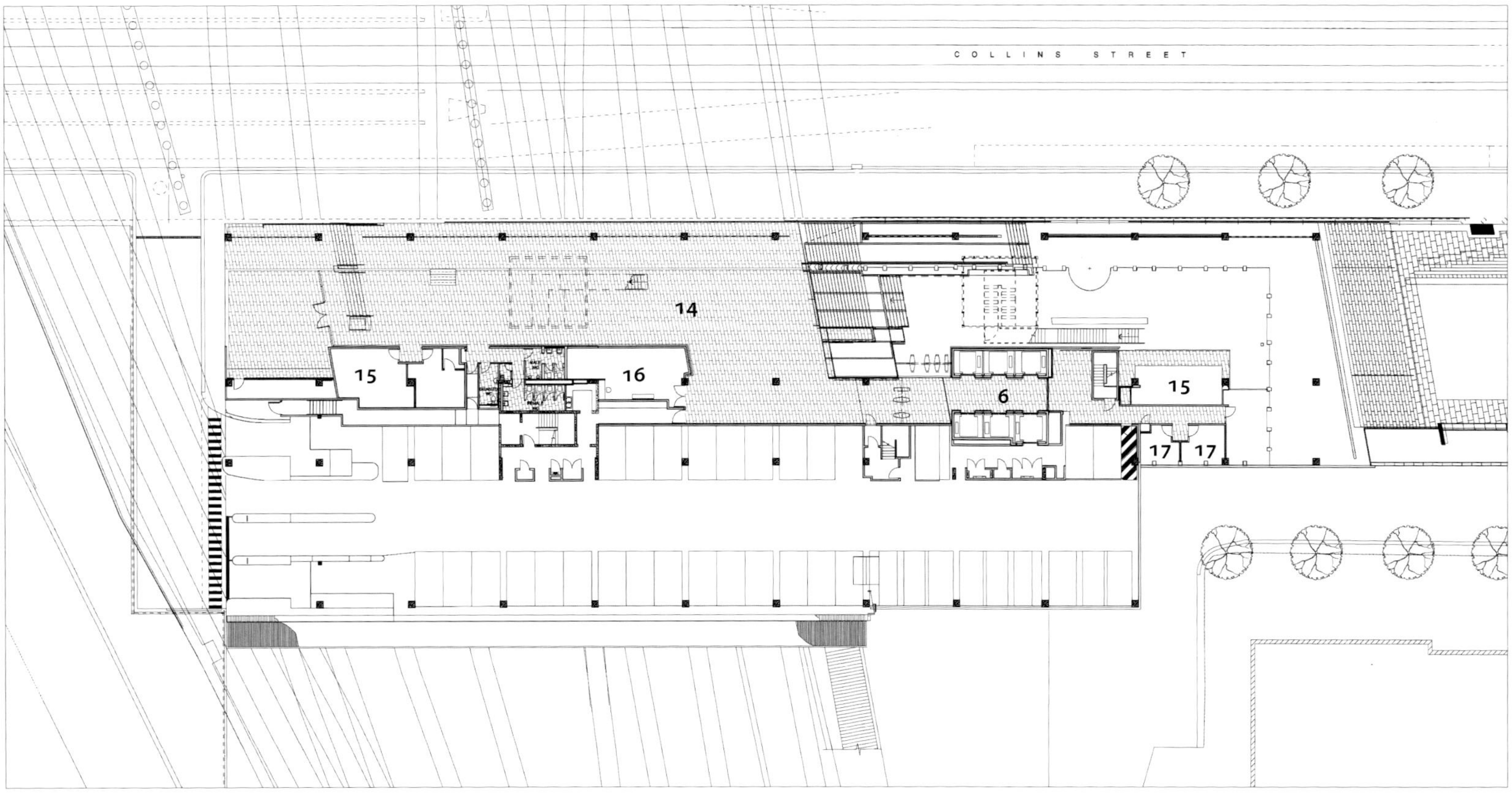

↓ → **Ericsson** • DEGW

The client's brief defined the Ericsson Experience Center (EEC) as a flexible space designed to experience new facilities and solutions that anticipate the future of telecommunications. To resolve the project a curved sign was inserted to organize and integrate the various functions it is required to contain. The ease with which this can be reconfigured will guarantee more comfortable uses of the space for the various activities likely to take place there.

The determining position of the sanitary area and the length of the available space suggested its division into two zones: Reception area/ open lounge and demo and exhibition area.

Located on opposite sides of the sanitary facilities, both zones are conceived as multiple use areas. When there are no visitors, the reception area can also be used by the Ericsson personnel for their breaks. The Demo area is divided into 4 zones, each dedicated to a particular theme, though it can also be used as an auditorium or TV studio. One side of the space is characterized by the "Memory wall", where glazed niches display historic Ericsson products.

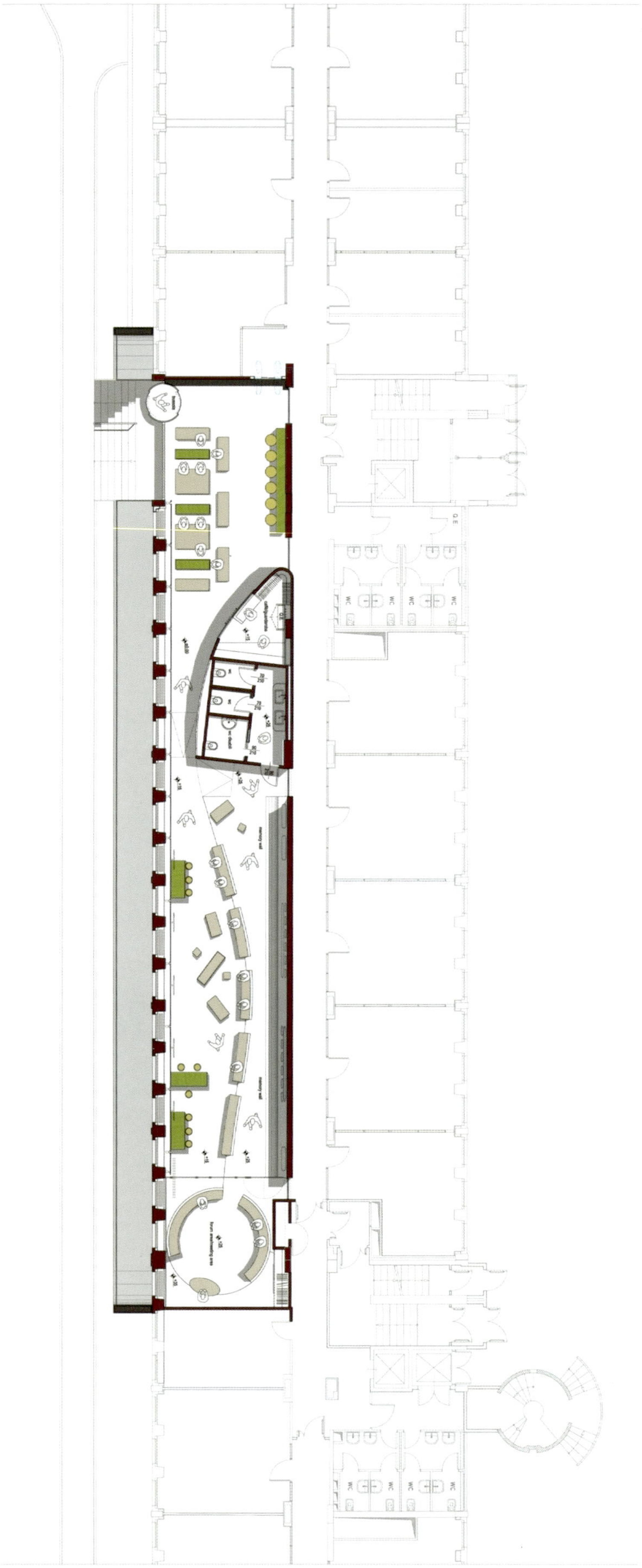

↓ → **Ecomplexx** • xarchitekten

Terms and concepts that vertebrate how the Ecomplexx network functions such as "Plug in" or "Backbone" were to play an important role in the company's future architecture to support and develop its own identity. No changes were made that would affect the attractive windows in order to retain the impressive generosity of the "loft feeling". The corridor and operating space follow a façade that is suffused with light. The concept of the central "Backbone" tries to focus all the changes into this connecting core area which has the potential for many different uses. Numerous workstations are connected to the "Backbone", which creates an open and communicative office structure.

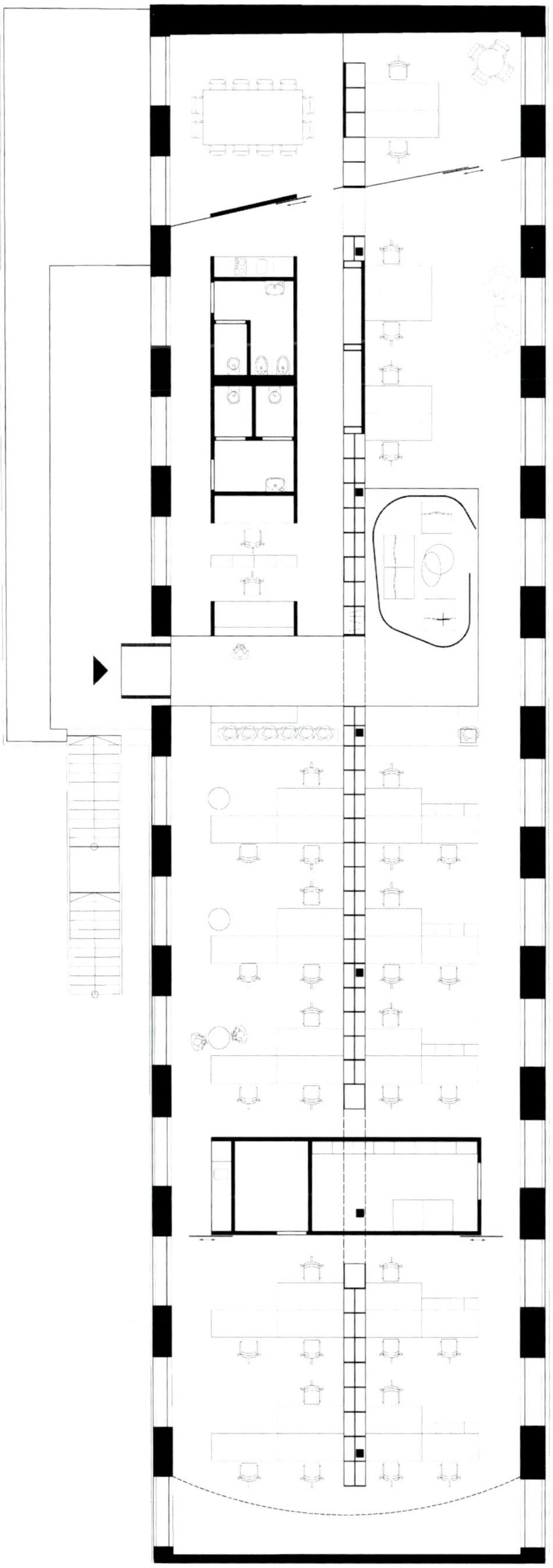

↓ → **Torre Cube** • Carme Pinós

The project for this striking office tower, situated on a 2520 sqm (27 125 sqft) site was born from the desire to create a building whose workspaces are all ventilated and lit naturally. Furthermore, given Guadalajara's good climate, another of the aims deriving from the possibility of having natural ventilation in all the offices is to dispense with the air-conditioning, thus reducing energy costs as well as improving the air quality in the workspaces. Given the exclusiveness of the area where the tower stands and the consequent competition to rent its offices, one of the requirements asked for by the clients was the creation of a singular building. This singularity is reflected in the spatial characteristics in the tower's interior, but is also evident from the particular volumetry generated by the construction's upward development and from the combination of materials used for the façade. The tower's exterior texture is characterized above all by a wooden lattice skin with sliding doors that acts as a brise-soleil.

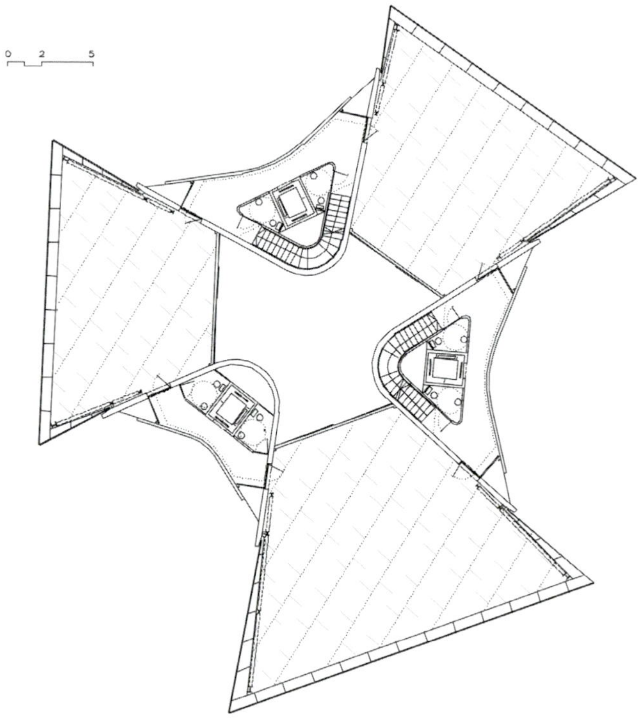

↓ → Banc Sabadell • Bach arquitectes – Jaume Bach, Eugeni Bach

In accordance with the law and the program requirements, the project proposed a building divided in two parts. One part composed of a warehouse, with access from the northeastern part of the site, which, if it were needed, could function independently from the rest of the building. The distance between the building and the limits of the site allows for loading, unloading and maneuvering lorries. Its shape is rectangular, with the exception of the western end, which traces a semi-circle that follows on to the rest of the building and adapts to the site's geometry. This warehouse has four mezzanines on the loading / unloading façade to facilitate the control, entry and dispatch of goods and to locate the space necessary for administration. Running parallel to the warehouse is the office building. This have no pre-established interior layout with the exception of the stairs, the hallway and the installations, which form compact spaces in the central part and on the northeastern façade of the offices. Between the volumes of the warehouse and the office building is an access road located at basement level, giving access to the car parks, also at this level as well as two other underground levels. The road passes below four bridges that join the two parts of the building at ground floor level.

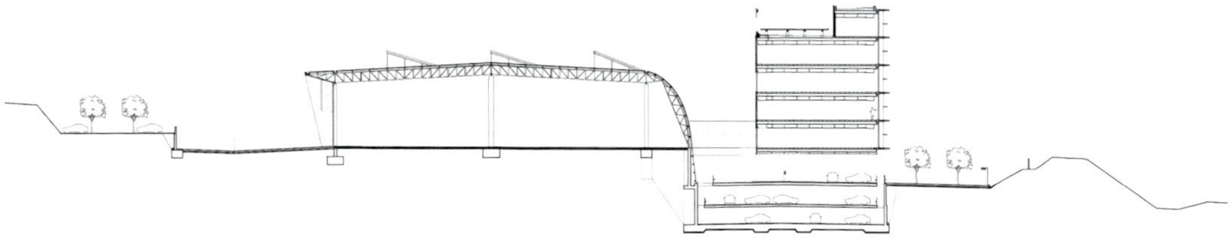

Section

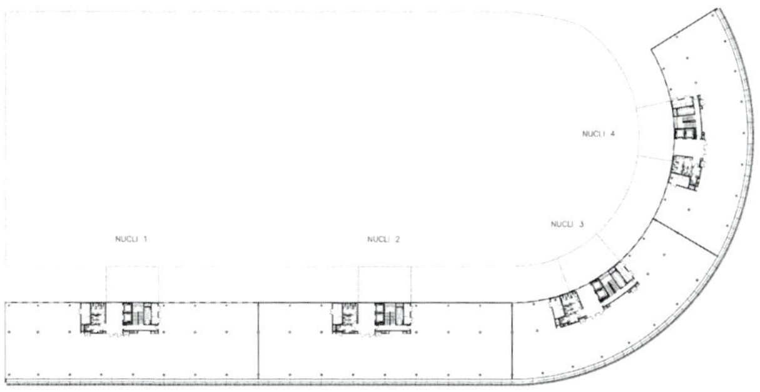

Typical floor

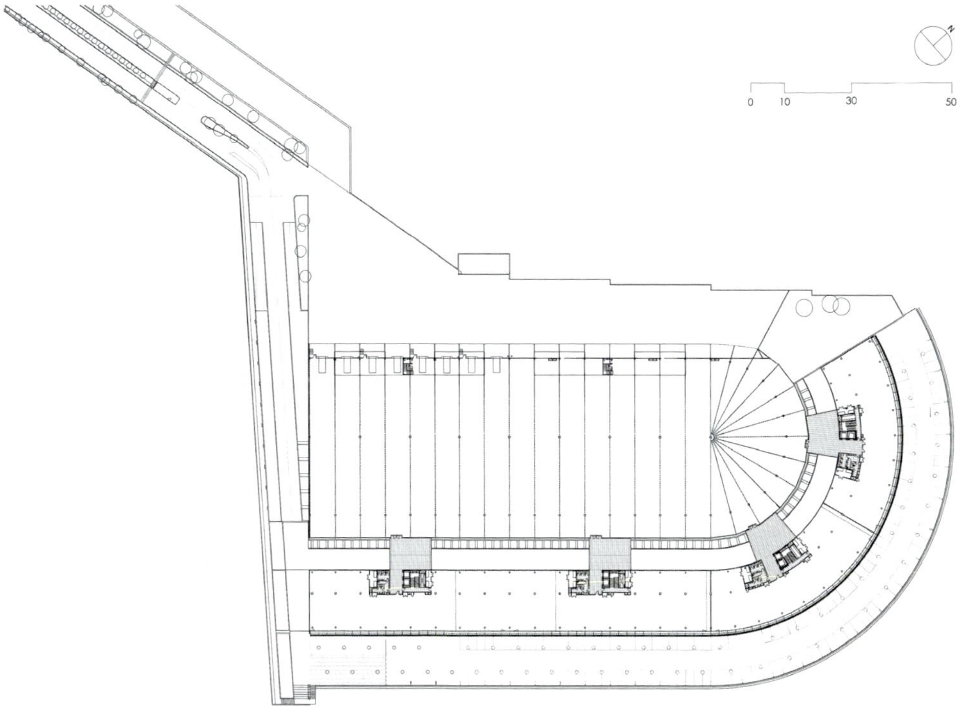

Ground floor

↓ → **Gas Natural** • Miralles Tagliabue EMBT

Planning constraints and size requirements – a maximum height of 80 m (250 ft) and floor space totaling 56,000 sqm (600 800 sqft) – affected the traditional notion of a tower. The architects sought to shape a slender tower in a rather high-density, low-rise environment. One of the project strategies was therefore a sort of division of the floor spaces into two blocks, one slim and in contact with the sky and the other stretching out towards the sea and its horizon.
In between the two is a large hall similar to the lobbies found in large U.S. skyscrapers from the '20s and '30s, which offers passers-by a glimpse inside this curious space. The construction's fragmentation allows it to respond to different scales and gives it a clear relation with the nearby apartment buildings. Furthermore, the building includes an original public space that brings the construction to the ground thereby becoming part of this urban landscape of different dimensions. The 'tower' is basically composed of four pieces: a 90 m (300 ft) 22-story tower; an impressive cantilevered body -nicknamed "Portaavions" (Catalan for "aircraft carrier"), a smaller, polygonal cantilever between the other two, and a 4-story base at the other side, which already existed and was rehabilitated for the occasion.

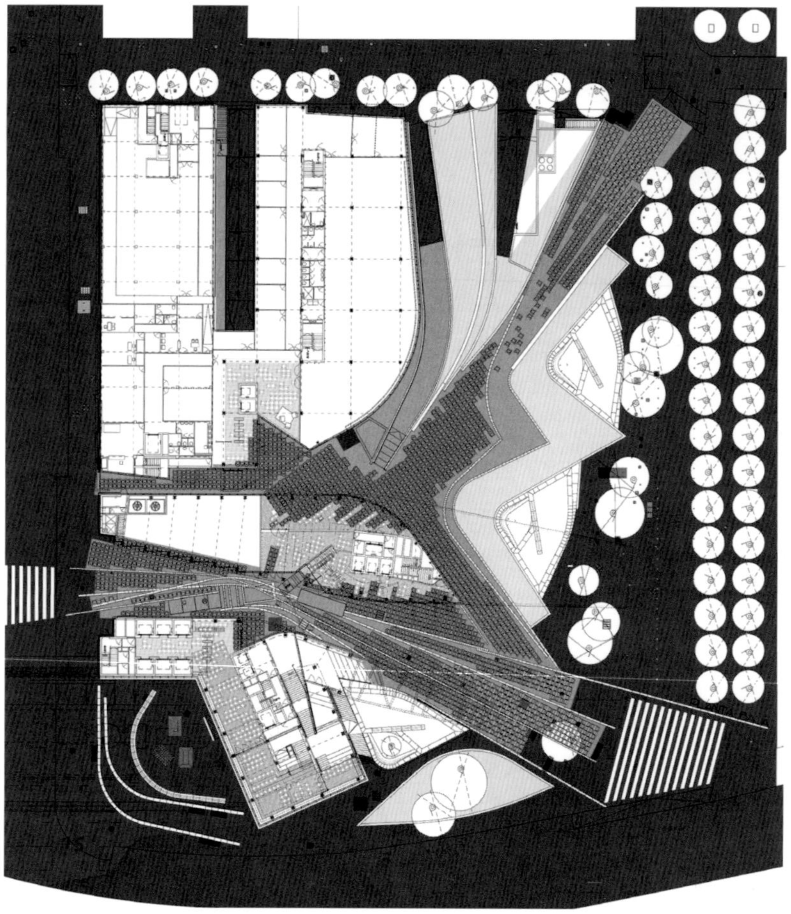

Ground floor

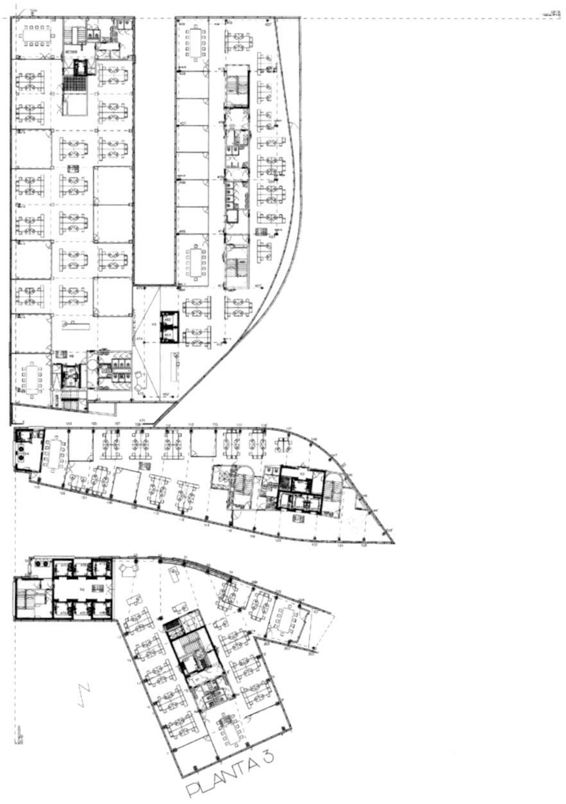

3rd floor

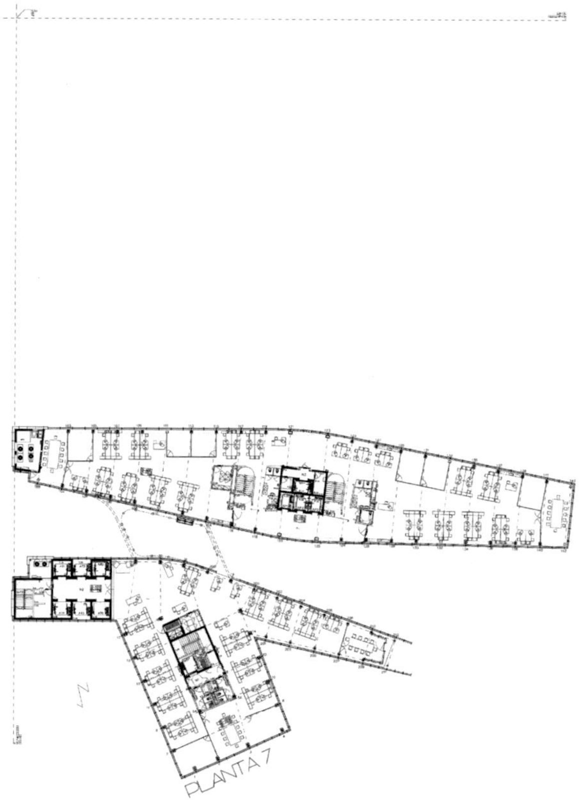

7th floor

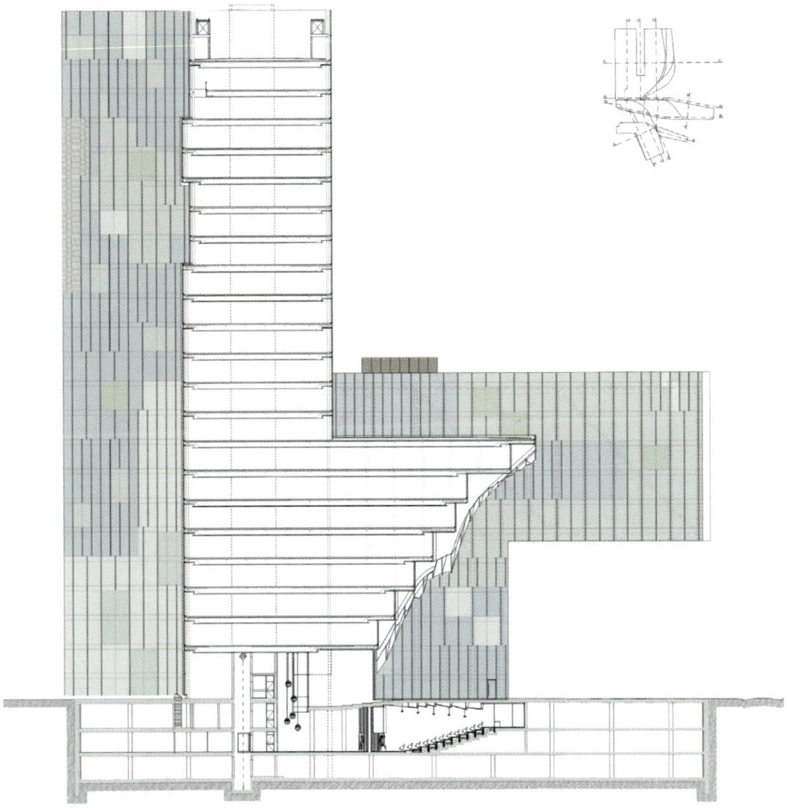

Section

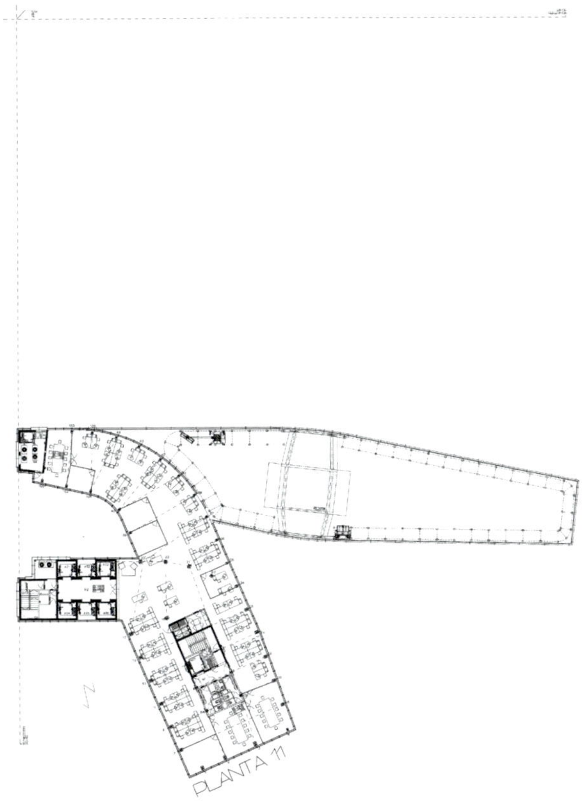

11th floor

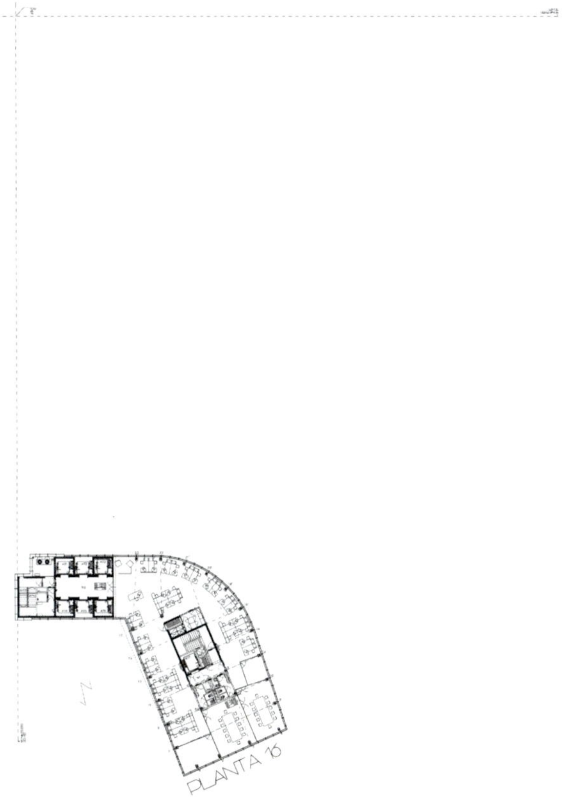

16th floor

↓ → **DMG** • Oskar Leo Kaufmann + Albert Rüf

The scheme of "DMG Headquarters" embraces representative exhibition area for the products of the company Deckel Maho Gildemeister (high tech machine tools for turning and milling) as well as administrative zones (office space, communication- and sales areas, teaching and meeting rooms, archives, service technician areas etc.)
The allocation of the building to a lowered level of the exhibition area accessible by lorries takes advantage of the existing declining ground level from east to west.
Lecture rooms and rooms for service technicians with metal workshop and material storage for exhibitions and teaching establish the necessary typological connections to the exhibition hall. The entrance for employees guarantees a stage-less shortcut to the office zones.
The typological raising of the boulevard area as a visual interface between administration and exhibition extrapolates the representative entrance to DMG Headquarters. The double-height reception area featuring a glazed roof guides the visitor to the cafeteria with adjacent patio area, to meeting rooms or directly to the central focused exhibition hall. The multi-transitorical, divisible and mergeable meeting rooms orientate towards the exhibition area. They are accessible from the office space as well as directly by the reception area situated at the central boulevard. Management, controlling, marketing and support are arranged adjacent to this space.

Ground floor

First floor

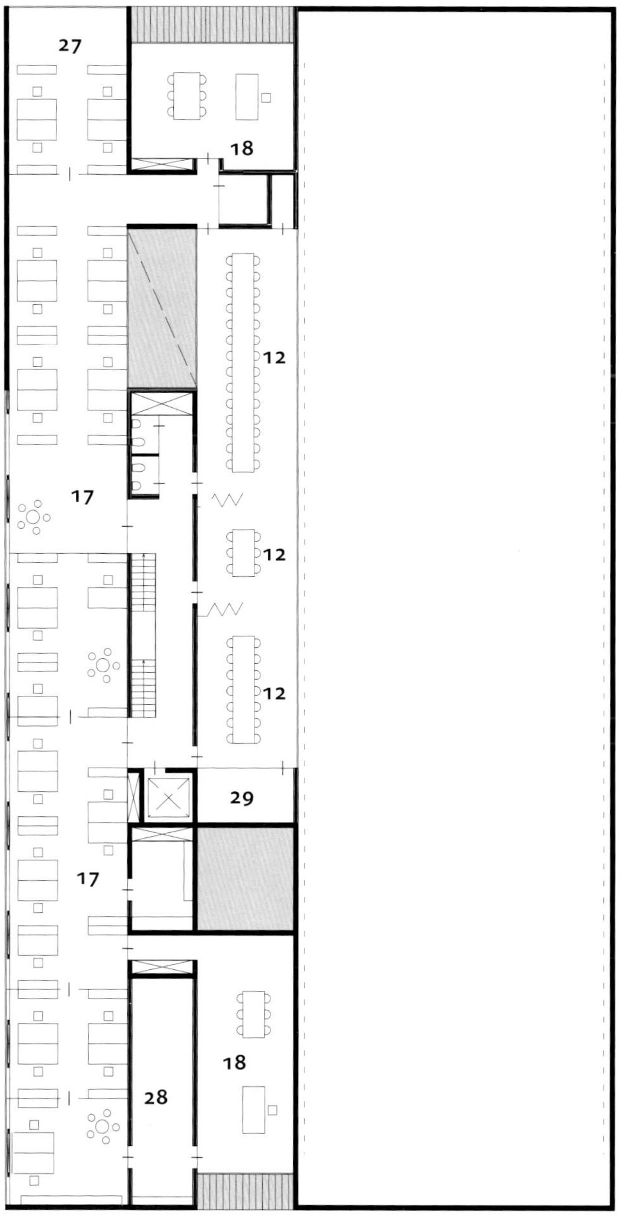

Second floor

1. Staff entrance
2. Changing room
3. Catering
4. Cleaning
5. Caretaker
6. Logistics
7. Open warehouse
8. Server
9. Warehouse
10. Seat storage
11. Lecture room
12. Meeting room
13. Technicians
14. Working room
15. Exhibition hall
16. Loading platform
17. Open offices
18. Private office
19. Secretary
20. Terrace
21. Development office
22. Photocopies
23. Client entrance
24. Reception
25. Cafeteria
26. Kitchen
27. Marketing office
28. Archive
29. Media room

Exterior

↓ → ING •

(EEA) Erick van Egeraat associated architects

The facade, in succession to the adjacent modernist building, is free from the traditional placement of openings. Composition, detailing and treatment of materials, -as well as the craftmanship quality-, are truly contemporary yet recall the richness and complexity of the historic facade detailing evident in the city. Undulating slightly, the facades become an instrument of light, giving an always-changing composition of visual effects: contrasts of brightness, reflection and transparency.

↓ → **Banc Sabadell** • Bach arquitectes – Jaume Bach, Eugeni Bach

The façades of the office building have been designed with different types of precast concrete pieces: the façade that faces the highway uses white precast concrete which juts out and is full of holes, while the façade facing the estate uses white and gray precast concrete creating an interesting combination of different shades on its surface.

↓ → **Saegeling Medizintechnik** • GPAC

The spacious and open character of the new building manifests itself on the east side where the curving glass façade envelopes a secluded outdoor space which visually flows into the indoor space. The glass façade dominates and communicates a heightened sense of openness and light-flooded space.

← ↓ **The Black Box** • Neri & Hu Design and Research Office

The Black Box is a five-story office building located in the former French Concession in Shanghai, which also includes a street-level storefront space. On the ground level, two wooden façades make up the base of the building, one comprising the new Design Republic store and the other leading up to the Design Republic and Neri&Hu Design and Research office. Above this glass and wooden exterior, a four-story dark façade is extruded and "cut" to reveal windows into the building.

The idea of the "Black Box" is the guiding concept behind the design, interpreted as a "black box" flight data recorder; it is used to represent the "storage" of conversation, ideas, thinking and research in the creative studio office. The black box also serves the function of protecting that recording in the event of a crash, fire or tragedy, analogous to the role of a design office servicing as a container of its intellectual production and protecting it from outside damage. The black box offers poignant, relevant and passionate design ideas with meaning and purpose to clients who may have had to face design tragedies in their lives. The ground floor in the form of a retail store displays some of these designed objects produced in the offices above, rendering it a window into the contents of the black box.

← **Media House** •
Bates Smart Architects

The design concept was based on the process of the media and how information is perceived and processed. This led to the idea of the virtual and reality, or virtual reality. Translated into the design, perceptions were explored through transparency, pattern and distortion as well as scale, materiality and texture. The idea being that things may not always be as they seem. The permeability and transparency of the fit out reinforces The Age's connection to the city of Melbourne and its people, with physical access into the public areas of the building as well as transparency into the drama and energy of the newsroom and supporting workspaces throughout the building. The direct line of sight from the street into key areas was designed specifically to convey messages of transparency, honesty and activity. This is visibly the hub where Melbourne's beloved newspaper is created.

↓ → **Torre Cube** • Carme Pinós

For this construction, while the number of square meters was pre-established, the height was not. Due to this condition the architects took the decision of projecting a high building based around three concrete cores, which would contain all the installations and vertical circulation. These nucleuses are in fact pillars and constitute the only supporting structure in the entire tower. Girders that vary in thickness cantilever out from these pillars to form the different floors. The prestressed floor framework is supported by these girders without the need for any pillars. This allows the 10 000 sqm (107 600 sqft) parking area to develop freely and offers open-plan office modules with no physical or visual obstacles.

The building's center, i.e. the space between the three cores of vertical circulation, forms an open shaft which is lit laterally due to the alternate removal of three floors of office modules. This also makes them into windows for this central space allowing air to circulate freely and offering the possibility of doing without air-conditioning.

↓ → **Hodgdon** • El Dorado Architects

The program for the company's new 790 sqm office was in part responsive to the hazardous nature of gunpowder manufacturing. Rather than design a singular structure, El Dorado proposed a series of Quonset Hut structures, all connected by an overhead canopy. Intimate courtyard spaces were developed as an integral part of the design, allowing the opportunity for outdoor dining, as well as creating a strong connection to the surrounding landscape. Additionally, these exterior spaces serve to buffer and organize varying aspects of the design program. Due to the remote location of the office facility, the architects ultimately conceived the Hodgdon "campus" as a community center of sorts, capable of hosting casual BBQ's, employee birthday parties, and family-related events. At night, careful attention to lighting allows the sequence of indoor and outdoor spaces to remain animated and intact.

↓ → Forum 3, Novartis •
Diener & Diener Architekten

The 'Forum 3' office building has two glass façades which are made up of a variety of differently sized overlapping glass panes, in more than 20 different colors. They are seemingly randomly arranged around the building alongside clear glass. Each pane is held in place by stainless-steel tension rods with each unique glass element being secured to the rods by clamps and spacers. The intense colors are intended to remind people of the beginnings of the chemical industry that began in Basel with dyestuffs. They also help to give the building a cheerful and striking appearance, while its transparency allows it to integrate with the surroundings constructions.

↓ → Pack Line Headquarters • Lea Katz architecture

The building's new exterior has the appearance of packaging material reinforcing the identity of Pack Line as manufacturer of Packaging Machines. Light aluminum panels wrap around it leaving a 20-cm (8-in) gap that creates an air barrier. This aids insulation and houses all the systems that connect the building to the outside, such as drainage, main electrical and telephone cables, and sewage and vent ducts. To reinforce the packaging identity, the doors and windows are hidden. The windows are behind perforated panels, which protect the interior from the strong southerly light meaning no internal curtains are required.

↓ → Centre ESPLAI • Carlos Ferrater & Núria Ayala

The design for the Centre ESPLAI project sought a balance between an austere, functional and practical building that solves the program's set of needs, and a construction that acquires the symbolic and emblematic character of an institutional building.
Given the heterogeneity of its uses, the project attempts to define a single enclosure that groups the different parts of this complex program, offering a unitary image to the exterior that makes it a landmark; an urban and civic reference point, due to its position in the neighborhood and since it generates both an urban appearance and a public space.

← Z58 • Kengo Kuma & Associates

The façade, clad in green louvers, separates the atrium from Fanyu Road and has been created with mirror finish, stainless steel planter boxes, which serve to provide an evergreen barrier of ivy between the interior and the exterior. From the inside this barrier gives visitors the sensation of being in a secluded forest. Outside the mirror-like finish on the metallic elements reflects the colors and shapes of the leaves, perfectly blending greenery and architecture, creating a harmonious effect.

→ Office in 't Gooi • Koen van Velsen

Koen van Velsen built these offices in 't Gooi to echo the farmhouses that are scattered around this part of Amsterdam, thereby preserving the rustic quality of this neighborhood. Strict construction regulations meant the building had to include a pitched roof and fired clay façades and that neutral colors had to be used throughout. The building basically had to integrate as smoothly as possible with its surroundings. The exterior of the building is clad in yellow gold-colored tiles that create stunning façades yet comply with the strict construction directives that the architects had to follow. What is perhaps most eye-catching regarding the appearance of the building is the number of windows. It appears as if more of the surface area of the building consists of window than brick. The result inside is the amount of natural light that enters during the day and, furthermore, being able to see outside from almost anywhere in the building prevents workers from feeling claustrophobic. There is, however, also an attractive aesthetic afforded to the exterior when, at night, all the lights are on and the building can be seen through the trees like a box of light. A large pond positioned adjacent to the building allows for a more homely and countrified aesthetic.

↓ → Highlight Munich • Murphy/Jahn

The building's technologically advanced and ecologically friendly façade gives the building a modern, crystalline-smooth appearance. A structure of unique and consistent transparency has been created by combining an innovative, interlinked steel framework with a glass and stainless steel façade. This single sheet curtain façade is made of heat reflecting, high performance triple glazed glass panels and incorporates an innovative window system that allows the windows to be opened individually providing natural ventilation. The 4.5-foot façade modules consist of these narrow operable windows behind vertical perforated stainless steel panels, which provide protection from the sun, wind and rain and contain soundproofing elements. From the inside the stainless steel panels give an interesting modulation to the views, while on the outside they reinforce the verticality. This single-layer façade was developed primarily to reduce construction costs and energy consumption.

← ↑ **Telefónica** • Felipe Pich-Aguilera, Teresa Batlle

Awarded First Prize in the open competition for the commission of a building for Telefonica Mobile phones, this project addresses the subject of the environment and the use of energy, not as an extra but as a fundamental determining factor of the architecture and the choice of building materials. The great container, built of industrial looking materials, consists of two three-dimensional nuclei and a structural frame that supports large slabs, like the infrastructure of a bridge with different heights. The system is intended to avoid later finishes and claddings, allowing the materials to display all their plastic power. Color plays a significant role throughout.

↓ → **Gas Natural** • Miralles Tagliabue EMBT

This skyscraper, commissioned by the national Catalan gas company Gas Natural to house their new headquarters, is located along the coastal ring road in the seaside district of the Barceloneta and constitutes one of the city's newly arrived tall buildings which have begun to alter Barcelona's skyline. The singular character of this new building coupled with its relationship with the urban periphery, makes this skyscraper different from the others. The design expresses a clear desire for the building to become compatible with its urban surroundings; the small scale of the district of la Barceloneta, the surrounding houses and the nearby park. The broken volumetry, more in consonance with the form of a shattered rock, is wrapped in tempered glass. The building's glazed facade is the key to understanding the building and its strong urban impact. The tower takes on a hue that lies somewhere between silver and blue, depending on the sort of light on the day, and it tends to disappear among the surrounding clouds, also depending on the highly variable weather conditions that either make it visible or disappear. The building has very little to do with your prototypical, corporate office tower -or with a tower at all-. Firstly, the complete lack of hierarchy between the façades immediately sets it up as an outsider among other buildings of this typology. Entirely clad in mirrored glass of different colors, there's no main façade, and there seems to be no main axis either. It is not an easy space to understand from just one perspective, the building looks different from each side, you need to walk around it to comprehend its geometry and recognize its relationship with the sky.

↓ → **Agbar Tower** • Jean Nouvel

The surface of this striking 142-meter high construction evokes water, rising out of a pool with waterfalls. Like a film of water, the exterior is smooth and continuous, shimmering and transparent. Set against the ever-changing Spanish skies, the facade possesses mirage-like qualities, as shades of colour, angles of inclination and degrees of opacity combine to mysteriously freeze the skin in liquid form, with depth, luminosity and reflectivity in constant flux.
The cladding is made up of aluminium panels in 25 different colours behind glass louvres. Red, earthy colors form the base, from where the green emerges, followed, finally, by blues at the upper levels, like those of the clear Mediterranean sky. However, although this architecture comes from the earth, it does not have the heaviness of stone. It could be a distant echo of old, formal Catalan obsessions, carried by a mysterious wind from the cliffs of Montserrat.
An exterior concrete bearing wall rises to almost the entire height of this bullet-shaped building's 31 stories, from which openings for the construction's 4,500 windows have been punched. The glass for these is transparent, or otherwise etched to be merely translucent. These details are all part of the multi-colored facade's elaborate solar protection system.

↓ → Siamese Towers • Alejandro Aravena

The problem that building a glass tower in Santiago presents, is that of dealing with the resulting greenhouse effect. The budget did not allow for a single energy-efficient glass structure so a series of skins was chosen, each with its role to play: an outer single-glass skin, bad in energy-efficient terms, but good in terms of weathering, and an internal building clad in fiber-cement, bad against weathering but good energy wise. The space contained between them acts as a perimeter chimney due to an air entrance space at the lower end of the outer skin and a similar exhaust at the top. The result is a constant convective flow of natural air, enhanced by the Venturi effect generated by the 'waists' created at the seventh floor, which counteracts the greenhouse effect. Finally, there was the problem of constructing a tower, on a site of just 53 800 sqft. No matter how much the surface was reduced the result was a "stocky", high building and not a tower. For each of the resulting parts almost width-less aluminum pieces were used of slightly different colors. If seen from the front, the building presents a unique "bi-cephalous" volume, but seen as a foreshortened figure, the color difference gives rise to truly vertical figures, that share a large section of their bodies, as if they were Siamese twins.

← ↓ Lev • Andrej Kalamar

The Lev Office Building stands on the corner of Tivolska Street and GosposvetskaStreet, one of the most frequented intersections in the Slovenian capital of Ljubljana. The program addresses the re-development of a site with 4200 sqm of available space, for offices, retail space and an underground car parking facility. The main defining qualities to be considered in this urban context were the impact of heavy traffic and the typological diversity with which the surrounding physical space is occupied.

Although one of the functions of the new building is to shield the inner courtyard from aggressive traffic of the busy intersection, it doesn't do so by facing the streets with a correspondingly aggressive impermeable rampart. On the contrary, its high-gloss minimal form interacts with drivers passing by, echoing their movement by reflection. The "chromosome image" of the vertical window openings provides rhythmical movement at a large scale, the layer of creased metal in two contrasting hues interacts with motion by changing color, the outer layer of printed glass softens the volume by answering the street with a shimmering rhythmical small scale code-like movement.

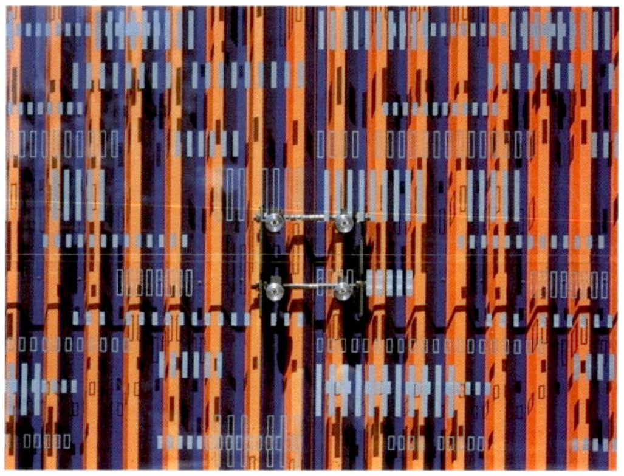

↓ → Ex Ducati • MC A - Mario Cucinella Architects

The building is "L" shaped, facing a major road junction, with the entrance at the point where the two wings meet. Facing the intersection, the entrance features a deep fracture that captures attention, counterpoised against the sheer surfaces of the façades. A trellis cladding the street side of the façades presents a compact urban frontage of climbing vegetation. The rear façade is clad in wood. The trellis consists of a 60 × 60 cm (2 × 2 ft) stainless steel grid anchored to the cantilevered galleries that provide access to the offices. The steel grid supports a growth of Star Jasmine, reminiscent of ivy covered buildings.

← ↓ **Inotera** • tec Architecture

In contrast to standard office all-glass facades the architects referred to the Taiwanese tradition of tile construction. Using the latest technologies in CAD and CIM hundreds of shapes and colours portray the formal complexity of natural elements such as the leaves of trees or ripples of water. An intricate combination of printed glass using the latest glass printing technology, structural glass and glass curtain wall systems articulates the building helping it to seek its own unique identity, while also assimilating local customs.
The V-columns which tie the building to the ground are aluminium wrapped steel for earthquake stabilisation. In the office area large glass cones bring light into the building as well as giving a three-dimensional depth to the zone.

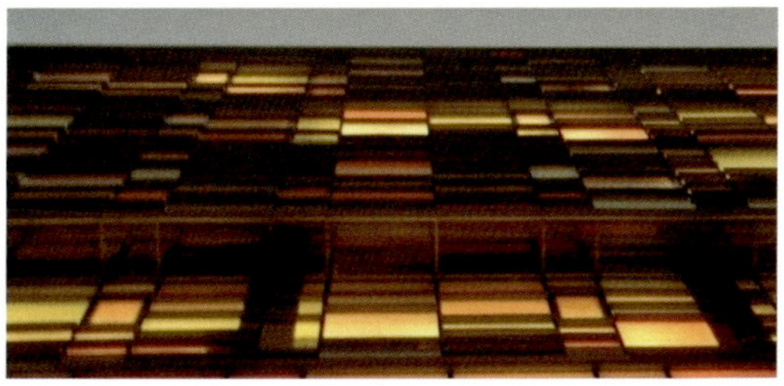

← **WWF** • RAU

Architectural studio RAU won the competition to build WWF's Dutch headquarters in the Schoonoord Nature reserve. The organization decided against a new building, opting instead to renovate an old agricultural laboratory complex dating from 1954. Since the original building was austere, impersonal and grim, the intention was to 'reanimate' it. The architects decided to preserve the frame of the building, reuse the rubble and add a warm, pulsating heart in the middle, while simultaneously returning the grounds to nature. The crystalline uniformity of the existing building demanded a dynamic enlargement. The middle part was broken away, and a new amorphous building block was put in, providing space for the main entrance, which was removed from north to south. A bridge crossing a pond leads to the main entrance.

↓ **Baufritz** • a. ml und partner

The new building seems to float lightly upon the landscape. The two longitudinal façades are closed surfaces. The staggered façade addresses movement and change, new perceptions of space and architecture being a main theme of the new building. The main access façade is fully glazed and, weather permitting, offers an uninterrupted view of the Alps. The various function-oriented areas receive natural light from five inner courtyards, each one installed in a theme-related manner. The links between architecture and nature are a prevalent subject throughout, and indoor and outdoor spaces become part of a single unit. Indicator cubes help customers to find their ways between the show-spaces that illustrate different facets of domestic life.
The 60 meter (197 feet) long side elevations take advantage of the roadside location; a double layered façade of wooden slats creates interference patterns in the eye of the rapidly-passing beholder, who perceives a structure apparently in a constant state of change. The shell of the building re-enacts the theme of "movement" as the pattern changes according to the beholder's speed, and even the Baufritz logo, perceived while driving past, disappears into the slatwork at slow motion and close-range. The north elevation, facing the freeway, is an eye catcher in giant concave frames that present the various themes of the Baufritz enterprise, telling the traffic what the building contains.

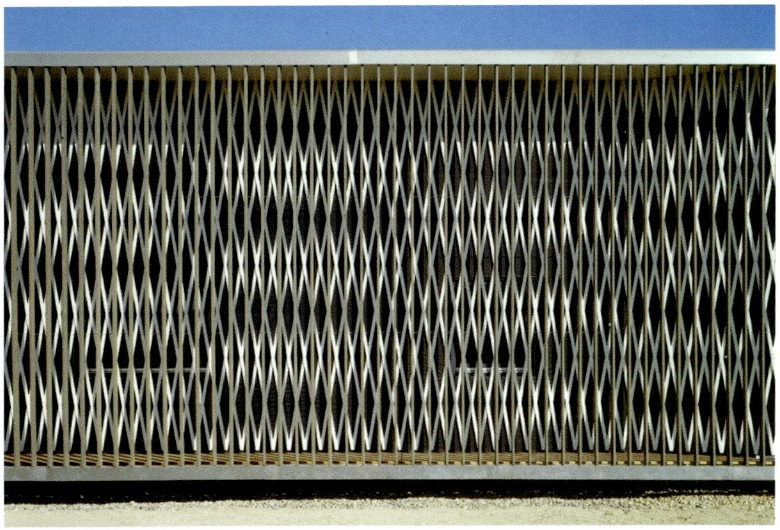

↑ → Ferrari Research Center • Massimiliano Fuksas Architetto

The project is born out of the desire to bring nature into this highly technological complex in order to create a comfortable working environment. Light, water and bamboo are used in such a way that building becomes landscape. This project represents the development of a new poetry of lightness. The overall image is dominated by an overhanging volume, detached from the rest of the building and suspended above the surface of the water which covers the lower volume, extending outwards over the entrance area by 23 feet. Brightly lit crystal boxes and a minimum structure are the only physical connections between these volumes. Above the surface of the water various walkways create a network of connections between two meeting rooms, marked by their respective colors, i.e. red and yellow. Water and light are the kinetic elements of the building, giving rise to reflections that give the upper volume the appearance of a container made from some kind of precious metal. In the middle of the building, a precisely ordered rectangular bamboo forest filters light and reflects it in a thousand different directions, while several staircases snake their way from this internal courtyard up to the upper levels of the building.

↓ → **D&G** • Studio Piuarch

Synergy between the classic and the contemporary is one of the core features of this design, which sets the early 20th century block with its historic frontage off against the 1960s structure, now new-built in glass. This glazed facade is in fact one of the work's most characteristic features, running unbroken around three sides of the whole building so as to provide total illumination inside at any time of day – and stunning visual impact. A wholly transparent prism, enlivened by a set of vertical shade-giving sheets of opaline glass arranged in a particularly tight pattern, which receives the sunlight at different angles from minute to minute, makes the D&G headquarters kaleidoscopic, seductive, almost incorporeal. A filter diffuses the light inside the building with an expansive softness, giving it a varied range of colours where the feel of no two moments is the same; in the evening it remains alive, shining by the artificial light inside and looking like a huge lantern of diffused light.

↓ → Lindberghatelier • Nickl & Partner Architekten

The alternating pattern of industrial glass and rough steel lamella defines the look of the building – a unique and, with varying light conditions, constantly changing skin. Each block of lamella is unique in its pattern of glass and steel elements, reflecting the individuality of the work spaces hidden within. Each lamella field can be adjusted manually by means of a rod rather like a french window shutter. Horizontal order combined with vertical rotation make the shimmering skin of the building appear both open and closed at the same time.

↓ → **Trutec** • Barkow Leibinger Architects

The exterior cladding is a mirrored fractal glass articulated into a series of crystalline-formed bays which project 20 cm (8 in) outwards. These three-dimensional forms refract light and image, rendering the façade as a fragmented and abstract surface. Any contextual image, any neighboring building will be reduced to fragmented pixels upon its surfaces. Reciprocally from the interior, window bays act as kaleidoscopes offering multiple views and orientations through the façades. This way the building acts as a phenomenal filter, effecting both vision and how it is viewed. Each individual window module includes sun and thermal protection.

↓ → **Relfo S.p.A.** • De Carlo Gualla Studio

This new architectural mix is expressed in three volumes, each one standing out with its own physical and functional characteristics.
The main body was conceived as a structure of reinforced concrete enveloped by glass surfaces. At both sides of it, the other facilities have been "hooked" onto the building like arms. On one side stands a compact figure of plastered brickwork in deep red, which houses changing rooms, restrooms etc., and on the other a light unit that is completely covered in glass, which encloses all of the vertical circulations. The first and second level of the building have been covered by a "second skin" of perforated steel sheets, while on the first floor the structural pillars form a shallow portico.
The skin of steel plates was made by Relfo following their own design, turning the building into a type of living advertisement. The architecture is converted into a vehicle of communication through which the business is represented and published.

↓ → **Bureaux-Habitation, Gand** • NU architectuuratelier

The Belgian team of architects 'NU architectuuratelier' has transformed this site, which previously hosted a mid-century bungalow, into an office/house. Erected on the foundations of the previous building, the present development was required to have an ambivalent function. It was to be an advertising agency today with scope for conversion into housing in the future.

The building stands in an area which is subject to early floods, and has therefore been placed on a white concrete plinth that forms both a literal and metaphorical island. Above the pedestal is a complex form whose character is neither recognizably commercial nor domestic. The black sculpture is reminiscent of a modern villa, yet the north-light roof construction has the character of industrial architecture. Daylight enters not only through four north-light roofs, creating a diffused lighting mood in the white internal space, but also through four large areas of glazing, each and every one positioned at the end of a wall. The entrance façade is entirely glazed allowing light to flood into the interior.

Concealed behind the zinc cladding is a steel-reinforced timber post-and-rail structure. The skin of the building is characterized by very refined detailing across the complex geometry. The detailing and geometry applied does not only control the physical and structural characteristics, but also especially the aesthetics of the building. The use of natural materials (concrete, steel, aluminum, black zinc, wood) supports the timeless and monolithical character of the building.

↓ → **Horten** • 3XN

3XNs design for Danish Law Firm Horten's new head office reflects the duality between the classic and the modern, combining solidity with an advanced choice of materials that express the profile of Horten's practice.

The volume's travertine-clad facade represents a reinterpretation of the classic concept of a corporate head office. Depending on the angle, Horten's facade gives the impression of being a craggy cliff face, an ocean blue glass facade or an intricate geometrical pattern of chunky diagonal, vertical and horizontal friezes. The facade elements were developed especially for this building's complex geometry while taking on board the requirements for sustainability. The elements were designed to ensure a pleasant working climate with maximum daylighting conditions while avoiding direct sunlight. The window sections are north-facing protecting against direct heat gain with their glass panes forming a 3D figure facing the water.

↓ → **ThyssenKrupp Quartier** • JSWD Architekten | Chaix & Morel et Associés

All of the building façades on the campus have been designed according to the "Shell and Core" principle, which is expressed in two façade types: while the "shell" defines the façades of the building volumes towards the exterior and the open spaces, the "core" is oriented towards the interior courtyards and atriums. The objective of these design leitmotifs is to underline cohesion between the buildings and thus the architectural homogeneity of this campus beyond the shared formal language of its building volumes.
The "shell" type consists of a thermally effective floor-to-ceiling metal-glass façade in post, beam, or elemental building structure. A metallic shell has been placed in front of these at various distances to bear sun-shading systems, which differ from building to building. The material "stainless steel" defines the outer appearances of all of the building envelopes, to express a uniform corporate architecture. All of the façades are characterized by a dominantly vertical structure, so that the horizontal lines of the story levels fade into the background, making the façades look homogenous in appearance over the whole height of each building; these multi-layered façade surfaces thus make the campus buildings look like abstract metal volumes. The individual buildings' partly recessed glazed ground floor façades and the glazed floor-to-ceiling building joints represent a further connecting element within the campus architecture.

Common Working Spaces

↓ → Raiffeisenbank Zürich • NAU + DGJ

Raiffeisen's flagship branch on Zurich's Kreuzplatz dissolves traditional barriers between customer and employee, creating a new type of "open bank," a space of encounter. Elegantly flowing walls blend the different areas of the bank into one smooth continuum, spanning from the customer reception at the front, to employee workstations oriented to the courtyard. The plan carefully controls views to create different grades of privacy and to maximize daylight throughout. The walls themselves act as a membrane mediating between the open public spaces and intimately scaled conference rooms.

↓ → Forward Media Group Publishing House • za bor architects

In addition to several popular and well-recognized magazines such as 'Hello', Forward Media Group publishes the largest and the most popular magazines on interior design in Russia.
The project was clearly going to be fairly complex from the outset – the premises comprised a huge loft of 4200 sqm with a narrow, elongated plan, located in the mansard level of a new business center. The situation was further complicated by the particularities of the program – the need for open plan editorial offices as well as commercial and retail departments, separate offices for directors and editors-in-chief with a conference corner, conference rooms, an archive with a library, storage rooms etc. All of these facilities were placed along the corridor which runs the length of the space. Open plan workstations have been concentrated on one side, and cabinets located on the other side of the corridor.

↓ → JWT Headquarters • Clive Wilkinson Architects

To promote interaction, mobility and collaboration, the isolated divisions within JWT would be opened up and reconnected. The new space would be 'open architecture', with no private offices, and vertical movement between floors would be facilitated to unite the JWT community. Separate businesses, such as the post-production facility JWTwo, would be expressed as distinct but integrated companies, adding character to the space.

↓ → **Cargo** • Group 8

The offices are housed within a former industrial warehouse, close to the center of the city. The white and luminous warehouse space contains a hidden treasure: 16 recycled shipping containers, all of which have traveled thousands of miles around the globe. Following the concept of artist Marcel Duchamp's "readymades", these monumental objects have acquired a new function.
The other half of the scheme is in opposition with the containers' structured zone: an open space enlightened by natural light that pours in through the glass-roof. This informal meeting space gathers all the employees together, thereby generating a strong sense of synergy in the workplace. This second zone is composed of informal meeting spaces (exchange spaces) that are radically differentiated from the containers' intimate interiors.

↓ ← **Ynno Workplace** • Sprikk

Since their consultants spend more time at their client's place of work than in their own office, YNNO asked for a workplace that functions as a home base rather than a conventional office. A working environment was created that suits the nature of the consultant's way of working in which communication and networking play a vital role. The floor plan is kept entirely open with the exception of two acoustically separated glass volumes. This stimulates free movement, spontaneous encounters and flexible uses while allowing for lots of natural light. In this open plan, organically shaped birchwood structures were placed that form partitions, niches, storage spaces and bookshelves.

↓ → **The Moving Picture Company** • Patrick Tighe Architecture

The Moving Picture Company is a UK-based visual effects post production company, a forerunner in the visual effects and animation fields for the feature film, advertising, music and television industries. The company is highly regarded for its work in the field of color manipulation in film. With this in mind, the project explores the notion of light as it relates to color. The forms and patterns employed in the design have been generated through analyses and three-dimensional modelling of light patterns. Frames from the resultant animation sequence have been selected and layered to organize spatial qualities and movement through the office environment. An organic, sinuous spine weaves its way through the suite. An appendaged soffit grows from the serpentine walls and serves as an armature for cable trays, mechanical and electrical systems.

↓ → **WongDoody** • Shubin + Donaldson Architects

The Los Angeles office of WongDoody is the adaptive reuse of a former warehouse. While the shell of the building was mainly left unchanged, the interior construction partitioned the space to accommodate the company's needs. The space is organized into three wings: a public wing flanked by two private work wings. All four of the public meeting/war rooms—the cork room, green room, black room, and silver room—are in the center of the space, marked by rectangular enclosures of different materials. The private work wings include the creative zone, interactive zone, communications, administrative, and account executives areas.

↓ → Yandex Kiev • za bor architects

The offices occupy the sixth and seventh floors of the top-class Leonardo Business Center, a two-level space with a void. The space is well lit with natural daylight through a huge arched window which offers a wonderful view of the Kiev Opera House and the square in front of it. The internal distribution is very fluid and the space is not overloaded with workstations. On each of the two levels there are about fifteen workstations. There are also two meeting rooms, the lower one used principally for meeting with clients while the upper meeting room is used for internal meetings. The upper, mezzanine level, is fully glazed and connects to the lower floor via a staircase. The gallery and staircase were designed as a single sculptural form with particularly complex geometry.

↓ **Obscura Digital** • IwamotoScott Architecture

Obscura's work involves design, r&d, fabrication and installation across a range of digital media, including architectural projections and large interactive touchscreens. Programmatic requirements for the space included an office and meeting space for the partners and staff, a large multi-functional showroom and exhibition area, workstations for digital production, and prototyping workshop spaces. The prototyping workshop and showroom are located on the lower level, the reception, main offices and meeting spaces on the middle level, and production on the top level. A broad new staircase at the entrance allows an easy spatial flow into the reception area, partners' offices and central meeting space. Partner and staff offices are defined by twisting polycarbonate screen walls that allow filtered views as well as the transmission of natural light from perimeter windows and skylights above.

↓ → United Business Media • Gensler

To relieve the density, there are two large communal spaces: the Town Hall and the Junction. They are strategically located to encourage gathering: the Town Hall opens onto a large outdoor deck and the Junction is placed at the knuckle of the floor plate. The Town Hall incorporates a café and elevated platform with a conversation pit that has jokingly been named the "dry hot tub". The platform leads out to a large deck that is surrounded by the views of the Bay and the downtown San Francisco skyline. It is a great place to relax or get fresh air on a nice day. The Junction features a second coffee bar with casual meeting places and spaces for relaxing.

↓ → Nije Gritenije • FLATarchitects

The Nije Gritenije foundation is a Rabobank initiative to stimulate local and regional entrepreneurship. The foundation asked Amsterdam based FLATarchitects to design twenty workstations and a conference room on the ninth and tenth floors of the brand new Rabobank building. Four of the workstations were to be used by the permanent staff of the foundation while the remaining sixteen were to accomodate a continuously changing group of start-up entrepreneurs and artists. FLATarchitects devised a simple interior design which could be customized and completed by the users so that they could adapt their space to their specific needs. In this way temporary users are able to appropriate their place of work in a relatively short period of time. Also, the interior is designed to encourage innovation and discussion among users and visitors.

↓ → **Dentsu London** • Essentia Designs Limited

Essentia Designs were approached to work on the offices for Dentsu London, a creative agency based in the UK. The offices are located in a building in an award winning development by Amanda Levete. The brief was to create a high-tech minimalist interior that would be in keeping with the curvaceous exterior of the building. In addition to the main agency studio spaces and the European head office, the brief included working space for Attik, an associated multi-award winning branding agency. The decision to relocate Attik in London meant the solution needed to encourage integration and cross-fertilisation between the two businesses. In addition, the European headquarters team were moving from separate offices in Mayfair so this would be the first opportunity for the business to function out of a single location.

← ↓ **Cubion** • Jackie-B

Located in the heart of Copenhagen, the consultant company Cubion a/s occupies the lower floor of a listed house dating from 1793. The house is on one of the principal pedestrian streets in the oldest part of Copenhagen.
Cubion contacted the Danish designer Jackie-B and asked him to create a creative oasis where customers would find a place for inspiration and understanding and a place where solutions were designed, rethought and questioned. Jackie-B took the challenge and turned the office into three different rooms for the exchange of knowledge and conversation with the design emphasis on simplicity of both forms and color.

↓ ← **No Picnic** • Elding Oscarson

The client had found a group of 19th century buildings in central Stockholm of which the two principal volumes – a former exercise hall for troops and a stable for police horses – were listed in the historical buildings register with the highest degree of protection. They had been converted into showrooms in the 1980s and were in a sad state of repair. Their conversion had to be realized with extreme sensitivity, so much so that the architects have evaluated every step with a historic buildings specialist, literally down to each new screw hole. The buildings have been stripped of all additional layers down to the original building fabric. In the old stable block they were able to strip the room, and added only a custom designed acoustic treatment along the walls, but in the exercise hall, economy and function demanded that a mezzanine constructed in the 1980s was kept.

↓ → **Gummo** • i29 I interior architects

As the space on the first floor of the old Parool newspaper building in Amsterdam was only going to be rented by Gummo for two years, i29 convinced Gummo to embrace the mantra of "reduce, reuse, recycle" to create a stylish office space that would have as small an impact as possible on the environment or on the client's wallet. The architects developed a theme that would reflect Gummo's personality and design philosophy – simple, uncomplicated, no-nonsense, yet unquestionably stylish with a twist of humour. Everything in the office conforms to the new house style of white and grey. The new office is a perfect case study of a smart way to fill a temporary space stylishly and at minimal cost.

↓ → **Media House** • Bates Smart Architects

The Age Gallery is an inside-outside space that is stepped to follow the gradient of Collins Street. Overlaid with strongly contrasting colours, bold patterns and warm timbers, the result is undeniably Melbourne. The gallery wall is constructed of punched white metal and uses a pattern of positive and negative shapes to convey a binary code, representing the digital direction of The Age. The northern face is fully shaded and fitted out as communal space; a linear breakout and reference zone open to all. Colorful staff hubs are located next to the dramatic stairs on every second floor, encouraging migration and collaboration.

↓ Saegeling Medizintechnik • GPAC

In configuring an effective office and work area, the strict partitioning of user and circulation space was discarded with the aim of creating a flowing, efficient and practically support-free architecture. Internal office processes are mirrored in the building's structure in the form of optimized workstations, short communication and circulation paths, as well as established visual relationships between the interior and exterior of the building. The efficiently designed office units in turn enabled the expansive configuration of the public spaces.

← Uniflair • Mario Cucinella Architects

The interior is a 200 m (650 ft) long open plan structure where the various workplaces are brought together along one single table that stretches in a continuous line through the entire space, a visible backbone that is an explicit representation of company procedures. The space is lit by a system of indirect lighting positioned in the central part of the table. Next to the long table a series of cylindrical spaces provide meeting rooms, areas for relaxing, and communal areas. They look like circular pavilions and are lit from inside.

↓ Study Residence in Omaha • Randy Brown

This building includes the studio of three architects and the dwelling of one of them, Randy Brown with his wife, Kim. The building dates from the late seventies and was originally a nursery school.

The heart of the building was occupied by a container-structure that gives the interior of the dwelling a powerful personality. It is a collage of wood, metal and glass that forms several elements (bookshelves, wall, dressing room, closet, glass table) and creates a common space on the ground floor (dining room/meeting room) and the bedroom on the first floor. This sculptural element also serves to divide the ground floor into two environments. On the left of the entrance is the studio area, on the right several spaces of the dwelling, although they are also shared by the employees of the studio: the kitchen, the bathroom and a small storeroom.

↓ Oktavilla • Elding Oscarson

Dividing the space with a wall created a large and bright meeting room, as well as a clean rectangular room for the rest of the program. This large space is softly divided with a box containing service functions and a kitchen. By compressing the contents of the box and positioning it carefully, the program effortlessly falls into place without breaking the impression of a single large room. The lighting solution and interior design, which uses Elding Oscarson's own furniture designs mixed with vintage pieces and staples already in the client's possession, highlight the nakedness of the space and the raw, largely untreated building fabric. By adding only two clearly defined architectural elements, the client's wish list could be met while keeping the beauty of the industrial atmosphere of the original building.

← ↓ → **The Power House** • Cannon Design

After standing vacant for nearly 30 years, the St. Louis Municipal Power House building in downtown St. Louis opened as the new regional offices of Cannon Design in September 2008. Although the building's exterior shell and original steel structure were fundamentally sound, reuse for a large architecture and engineering practice required a creative spatial solution that exploited the building's massive volume. Two new floor plates have been inserted inside the tall volume, thereby creating two extra floors and ample collaborative meeting space and workspaces for approximately 120 employees. The floor plates are separated from the external walls on two sides to preserve the full height of the arched windows on the north and east elevations, generating a partially full height gallery and exhibition space on the ground floor for use by the firm and the larger community. An elevator shaft, kitchenettes on each floor and two staircases have been inserted against the back wall in the northwest and southwest corners of the building. A model shop and materials library plus a boardroom have been excavated in the basement. On the roof, an oblong structure originally used to store coal conveyor equipment now houses another boardroom and staff lunchroom.

↓ → Bruce B./Emmy B. •
Ippolito Fleitz Group

The atelier itself is an open-plan room. Shelving units hanging from the ceiling are aligned with the ceiling joists, delimiting the workstations. The workstations themselves are solid oak tables, most of which the client already had at his disposal. The furnishings create individual units with plenty of free space in between. The units are placed together in groups of two or three to form islands within the space. The resultant effect is a mix of open-plan office and semi-enclosed cubicles. This layout is emphasised by the circles of carpet that reinforce the island groupings.

↓ → **CheBanca!** • Crea International

Crea International has designed the new and surprising retail format for the Mediobanca group, CheBanca!, a multichannel distribution model based on internet banking, customer service and new generation "light" branches. The design of the new branches emphasizes the consultancy, DIY transaction and self-education activities, placing the consumer at the center of the process. The "Natural Tech" of CheBanca! is intended to convey an ethical and transparent financial institution, an apparently technology free environment where direct human contact is at the forefront. The innovations in this project are various: first of all, the layout with a central base point and perimeter connection booths. An open and fluid space is generated at the center of which is a counter from where the store staff move to attend the customers. At the entrance, the consumer is directed to the multitasking connection booths where any banking operation can be performed either in DIY mode or with the support of store staff, upon request.

↓ → **DATA** • Randy Brown Architects

The designers were immediately struck by the close personal relationships between all the employees. In order to encourage this culture they designed the working area as a large open plan space with workstations, a café and a gaming lounge. The second strategy of the design was to create a centrally located circulation element that would generate a distinctive atmosphere for the office and connect all the spaces. This was materialized as the porous central corridor formed by folded, fragmented green panels, which creates a diffuse space that leads from the entrance to the depth of the plan.

→ **HTC** • chadbourne + doss architects

Collaboration is an important part of their work-process, and wall mounted white-boards are the typical medium. A 48ft long work table with an adjacent 48ft long writable board allows for group work. A 32ft long work counter with a writable surface separates work and meeting spaces and provides space for informal gatherings and collaboration.

↓ → **LEGO** • Bosch & Fjord

Innovation begins at the entrance to LEGO Group's development department. The visitor steps directly into a dynamic reception area where the reception desk is part of a cafe area that welcomes visitors, and where employees are having coffee, informal meetings or lunch. It is a very lively and dynamic place, buzzing with activities and people. The cafe is divided into three areas, each with its own character and functionality, inviting different types of meetings and gatherings. There is the 'Dining Area' with a long black common table and a book case; the 'Cafe' area with white furniture and shadow decoration in the windows; and the 'Lounge' with long, red benches, white tables and wall paper with an organic design. The reception desk is part of a huge organically shaped high table winding through the room on the green floor, which acts as a reception counter, a buffet and a dining table. The table places the receptionist on eye level with the visitors, thus creating a direct and engaging reception situation to make people feel welcome.

← ↓ Facebook Headquarters • Studio O+A

The design of the space relied heavily on input from the users, appropriate for a flatly structured company that weighs every employee's opinion equally. O+A designers interviewed employees about what they wanted from their new headquarters. The Facebook platform was used to conduct company-wide polls about design decisions, post construction photos and updates, and keep everyone informed of the thought processes behind the project. Because the new facility houses employees coming from various locations, the company wanted to maintain each division's distinct identity. The design takes its inspiration from the patchwork nature of Facebook users and employees, bringing together seemingly disparate elements to form a cohesive pattern and using color and interior spacing to create neighborhoods within the open plan space. The company's executives sit in central areas, accessible to all employees. Large lounges and open spaces provide venues for the community to come together. A kitchen and café continue Facebook's tradition of providing gourmet meals to staff at all hours, while drinks and snacks are available at micro-kitchens throughout the headquarters.

↓ → Grupo Fornari • Giorgio Borruso Design

For the Fornari Group Headquarters on Via Morimondo in the Navigli area of Milan, a conversion of the famous historic porcelain workshops of Richard Ginori, the intention was to create a 35 000 sqft (3250 sqm) flexible space, with industrial concrete floors and exposed steel structures throughout, to house the showrooms, as well as executive offices, storage, and areas to be utilized for exhibitions and events for the various brands that comprise the Fornari Group.
To take advantage of this sequence of large open spaces in a severe orthogonal grid, the architects inserted a central spine that penetrates the entire volume, not only connecting the different levels in a fluid and organic way, but also forming a pathway to guide traffic inside the expansive volume of the building.

↓ → **Bugaboo** • RA-DA

RA-DA architects decided to approach the design from a practical and minimal perspective. The Bugaboo "strollers" are characterized by a simple no-fuss form and an intentional use of color. It was decided to use the work-area as a backdrop to the product so that the strollers would be the primary elements activating the space. This was achieved by keeping the layout simple and making most of the space white: white floors, white desks, white light fixtures, mimicking a photographer's product backdrop. The strollers are set on platforms that bookend each row of desks, for easy viewing and reference. Rather than separating the departments, the desks were organized around internally-lit, partial height walls so that employees would have some sense of privacy, but also be able to have visual access throughout the entire office and communicate readily with other departments.

↓ → GALCIT • John Friedman Alice Kimm Architects

The client wanted the space to reflect the innovative research being performed by the department's teachers and students. The program included a new lobby; new laboratories for teaching and experimental research; new exhibition areas; and new conference, office, and interactive spaces, configured to give GALCIT the strong, dynamic branding they desired to attract the world's best scientists, engineers, and students.

Given the variety of topics that the GALCIT faculty and students research, pinpointing a formal starting point was a challenge. Aerospace engineering includes everything from the way blood cells flow to rocket science, or a new Mars Rover vehicle in collaboration with a group from NASA. How to be inclusive? Ultimately the formal language derived from the notion of Flow. Almost all GALCIT research involves flow – understanding how solids, liquids, and gases behave under differential pressures. As a result, the existing building became a metaphorical wind tunnel a neutral container into which new ceilings and wrappers could be inserted. The resultant flow patterns became the basis of new spatial relationships and definitions.

↓ → **PostPanic** • Maurice Mentjens

Parallel to the façade but diagonally placed, the 16-seater (5m x 1.20m) table meant for reading and dining has a hollow middle to store books and magazines. Bar, grandstand, table and screen provide the office's 'recreation zone'. Occasionally the employees can sit on the grandstand, beer in hand, enjoying a film or a match.

↓ → **Goods Shed North** • BVN Architecture

The refurbishment of the Goods Shed North, in Docklands, a heritage listed railway goods shed, presented a great opportunity to renew an integral part of Melbourne's history.
Whilst the building's historical exterior has been restored, the interior has been designed to be an innovative, contemporary, office space. The design enables the organizations to foster a more innovative and collaborative work ethic through increased visibility and transparency and the creation of both active and passive project spaces within the building's central zones. By locating workspaces to the east and west side wings and retaining clear lines of sight through the building's spine, multifunctional project spaces were created centrally within the base of the voids to ensure greater staff interaction and connectivity.

↓ **Ogilvy** • Studio Ramin Visch

The entire staff occupies a single colossal open space of 115 × 50 m (377 × 164 ft). Under the high shed roofs, interior partitions and offices are noticeably absent. The only interruption in this enormous workspace consists of four large patios. To make the former factory halls suitable for housing a publicity firm, architect Georg Witteveen and interior designer Ramin Visch devised a strategy of 'light urbanism'. In other words, there was to be no fixed distribution of the interior space with a permanent infrastructure of corridors and services; instead a more or less provisional exploration of the floor area was adopted using detachable elements.

↓ → **Red Town** • Taranta Creations

The office is situated in a former metal factory. The distance between the existing steel structure and ceiling was too small to fit a much-needed second floor into the space. The architects resolved the problem by creating a horizontal surface just above the steel structure with four workstations placed in the space between the steel sections. This way the "floor" is transformed into one continuous desk, while the four recessed stations provide a more traditional workspace. The large 'work floor' invites the designers to use the open space for thinking, sketching, meeting, drafting, modeling, sitting and relaxing. This informal interpretation of office space encourages cross-pollination between the different projects and disciplines occurring within the studio.

← ↓ Thin Office • Studio SKLIM

The program brief was for an office space shared by two companies, an IT company and a multi-media setup. Located in a refurbished post-war building in Singapore's CBD outskirts, the space was long and narrow with split levels, offering the possibility of a raised space. Throughout the long and narrow office, the ceiling and wall conditions were left unaltered as much as possible, along with the existing light fixtures. The designed space was to reflect the ethos of the companies: flexibility, technology and creativity. The office space was loosely organised into eight clusters, namely: the Boss Boxes, Long Work Top, Discussion Table, Welcome Mat, Sanitary & Storage, Recharging Point, Twist Platform and Multi-media Corner. Each of these clusters was arranged around an open plan configuration, with the exception of Sanitary & Storage, to allow a multifarious overlap of working trajectories.

← ↓ Z58 • Kengo Kuma & Associates

The largest public space is the four-story high atrium, which serves as an exhibition and conference space, and gently connects the interior with Fanyu Road in front of the building. Since Feng Shui holds great importance in China, it was decided to incorporate water into this section of the building. A "glass waterfall" was created by painstakingly bonding approximately 5,000 individual glass bars with a sectional shape of 20 x 20mm (0.8 x 0.8in) to plate glass. Water continually flows down these glass bars, creating white bubbles. The waterfall is surprisingly loud, some people have even called it the "Niagara Falls of Shanghai." A Quiet living space awaits people after passing under this unique cascade.

← ING • (EEA) Erick van Egeraat associated architects

The dynamics of the exterior find their continuation when entering the building through one of the atria. Connecting all office floors, this communal space with slightly inclined, semi-transparent surfaces is surprisingly bright, yet without being overwhelming. The use of glass and steel drapery creates a layered effect, arousing a feel of intimacy and solace. The detailing again seeks relation to the traditional architecture.

↓ **Publicmotor Brand Communication** • Bottega + Ehrhardt Architekten

A loft space with an overall size of about 700 sqm in the center of Stuttgart was transformed into the new office space for Publicmotor. Rectangular volumes covered with a light gray carpet divide the space into separate workstations. The volumes serve as cupboards, acoustic insulation and have integrated lighting. Yellow vertical volumes, serving as the office library, separate the working area from the communication zone.

→ **MAXAN** • Abeijón-Fernández

The office is located one flight above street level and its connection to the street is a black stairway designed to contrast with the white, neutral space of the interior. The concept of the space is open; the different departments interrelate visually and spatially with one another, following the work method of the firm. Divisions are kept to a minimum and if they exist, tend to dematerialise through the use of glass. False ceilings, emphasized through the use of indirect light, and furnishings have been used as configuring elements for the spaces, achieving a high level of interior permeability. Custom-made furnishings were made by Distecar S.L, with chairs by Arper.

↑ → Mews House Studio • Geoffrey Powis

The studio occupies the lower level of a two-storey nineteenth century building and has been radically transformed from a garage workshop to create a single volume space in which to live and work. About half the floor area has been excavated to allow two levels at the rear and one at the side. The lower level accommodates a single stainless steel kitchen worktop, office and storage areas. An exposed steel frame supports an aluminum floor deck with workspace above. Sliding perforated aluminum and polycarbonate panels enclose a shower room and dressing area. Alternating steps folded from a sheet of steel provide access between the levels.

A four-meter high bed space is located externally at the front and is lit by a wall of sandblasted glass and skylight above.

The front façade is transformed into a mobile sculpture by three pivoting glass doors, which incorporate electric blinds to create an entirely open or closed face to the mews.

↓ → Office in 't Gooi • Koen van Velsen

The ground floor includes a reception area, work spaces and a conference room while the offices occupy the first floor. A staircase situated in the middle of the floor plan connects the two levels. The open plan interior is divided by glass walls on both levels increasing the amount of light entry throughout the space and offering a less hierarchical and friendlier atmosphere. On the ground floor the floors and ceiling are clad in wooden boards, affording the space warmth, while the second floor ceiling is the pitched roof, which is perforated by numerous skylights, again allowing light to flood into the interior.

↓ → **Glass House** • Shinichi Ogawa & Associates

The building is located in the western part of the Japanese city of Hiroshima, known as Nishi Ward. This area lies on the estuary of the Hachiman River where it flows into the Seto Inland Sea.
This is a very pure, geometrical volume, a minimal and open glass box that contains both the house and studio of the architect Shinichi Ogawa.
The project is based on a three metre, three-dimensional grid and takes the simple form of a 6x15x12 m box. The volume is divided into four parts along its Z-axis, with the two uppermost blocks (6x15x6m) forming the third floor, where the architectural office is located, while the two lower blocks function as the first and second floor living spaces.
The different living areas are divided by furniture and partitions, and the spaces have a neutral quality, allowing a flexible response to changing functional requirements.
The building is wrapped in transparent glass on all four façades, which strongly contributes to making the interior a very sunny and clean space during the day. All spaces can be enclosed if desired, however, using movable insulating screens that change the perception of the building from the outside as well.

↓ → Grip Limited • Johnson Chou

This is Johnson Chou's second project for the Canadian advertising agency, Grip. The plans for the new offices incorporated an array of different spaces into the building's first, fifth and sixth floors. The resulting space included a reception area, formal and creative boardrooms, meeting rooms, an atrium, creative offices, open workstations, studio spaces, kitchens, a lunch area, lounges, rooms for screening, editing, and photography and showers.
An atrium visually and functionally links the two main floors, the fifth and sixth, with a double-height space, within which the major gathering/lounging activities and vertical circulation take place. A staircase here relates to the bleacher seating, constructed from folded, hot-rolled steel and stained walnut veneer. This provides a gathering space for full office meetings, film presentations and an alternative workplace with a laptop. Vertical circulation is also provided by way of a slide, which has become the adopted symbol at Grip, and a fire-pole, which both connect the creative offices located on the two levels at the north wall. These surprisingly exhilarating and unique experiences of movement through the office act as a metaphor for the agency's belief in the importance of the creative process; a methodology centered on the notion that the journey is as important as the destination, and should be as enjoyable.

↓ → **Horten** • 3XN

3XNs design for Danish Law Firm Horten's new head office reflects the duality between the classic and the modern, combining solidity with an advanced choice of materials that express the profile of Horten's practice.
The emphasis is placed on a spatial experience with optimum daylight conditions in the individual offices as well as in communal areas. The main layout places the offices in two angled building volumes with open atria between them, creating visual contact between the two. Between the atria, distinctive sets of stairs criss cross up through the circular stairwell, the spine of the building, creating interaction and contact between storeys. Only twodecks are accessible to visitors, the reception area and the top floor, which contains meeting rooms, etc. The flexible office environment encourages knowledge sharing, informal meetings and interdepartmental communication which in means that employees benefit mentally and physically from their new surroundings.

↓ → **BP Refinery** • GROUP A

An elongated and organising atrium space is cut out from the man made dune, full of light and with constantly changing dimensions by the undulating cutting edge to the dune side. The wall on the cutting edge is covered with timber slats that differ in color and size, and evoke an association with geological layers; a reference to the business activities of BP RR. The extensive use of natural materials like wood, concrete and natural stone, again emphasise the 'nature' and robustness of the core business activities of the company

↓ → **PONS / HUOT** • Christian Pottgiesser

The starting point was a derelict industrial hall built in the late 19th century with a steel framework typical of the period, and a glass roof that was on the verge of collapse. Rumor has it that it was designed by none other than Gustave Eiffel.
To start with, the hall was completely restored. A new glass roof was fitted, and all the main features of the building was put back into their original state. Finally, the project itself consists of inserting into the existing shell a wooden unit made of solid oak, 1.7 m high, 22 m long and 14 m wide (0.57×7.34×4.67 ft). The entire program is embodied therein. Each individual workplace is incised into the wooden upper surface and covered by a "telephone"-dome in Plexiglas. The four lateral surfaces contain filing systems, cloakrooms and the kitchen. Completely embedded in the body are the meeting room, the recreational room and the restrooms. The remaining space is taken up by technical transmission systems (computer, electricity, air condition, heating and water) and also by 18.3 cubic meters (646 cubic feet) of soil, the bed for eight Ficus Panda trees.

↓ → **Anderssons Flat and Architectural Office** • Stig L. Andersson

The flat, located in central Copenhagen, is inside a block dating from the early twentieth century. It contains the residence and studio of the Danish architect Stig Andersson.
The restoration focused on intensifying the experience of the textural effect of the surfaces. "Reason is not interesting. It is all about 'contemplation of the surfaces', a meditation. (...) One learns from looking into walls", says Andersson, a great admirer of the Japanese tradition.
"My wish was to create a home in this spirit. Over the years many people have been lived in this flat. More than seven wallpaper designs were the signs of this long story. By removing all the superfluous designs I have achieved an impression rich in experiences.
So I decided to leave the walls entirely free of wallpaper, only asking the craftsmen to fill out some of the irregularities and gaps. This is the rawest impression one can create. Only where necessary I took a bit more care, for example on the walls where all the pictures are placed. The refined lines appear more clearly against the rustic impression of the background. By placing more refined objects on the rough walls the items look more elegant and delicate".
The colors in the flat are very vague. "In our country one will find many shades of gray, which change with the light all the time. The Danish landscape has many fine shades. There are no intense impressions to see as in the south. The colors in our part of the world are cool like our climate. In our light there are no deep contrasts, therefore the colors seem dustier. The light is often more diffuse. It is this ambiance that I was looking for in this flat. Therefore, I used Japanese paper roller blinds."

↓ → **Scherpontwerp** • RO&AD architecten

In planning a new office space for their clients Scherpontwerp, a graphic design company and De Boekenmakers, publishers, in the centre of Eindhoven in The Netherlands, RO&AD Architects drew inspiration surprisingly from the open spaces of Central Park in Manhattan. In their view it is a good example of a clear space, defined by a rectangle where no buildings are allowed. Their objective was to convert 200 sqm (2150 sqft) of dreary, disorganised rented office space into a pleasant and stimulating working environment within a limited budget.

They applied the urban concept as seen in Central Park to the office environment. First they defined the maximum rectangular space in the centre of the area, then filled the outer edges with cardboard. The functional items needed - shelves, desks, work stations, meeting areas, a canteen and walk-in cupboards - were then sculpted out of the cardboard, while a long low table was created out of cardboard in the central area. Just as the buildings around Central Park define the park, the interior cardboard edges define the open space in this office; the buildings have urban functions and the interior facades have interior functions.

← ↓ **Mother** • Clive Wilkinson Architects

Mother is a young but significant British advertising agency whose radical approach to the advertising business and contemporary culture has translated into their work environment. The company boasts a flat organization with no space privileges; everyone working around a single large worktable. As the advertising agency has grown so has the table. Clive Wilkinson Architects was awarded the project of redesigning Mother's work premises in a three-story warehouse covering 3900 sqm (42 000 sqft) in Shoreditch, London. The client elected to use the 2nd floor as their primary workspace due to the existing enhanced 13 ft floor height and a large 1300 sqm (14 000 sqft) open area. In order to achieve a strong connection to the loading bay lobby, two floors below, the team of architects proposed to build a new concrete staircase the width of a small road, which cuts through the building and connects the three floors. This 4.65 m (14 ft) wide staircase would turn into the Agency's cast-in-place concrete worktable and circuit the third floor room like a racetrack. At 84 meters (250 feet) long it has become perhaps the world's largest table with a maximum capacity of 200 people. Due to its enormous dimensions it has been broken in sections to aid circulation. The inspiration for the concrete table was the iconic 1920's Giacomo Matte-Trucco roof top race track for Fiat Lingotto in Turin.

↓ → St Joseph Media • Teeple Architects / Superkül Inc

The reception area is a strategic point in the corridor and large stairways at each end connect the floors, striking visual features in steel and acrylic. This space is wrapped with patterned glass, and felt is used to absorb sound and for magazine logos and signs. These new interventions form a sleek counterpoint to the raw materials of the original warehouse, though respect for the 19th century elements has been shown. The interior brick has been sand blasted, wooden floors sanded and sealed and some of the timber structures retained to give a sense of industrial loft space.

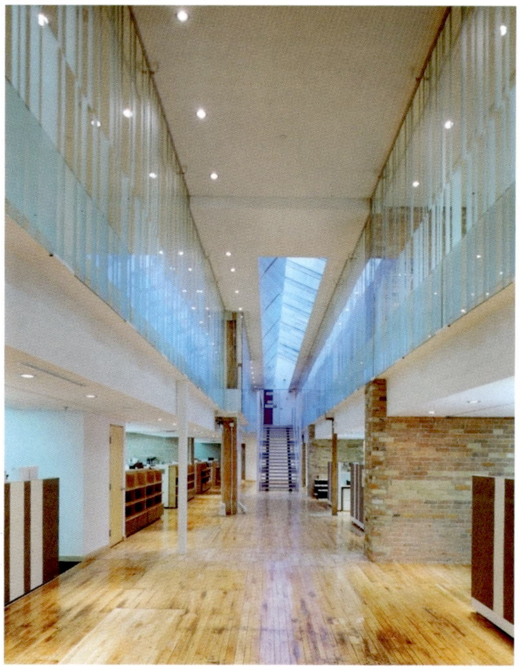

← ↓ **Rehauwork** • weber+würschinger

Rehauwork is a project that addresses the refurbishment of an obsolete but solid industrial building into office space for 150 employees. The existing building could not be altered as it is a listed architectural landmark. The intervention involved inserting all of the modern facilities into the existing structure without affecting it in any way other than restoring it to its original condition. The old factory has been adapted to the new requirements of the workspace, concerning data processing systems, atmospheric conditions, luminosity and ergonomics. The location houses managerial office space in each department, room for 150 employees, areas for copiers and printers, meeting rooms, relaxing areas, exhibition space and storage facilities.

The lofty appearance of the century-old industrial shell with its great window surfaces has been conserved. Based on the colors white and grey, a reductionist material concept developed, permitting porcelain, the product of the enterprise, to speak for itself. The scarce presence of color defines areas, with accents of orange, details of yellow and/or plants.

↓ → **Forum 3, Novartis** • Diener & Diener Architekten

The colorful impression that the building conveys outside forms a contrast with the light, solid elegance of the interior. To achieve an impression of softness, interior architectonic elements such as handrails, the glass walls of the meeting rooms and the lounge are equipped with metal profiles and wrapped around with synthetic leather. The design of the interior was intended to allow employees to have a large number of individual, joint, open-plan and closed work areas at their disposal.

→ **Red Bull HQ** • Jump Studios

The brief was to amalgamate two separate offices into one central headquarters building, located in London's Soho district. The new offices occupy the top three floors of an existing 19th century building, and include a recent roof-level extension in the form of a glass "box" surrounded by an exterior terrace, providing spectacular views of the West End.

This, according to Jump Studios' director himself, Simon Jordan, represents an ideal starting point for both employees and visitors alike, as a way for them to experience the building. They arrive by lift into the top-floor public reception and social zone, before descending through the building. This sense of descent is enhanced by voids punched through the building's fabric, providing vertiginous views. A three-story video wall occupies one void, while another includes a dramatic circulation system, consisting of a floating staircase and even a slide, aimed at encouraging free movement through the spaces.

The design team has succeeded in creating an open, efficient, dynamic and connected workspace. The top floor acts as a social hub, containing the main reception, bar, café, both informal and formal meeting areas, plus the main boardroom. They are all in continual use throughout the day, both for company activities and to encourage interaction. These top floor features are "stitched" together by a continuous, snaking carbon-fiber element, which runs from the exterior terrace (providing a wing canopy) through the building, encapsulating the main boardroom, forming the reception area, before disappearing through a void to form the enclosure for the slide and support for the staircase. It terminates on the lower floor as a platform, creating an informal meeting area. The feature evokes the trace patterns left by skaters, snowboarders, stunt planes, race cars and bikes, symbolizing Red Bull´s commitment to placing adrenalin sport at the heart of its business.

01
02
03

01

↓ → **Lindberghatelier** • Nickl & Partner Architekten

The objective of the program was to design a building whose structure and flexibility would reflect the needs and demands of the future tenants, whilst at the same time harmonizing outwardly with the as yet unfinished but essentially heterogeneous nature of the surrounding development.
The result is a simple cube. Anchored by its head –the entrance area– to the Lindberghstrasse in the south, the body of the building appears to almost float into the landscape. The rather raw industrial character of the outer skin has an optically defensive effect that belies the openness enjoyed by the occupants.
The entrance area contains communal facilities such as kitchen, staff room and foyer. The office and workshop area is openly planned to allow future tenants maximum flexibility to create their own working space.
The first floor in its entirety is home to the architectural offices of Nickl + Partner Architekten GmbH, these being composed of the architectural workshop with two special use areas, and a central area containing service and information facilities. The two head ends of the floor are occupied respectively by the management offices and competition department to the north, and reception and conference facilities to the south, the functional division of the offices being defined by moveable partitions and the illuminated boxes of the central area.

↓ → **Saxo Bank** • 3XN

In spite of the fact that Saxo Banks's clients primarily meet their bank in cyber space, the physical gesture of the head office is of great importance to the bank's management, who took a great interest in the design process. This was not only due to the client's interest in the creation of a building endowed with iconographic qualities, but also to the conviction that architecture and design plays an important role for staff performance and dedication to the company.

Inside, a transparent and inspiring environment enhances the sense of team spirit. The open plans centre round a softly shaped top-lit atrium with a winding main staircase. The trading floor located at the top of the building contains state of the art technology and a highly international staff of professional bankers.

The building consists of a structure of LVL (Glulam) timber porticos with 20 m spans placed at 5 m centers, clad with Alucobond aluminum panels. A coffered concrete floor slab supported on slender concrete columns has been inserted within this structure to divide the building into two levels. On the upper floor the structure is completed with angled tapering timber columns.

↓ → **Sony Music Sweden** • Claesson Koivisto Rune

Sony Music Sweden moved from the outskirts of Stockholm into the center of the city, into a six-story building that had formerly been used as a church. Music, music at high volume and one stereo per employee. No wonder a traditional record company is all closed offices and corridors. But the modern organization called for more direct internal communication. The solution was a hybrid between an open and closed plan (and headphones). The project combines closed conference, meeting and listening rooms with open-plan workstations. Half-height partitions, freestanding wall units or cabinets divide the open workspace into different departments.

The big, open space with two mezzanines enabled the architects to create an intricate spatial composition that works both horizontally and vertically. Two longitudinal staircases connect the floors. Most of the office storage was placed against the stair walls. When moving around the floors or up and down the stairs the spaces is constantly changing as lines of vision open and close.

↓ → **Jazztel Lisboa** • Carlos Manzano y Asociados

When the architects remodeled this 7,000 m former grain store, the project established the hierarchical structure of a city, with two districts – the urban extension and the garden city – an avenue, a square and a port. The structure of two inclined volumes forms the entrance to the city. The widest part of the office represents suburban expansion. A perpendicular arrangement of work positions makes up the blocks of house, only interrupted by the avenue.
At the end of this route is the square, a place for reunions and rest from the office. The garden city is the management area. White volumes with marked edges stand out against the slate floor and organize the space by creating different work areas.
Once the space on the ground plan was structured, the subject of height was considered. Here micro architecture has been the answer: small sections that interrupt the view and mark out the workspaces. On the ground floor, solid bodies hold the offices and on the upper floor they hold the meeting rooms: elevated open micro squares over the city.

↓ → Beacon Communications • Klein Dytham architecture

The newly formed agency, Beacon Communications, wanted to move into offices that reflected their unique approach to advertising and could accommodate new ways of working. Located in a new 17-floor office tower, the four-story, 56,300 sqft (5,200 sqm) office interior features wild curves, Day-Glo colors and open-plan offices.

Each of the column-free floors is divided into open workspace traversed by an undulating 15-ft wide "ribbon", within which shared function are lined up like train compartments. The lowest floor houses the reception, management and support area, while the other levels are devoted to ad development.

For individual workstations, the designers arranged an office system in horseshoe clusters that can accommodate up to 85 workers per day. Company directors have not only foregone private offices but also desks. Each director has a chair of his or her choice, a filing cabinet on wheels and a spot at a collective directors' work area. Clad in white plastic laminate, this station has an inviting openness. The ribbon's meeting rooms are accessible from either side, each of the four ribbons has a frame covered with plasterboard, rising to become the ceiling over a conference room, stepping down to form screening-area seating, or swooping low to provide a platform for a test kitchen.

↓ → **TBWA \ Chiat \ Day** • Marmol Radziner and Associates

The architects received the commission to renovate an 85-year-old four-story warehouse near the San Francisco Bay for the advertising firm TBWA \ Chiat \ Day. The architects sought inspiration for the design in the site's maritime history, and the architectural forms and materials are a reference to the ships buried beneath the building as well as the cargo crates that used to be stored in the building.

By stripping the building down to its existing brick walls, wood ceilings, timber columns and large glass windows, the space and access to natural light are significantly improved. A huge, upwardly curving wall of rough horizontal boards, recalling a fragment of a wooden ship's outer hull, draws visitors through the lobby. The upper floor has been cut away to reveal other curving laminated forms, which suggest the ribs of oddly configured ships. Only partially visible overhead, these elements form the structure of translucent polycarbonate-lined conference and project rooms on the second level.

↓ → **Snowcrash** • Tham Videgård Hansson

Tham Videgård Hansson were commissioned to remodel one floor of an industrial building in Stockholm as the headquarters of a Swedish-Finnish company that specializes in developing products for the home.
The building, measuring 28 x 42 x 3 m internally, had a column and slab concrete structure and light from the east, west and south. Apart from an open-plan office and showroom, the program also included a workshop, a prototype atelier and an apartment for visiting designers.
The new office layout combines an effective open office with defined rooms of varying size. The aim was to create an optimum work environment, and aspects such as acoustics, lighting and air were studied. The main design element is a continuous, free formed, glass wall inserted into the existing warehouse structure. The undulating glass core creates defined places within the premises: showroom, east office, kitchen, west office. Simultaneously it constitutes a link between all areas, both visually and logistically.

Belastingdienst
Dienst Uitvoering Onderwijs

← Education Executive Agency & Tax Offices • UNStudio

A new, 92 meter tall complex of soft, undulating curves marks the skyline of Groningen. This asymmetric, aerodynamic construction is set amidst small, ancient woodland, sheltering rare and protected species. The project includes the design, construction and financing of two public institutions; the national tax offices and the student loan administration. Accommodating 2500 workstations, parking facilities for 1500 bicycles and 675 cars in an underground garage, the building will be surrounded by a large public city garden with pond and a multifunctional pavilion with commercial functions.

The architecture aims to present these institutions with a softer, more human and approachable profile. Tall buildings are generally associated with mid-twentieth century modernism. Their harsh, businesslike exteriors contain powerful, inaccessible-seeming strongholds. By contrast, the DUO and Tax offices deliberately cloak a commanding public institution in an organic, friendlier and more future-oriented form.

↓ Middelfart Savings Bank • 3XN

The building is characterized by a dramatic roofscape accommodating multiple functions. 83 prism-like skylights compose the spectacular roof surface defining the geometry of the building – in reference to the maritime environment as well as the surrounding timber framed buildings. Thus, the new Head Office gently reflects and interacts with the dimensions, scales, roofs and cornice lines of the old town.

A bookshop, a café, a real estate agent and the cash desk are placed around a central plaza, resulting in the building forming an informal public meeting space at the ground floor level. The Savings Bank work stations are located on three open terraces internally connected by broad staircases encouraging interaction and informal meetings or breaks. All plateaus are endowed with plenty of daylight and an unhindered view to the water.

Private Spaces

↓ → JWT Headquarters • Clive Wilkinson Architects

As circulation off the stairs flow into distinctive 'neighborhoods' representing various departments within the agency, special landmarks such as meeting and conference rooms help create visual interest while facilitating way-finding. The creative area includes a mezzanine 'tree house' structure with several collaboration spaces and an adjacent multi-purpose café/bar space with an illuminated bar.

↓ → **Nendo** • Neguro Office

The firm wanted the usual spaces and functions -meeting space, management, workspace and storage- to be separated from one another while at the same time maintaining a sense of connection between them. To achieve this effect, the architects divided the space with walls that seem to sag and flop like a piece of cloth held up between two hands. Employees can move between spaces by walking over the parts of the walls that "sag" the most, thus emphasizing the contrast between the uses of the different spaces. Spaces that need more sound-proofing are enclosed with the kind of plastic curtains you might find at a small factory so that people can work without worrying about noise but not feel isolated. When you stand up and look through the whole space, people, shelves and plants seem to appear and disappear as though floating between the waves.

← Ynno Workplace • Sprikk

The floor plan is kept entirely open with the exception of two acoustically separated glass volumes. In this open plan, organically shaped birchwood structures were placed that form partitions, niches, storage spaces and bookshelves. The wood structures contain a number of ergonomic workplaces that embrace daylight and offer a view to the outside. Settings for the concentrated individual as well as active collaboration can be found. A vis-à-vis setting for casual discussions is placed on a platform integrated into the wooden structures. Groups of up to eight people can work on projects and presentations in an acoustically well-balanced room. The room is fitted with writable surfaces and high-end presentation equipment. Private meetings or presentations for clients are held in an acoustically separated room that offers a casual atmosphere and plenty of daylight.

← ↓ Studio Spec • Facet Studio

Three functions, two characters, one irregular office space: this demanding project cleverly integrates three separate programs – a graphic design studio, a graphic design school and a beauty consultation room – by creating spaces within the main space through the installation of two opposed wooden boxes.

↓ → **Yuras** • Sinato

New rooms were constructed in the middle of the floor plan for this office without touching or modifying in any way the existing floor, walls or ceiling including the lights and the air conditioners. The new rooms were required to be closed, intimate spaces because of the purposes they would serve. The upper part of the partitions that separates the rooms was therefore bent so that the section form of each room might taper off as it rises. Openings in these walls allow natural light to enter the interior and offer a connection with the surrounding office space, avoiding any sense of claustrophobia. The bending form of these new offices, which is designed to affect the inside of the rooms, also has a direct consequence on the form as seen from the exterior. An outward appearance similar to a connection of gabled cabins or a mountain range appears by placing the aforementioned section form side by side. In addition, this symbolic mountain range mass is arranged diagonally and becomes a thick partition which divides the site into work space and common space.

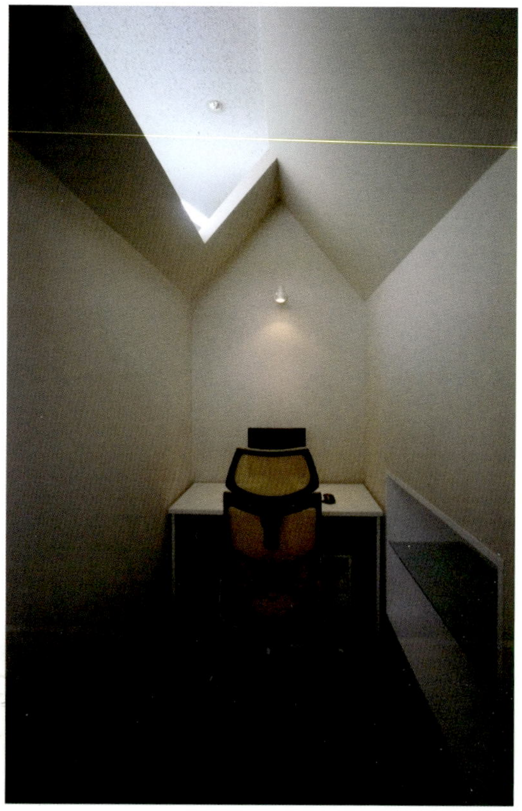

↑ ← **Z58** • Kengo Kuma & Associates

The newly added forth floor consists of four glass boxes, which contain bedrooms, a canteen and a lounge, intended for designers that come from cities around the world to attend meetings in Shanghai. Again natural elements play a fundamental role in defining the space. A large surface of water covering the roof of the building makes these installations appear to float, and establishes a visual connection between this area and the beautiful Sun Yatsen family gardens next to the building.

709159

← **Cargo** • Group 8

The offices are housed within a former industrial warehouse which contains a hidden treasure: 16 recycled shipping containers, all of which have traveled thousands of miles around the globe. These silent travelers are piled up like giant Lego bricks, left, in fact, as they were found, without any changes made to their exteriors. The aesthetic maintains the poetry of their former use and differentiates them from the immateriality of the large neutral space they lie in.
On a practical level, the use of containers represents a gain of 2,150 sqft (200 sqm), and makes excellent use of the ceiling height. Following the concept of artist Marcel Duchamp's "readymades", these monumental objects have acquired a new function. Modern objects and industrial space both recover a functional use which turns them into contemporary living and working spaces. The containers formalize structured collective spaces. Each container embodies a collective form or a work-related situation: meeting rooms, cafeteria, lounge zone, bathrooms and showers, etc.

↓ **North** • Skylab Architecture

A cantilevered think-tank module is elevated above the center of the space. It reveals a view of the West Hills through clerestory windows in the building. Similar to the North creative process that reveals something about a client's brand that may have always been there but had not been communicated, this view had always been there, it was simply waiting for the viewpoint to be created.

→ **No Picnic** • Elding Oscarson

The client wanted large, open office spaces, a prototype workshop, a prototype showroom, several project rooms and a customer area, separated from the other spaces in order to maintain privacy. The meeting rooms behind the metal membrane have large windows overlooking the hall. The flat reflection of the glass flush with the distorting metal surface makes the glass seem like a mirror while the metal appears transparent: the wall is there, yet it disappears. It is bold, kaleidoscopic and illusory with its trompe l'oeil effects. At the same time it allows the main act to take center stage: the light and space of the exercise hall and the old building's straightforward display of materials, construction, imperfections, and the passage of time.

← **Publicmotor Brand Communication** • Bottega + Ehrhardt Architekten

The management workstations and the meeting room are divided by floor to ceiling glass partitions and their degree of privacy can be individually controlled with bronze-colored semitransparent curtains.

↓ → **Thin Office** • Studio SKLIM

The flexible working environment was kept in mind with the possibility of hot-desking, informal working clusters and also semi-private cubicles. The Boss Boxes were an option for more privacy as some work required a certain level of seclusion. The unconventional form of the Twist Platform in an otherwise sleek and straightforward office space added a dynamic backdrop to the Recharging Point and provided privacy to the independent operation of the multi-media setup. The giant overhead light fixture was a final touch to the suggestion of this event space.

→ **Cubion** • Jackie-B

The kitchen is designed as a social meeting room with a bright yellow table that centers the room. A forest of Photostats leads into the back office where a representation of a child's playhouse with small lamp flowers stands as a shining white homage to play and imagination. The sofa house offers space for deep thoughts and loose conversations.

→ **Onesize** • Origins Architects

The program included standard workspaces together with dark rooms for editing and projections. The existing building, a top-lit industrial hangar, was an open and airy space which the architects saw would lend itself to the insertion of a central volume around which the work of the company could be carried out. Whereas projection rooms and editing suites are often segregated from other activities and located in basements or residual spaces, in this project they have been placed in the very center of the plan, representing their position and importance in the firm's activities, aligned along the central axis of the space within a striking secondary structure. This structure, inspired by the visual modeling activities of the firm, is a series of polygonal sculptural forms realized in low-grade timber multiplex board which transforms the program into an interesting shape while subdividing the space to create a clear layout.

The three central structures house, respectively, the meeting space, projection room and editing suite, with degrees of permeability of their outer shells which vary in relation to the activity housed within. Thus the editing suite and projection room volumes are opaque on three sides with glazed end walls permitting visual connection to surrounding spaces, while the meeting space is defined by series of porticoes which suggest, rather than enclose, its volume.

←↓→ **Red Bull Canadian Headquarters** • Johnson Chou Inc.

The architects decided to modify the original building fabric as little as possible for cost reasons in order to focus on improving the existing services and implementing new architectural elements. The Music Academy encapsulates Red Bull's corporate philosophy of mentorship instead of sponsorship. The new space, both as the Academy and later as the Canadian Headquarters of the brand is intended to function as a forum for the exchange of ideas, an inspirational hub where knowledge and experience is gained and disseminated and the participants transformed through the experience. The design concept used for the Music Academy and Headquarters was a metaphorical representation of the spaces as vessels for transformation: both as significant events in the lives of the participants and experientially, with engaging, interactive architectural elements.

The notion of "vessels" and "transformation" is represented at many levels, from the smallest detail to the overall space.
The architectural elements of the space are "vessels" created to support the activities within, designed to stimulate creativity. Gathering spaces from enclosed, private rooms to open casual areas for impromptu meetings provide opportunities for the exchange of ideas.
The wing-like curved glass partition walls of the private offices animate the space, creating pattern and repetition. A new double-height atrium space with a custom-designed perforated steel spiral stair was created to link the two floors. Second floor meeting rooms contain bar-like, sunken, and formal meeting areas.

↓ → **BP Refinery** • GROUP A

The atrium is flanked by two parallel office wings. Office floors, each linked by bridges, are in open connection with each other and the atrium space. Meetings take place in box-shaped volumes, pushed into the atrium as 'sky-boxes'. The entire BP RR organisation operates in one open space according to 'The New World of Work' principles, resulting in an interactive environment that encourages communication, collaboration and creativity amongst staff.

service desk
service desk
post & copy room
postkamer & repro

↓ **PostPanic** • Maurice Mentjens

Large pivoting wooden doors separate the meeting room from the hall. Carpeted as a single object, the fluid lines of the floor, walls and table create a futuristic grotto.

↓ **Bugaboo** • RA-DA

The private offices along the south edge of the main space are separated only by a transparent glass wall in order to avoid the visual separation that private offices often generate.

↓ → **HTC** • chadbourne + doss architects

The owner of HTC wanted an open-plan office, but with the addition of spaces for more private, silent, contemplative work.
Six drywall pods lined with plywood have glazed façades that look onto the main space and define the entry hall. Each pod contains a writable laminate desk and a chair, providing the company's staff with a place of retreat when extra concentration of the more individual sort is needed.

↓ → **LEGO** • Bosch & Fjord

In LEGO Group's development department, Bosch & Fjord also designed 13 meeting rooms, each with its own unique identity. There are rooms for all kinds of meetings: large and small; long and short; development and brainstorming meetings; confidential and intimate; formal business meetings, etc. The design and the creative solutions stimulate more than just the work processes. The employees are personally challenged and motivated, which in turn contributes to a healthy and comfortable working environment and boosts the ongoing development process within the company.

← Goods Shed North • BVN Architecture

The refurbishment of the Goods Shed North, in Docklands, a heritage listed railway goods shed, presented a great opportunity to renew an integral part of Melbourne's history.

Whilst the building's historical exterior has been restored, the interior has been designed to be an innovative, contemporary, office space. The design enables the organizations to foster a more innovative and collaborative work ethic through increased visibility and transparency and the creation of both active and passive project spaces within the building's central zones. By locating workspaces to the east and west side wings and retaining clear lines of sight through the building's spine, multifunctional project spaces were created centrally within the base of the voids to ensure greater staff interaction and connectivity.

↓ dtac • HASSELL

HASSELL designed the new workplace for dtac, one of Thailand's leading telecommunication providers, to accommodate 3500 staff members occupying 62 000 sqm over 20 floors.

The design successfully reflects dtac's corporate philosophy of 'play and learn', challenging conventional notions of arrival, meeting, concentration and relaxation spaces. The team-based environments created by HASSELL encourage dtac staff to be mobile and creative in their selection of a work space, enabling them to choose between their regular work point, a meeting lounge, or the open terrace overlooking Bangkok's skyline. Open workspaces are supplemented with indoor plants, and the incorporation of a floor dedicated to relaxation and fitness, further enhancing staff amenities and promoting a healthy work environment.

← ↓ **Obscura Digital** • IwamotoScott Architecture

The new space is within a three-story 1940s concrete and steel framed warehouse in the Dogpatch neighborhood of San Francisco. An important aspect of the redesign was the removal of three bays from the center of the building to form a spatial connection between the lower and mid levels. This move also allowed the installation of one of Obscura's hemispherical projection theaters housed within a 30 ft diameter geodesic dome.
Overlooking this new double height space is a conference room designed as a freestanding object peering over the end of the new void, oriented towards the dome. One side of this 'meeting box' is kinked inward to adapt to the seismic bracing of the existing structure and create room for a stair that connects the two levels at the edge of the void.

↓ → **Autodesk AEC** • KlingStubbins

The design solution expresses the Autodesk mission and values by exposing and featuring the building systems. A three-story floor opening visually connects the activities between all floors and provides a dramatic demonstration of the energy of the space to Autodesk visitors. Open workspaces and glass conference rooms provide visual connections and encourage collaboration. Open ceilings expose the building's structural and mechanical systems.

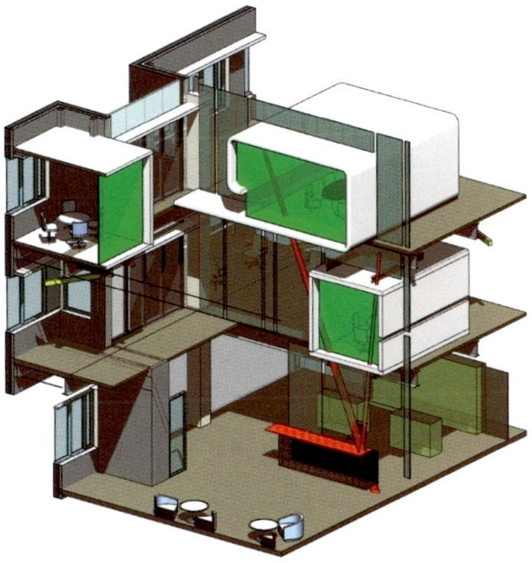

↓ → **Ogilvy** • Studio Ramin Visch

In many regards the Ogilvy office has the character of a covered exterior space. Little pavilion-type buildings can be seen here and there between the long rows of work tables. There are two glass boxes on pillars for meeting rooms that are reminiscent of the famous glass houses of Mies van der Rohe and Philip Johnson in their design and detailing. And there are four black boxes of untreated steel, with raised work floors, which are built on 'cocoons' containing small offices. Two wooden sheds with red boards form an entrance portal and company kitchen respectively.

The pavilions are exceptionally neat and minimalist in their detailing. They are not placed free-standing under the roof, but have good solid foundations underneath the concrete floor, which is located 35 cm (14 in) above the original factory floor to provide room for invisible floor insulation, services and cable ducts. Reverberation is reduced by applying a strong sound-absorbent layer on the underside of the shed roofs.

↓ → Artistic Image / Artemis Creative • ai3

Artistic Image and Artemis Creative headquartered in Atlanta, Georgia, serve high profile clients such as the NFL, Coca Cola, The Golf Channel, Pepsi, and Ford Motor corp.

As both design studios work with clients that may be in direct competition with one another, it was a primary goal to maintain separate identities for each, while at the same time allowing them to collaborate and use the same resources.

Structured with plywood ribs and sheathed in translucent plastics, the tunnel allows for discrete passage from the main entry to one group's studio space on the lower level. The tunnel is lit from within, thereby also serving as a translucent stage that illuminates and projects the interior activity to the studios beyond. The bent plastic distorts the light, creating unique and ever-changing reflections within the space. A white epoxy coating on the concrete floors helps to reflect and bounce light into the inner areas of the space.

The other studio, located on a central mezzanine, is accessed by a "hidden" stairway located behind the feature wall that supports the tunnel. The mezzanine, itself, intended to blend with the lightness and loftiness of the upper clerestory, uses a minimalist approach with cable rail guards for continual light to reach the mezzanine from all possible levels and angles. From high above, the translucent tunnel's fifth elevation is revealed, which reflects light inboard into the space. This group is also given the ability to interact with the existing structural steel trusses, creating a space that is totally connected and immersed within the building itself, and reminds the group of the building's historic importance and presence.

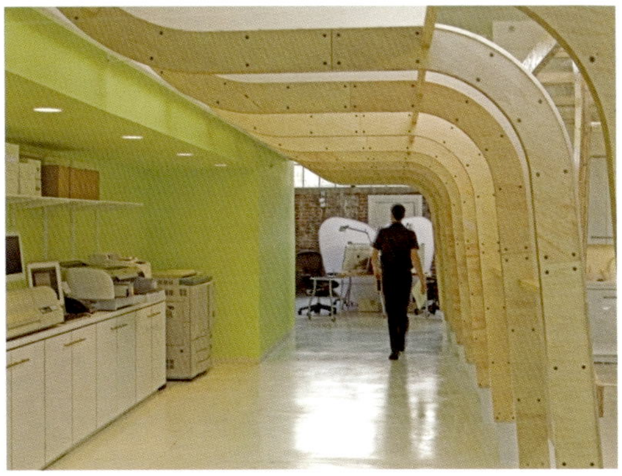

↓ → Grip Limited • Johnson Chou

The meeting/lounge area was designed to resemble a hot tub capable of seating ten people. This small pool offers a circular (and therefore democratic) seating format, and has often been used to disarm the most difficult of clients. A more formal boardroom, known as "the fridge", makes reference to Grip's beer industry clients. Clad in stainless steel, the interior is finished with white synthetic grass, used to absorb sound and because of its resemblance to frost.

↓ → Endeavor • Neil M. Denari Architects Inc.

The screening room consists not only of a high performance space for viewing films, but also a large pre function lobby area, a kitchen/bar, and a major façade to the street. The intention was to make what is essentially a private space become more public. This serves two purposes: One is to create as much spatial depth as possible in the entry sequence so as to break down the flatness of the "storefront" conditions surrounding it. The other is to create a public identity for Endeavor in a way that the offices cannot. The folded aluminum panel façade and the smooth, white undulating ceiling and wall surfaces that form the first 10 ft of the space allow passersby to catch fragments of the floor and ceiling surfaces inside. The exterior wall of the screening room is wrapped with wallpaper designed by 2×4, while the interior is a deeply saturated red world consisting of different materials and textures of paint, carpet, and fabric.

Furniture and Interior Elements

↓ **Prayer Rahs** • SUE Architekten

Stretched storage furniture separates the working area from the hall and communication zone. On one side there are generous cubicles and a meeting room, on the other side of the hall are seating niches, space for photocopiers and a common working area that is shaped by storage furniture. The layering between the entrance area and the central working space is additionally supported by varying material and colours. Sand-coloured walls and floor tiling dominate the friendly reception, while the furniture used to define the rooms are a dark oak. White room furniture with textile patches, custom-arranged in each room, dominate the central area. The generous impression of space provided by the loft is maintained, despite the visual and acoustic separation of the rooms from each other.

The spectacular buyers' lounge on the top floor is an informal meeting space, arranged as a fluid wrap of 3D elastic screen walls around a resin coffee bar. The plan allows those working there to pass through discreetly, and those doing business there to soak up the office atmosphere while finding privacy and refreshment. A smaller meeting room is defined by perforated concave 'wrap' wall. The combination of a limited palette of 'jointless' materials with Lensvelt furniture, make for extraordinary space and light.

↓ → Ynno Workplace • Sprikk

In the open plan, organically shaped birchwood structures were placed that form partitions, niches, storage spaces and bookshelves. By applying one material and a single construction method, a coherent appearance of the space is created that still offers a diversity of working places with gradations between open and closed environments. The natural, haptic qualities of these birchwood structures form a contrast to the high-end communication and presentation technologies that were applied throughout the space.

↓ → **Gummo** • i29 l

All the furniture was locally sourced via Marktplaats (the Dutch eBay), charity shops and whatever was salvageable from the old office. Everything was then spray-painted with Polyurea Hotspray (an environmentally friendly paint) to conform to the new colour scheme. The new coating has given the collection of old and repaired items an exciting new potential.

↓ → **Nendo** • Neguro Office

The firm wanted the usual spaces and functions -meeting space, management, workspace and storage- to be separated from one another while at the same time maintaining a sense of connection between them. To achieve this effect, the architects divided the space with walls that seem to sag and flop like a piece of cloth held up between two hands. People are able to move freely from one space to another while having the capacity to tell at a glance whether they are intruding or not in any given area. Adding to the office's flexibility, furthermore, the wooden panels are not permanent but can be rearranged or removed at any time. In fact, Nendo's designer, Oki Sato, considers these panels to be closer to furniture than to pillars or walls or part of the building's structure.

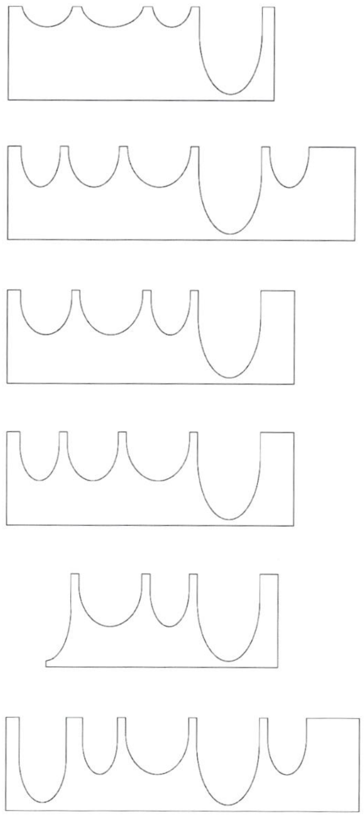

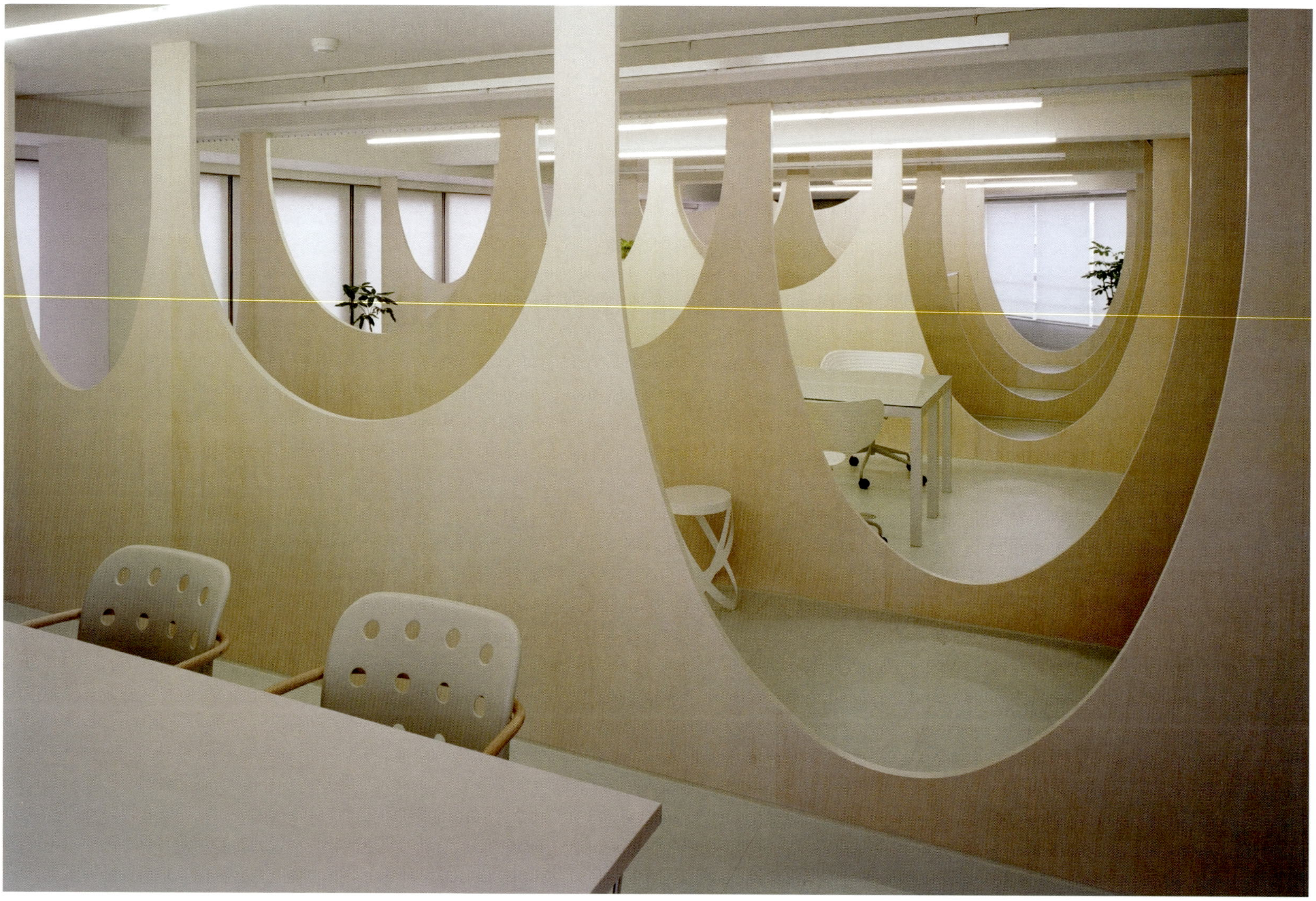

↓ → Dentsu London •
Essentia Designs Limited

The designers wanted to retain as much of the base build elements as possible, so developed the concept of a curved tensile fabric screen to separate the client reception area from the Dentsu Europe team. The reception is entered through a fabric tunnel which peels back to reveal the thermo-formed corian reception desk and client waiting area, a fitting introduction to this amazing agency.

↓ Thin Office • Studio SKLIM

The program for this office fit-out was for flexible working spaces which could be contracted and expanded as the size of the office's workforce varied. The result was the "Long Worktop" which incorporated an ingenious power strip of data points, power supply and telecommunication points to be accessible at any location along this table, expanding the number of workstations from 6 to 10 in a few minutes. This single piece of stretched work surface became part of a greater string of furniture transforming from tabletop, reception seating, storage and finally to pantry space.

← → Publicmotor Brand Communication • Bottega + Ehrhardt Architekten

One enters the office by passing through a "forest" of triangular, dark gray volumes, to an open space and the waiting area, defined by a golden circle on the white floor. Small LCD screens are integrated into the back of the triangular volumes, showing projects and works by the agency. Rectangular volumes covered with a light gray carpet divide the space into separate workstations. The volumes serve as cupboards, acoustic insulation and have integrated lighting. Yellow vertical volumes, ser as the office library, separate the working area from the communication zone. A long wooden table, where the office comes together for lunch, is connected to a small kitchen in the back of the space.

↓ → **Sandoz** • Delugan Meissl Associated Architects

NovaMobile, the flexible shelf system developed especially for Novartis, forms the basis of the interior design of the office spaces:
The shelf system's basic function is separation of access ways and office spaces, but it also forms zones of differing density and transparency – depending on the requirements and communication values of each given place. The combination of different module types, plus variable assembly possibilities permit the parallel formulation of closed-off areas, semitransparent zones, and areas of absolute transparency in different communication and work spaces. All in one, NovaMobile is a space-defining element and visual guideline.
The graphic linearity of the module system, as opposed to the organic patterned screen lit from behind, makes the hallway into an energy-charged place whose impact emphasizes the vastness of the spatial impression and goes beyond the functional. In the lobby, the linear module system takes on the distinct contours of an object – the reception desk – allowing a transition from the hallway's tight clarity to an open gesture of arrival.

↓ → Kapero • N59 architects

Custom made white lacquered MDF furniture pieces separate the functional zones of the office: the service area behind the reception desk, a creative area for group work and the workstations zone. The heights of the furniture pieces vary between 90 and 210 centimeters to create different degrees of transparency or privacy between the different zones, while 80 cm high yellow cabinets separate the individual workstations but are sufficiently low to allow spontaneous communication.

↓ → **Oktavilla** • Elding Oscarson

The construction of the dividing wall creates the sensation of it being both temporary and solid, while the window inserted within it allows the continuous row of windows in the external wall to be read as a whole. Besides the reference to the client's business, the wall made of stacked bundles of magazines is not only a natural conversation piece, but also works as an acoustic absorbent.

↓ **HTC** • chadbourne + doss architects

Several pieces of custom-made plywood furniture are also integrated into the space including a coffee table made to measure. The contractor, Fackler Construction, designed and built a customized dog bed for the office mascot. A 60ft long work table to accommodate further growth is currently in the design stage.

→ **Ruales Izurieta Publicidad** • arquitectura x

This small intervention for a young advertising agency is based on the requirement for a flexible and expandable space, adaptable to the multiple tasks and changing needs that will arise through the enterprise's activities and expansion. An important condition was that the budget had to be kept low, as a major proportion of the clients' overall investment was to be for the specialized tools and equipment required by the clients' work. In response to the challenge, the architects' first move was to take out all the dull finishes and claddings typical to a standard office in an office block, leaving all the ductwork and the steel and concrete structures showing; this enabled them to strip the space down to its bare constituents, to achieve a raw and flexible container in which to insert the furniture and the containers for the various activities that are likely to vary with time and may require occasional modifications. These "pieces of furniture", made of plywood and floating parquet floors have been "plugged in" to the various corresponding networks, all of which are entirely visible. The same maple finish has been used throughout (floors, walls and ceilings), achieving a strong result at minimal cost, providing a work environment that has been easy to install and offers the possibility of uncomplicated alterations in the future to adapt to a variable work context.

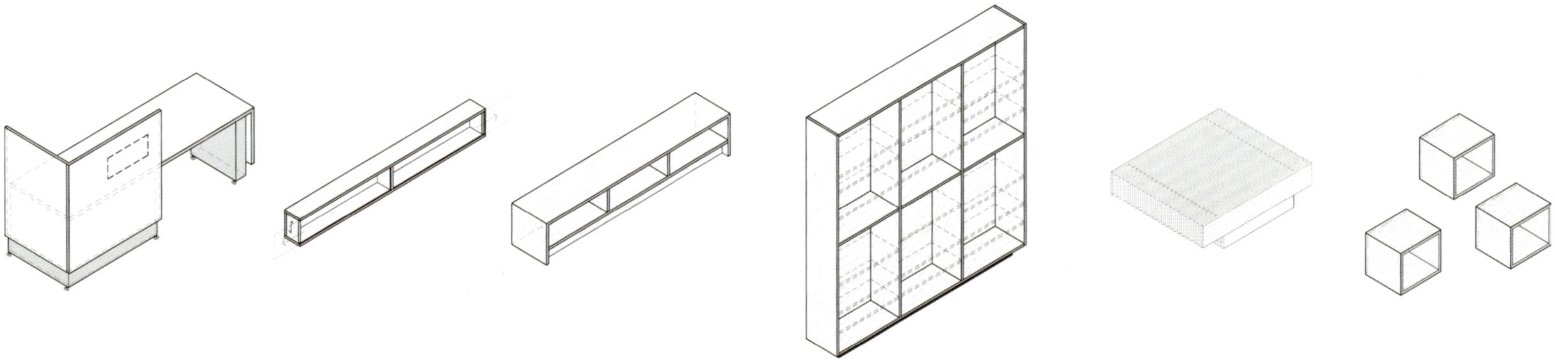

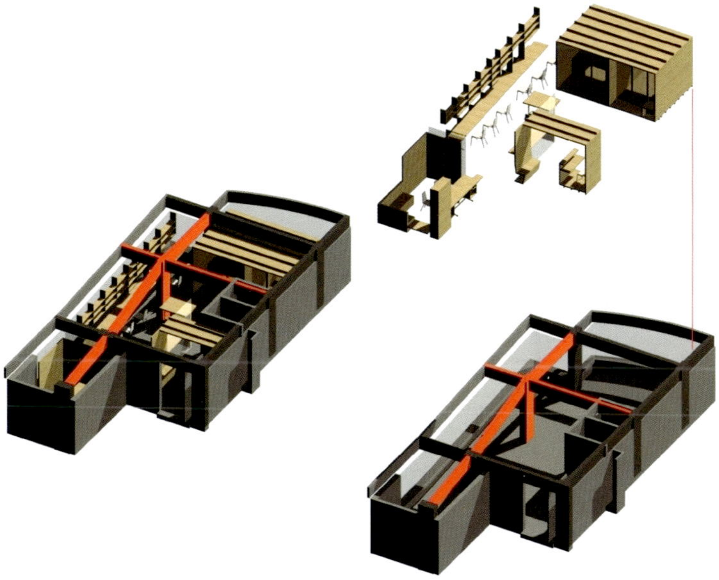

ENGINE
ARENA

← Engine • Jump Studios

Jump Studios designed an animated but suitably slick new office for London-based communications group Engine. With 12 different companies operating under the Engine umbrella, the challenge was to create an environment that would appeal to a broad range of tastes while respecting and upholding the individual brand identities. 'We really wanted the office to look like it was machined rather than constructed,' Jordan explains. This idea is most clearly manifest in a series of perfectly formed elements that run through the building, essentially forming a backbone that links the ground floor to the fifth. Among the many 'talking points' in the building are the seating pods on the fifth floor with their Corian shells and Barrisol light ceilings. Here employees are encouraged to interact, serviced by a café offering spectacular views across the city's rooftops and a series of conference and meeting rooms ranging in design, size and style. The idea was to offer a more refreshing alternative to the conventional table and chair.

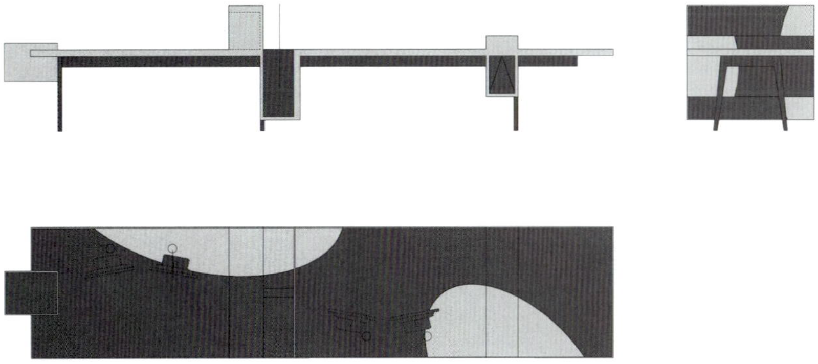

→ Herengracht • i29 l interior architects

The design of all three boardrooms and the lounge are firmly submitted to an overall design concept. Large round lampshades, spray-painted gold on the inside, seem to cast oval areas of light and shade throughout the entire space. This playful pattern of golden ovals contrasts with the angular cabinets and desks, which are executed in black stained ash wood. On the floor the oval forms continue by using light and dark gray carpet. Also, these ovals define the separate working areas.

← ↓ **Syzygy** • eins:eins architekten

Syzygy moved its central offices into a monumental building located on a prominent corner in the immediate vicinity of Hamburg's town hall. The clients envisaged a working environment in which all employees would be seated together at a single desk. eins:eins architekten took this idea to another level and developed an item of furniture that allows all employees to effectively sit "in" a single desk. The single desk-units can be arranged in various configurations but always result in a whole. This allows a great variety of arrangements, which would be impossible to achieve with conventional desks. The major benefits of this innovative office furnishing is that it can establish a highly communicative constellation of workstations, and, in addition, presents an opportunity to furnish oddly shaped spaces, which may otherwise be hard to utilize.

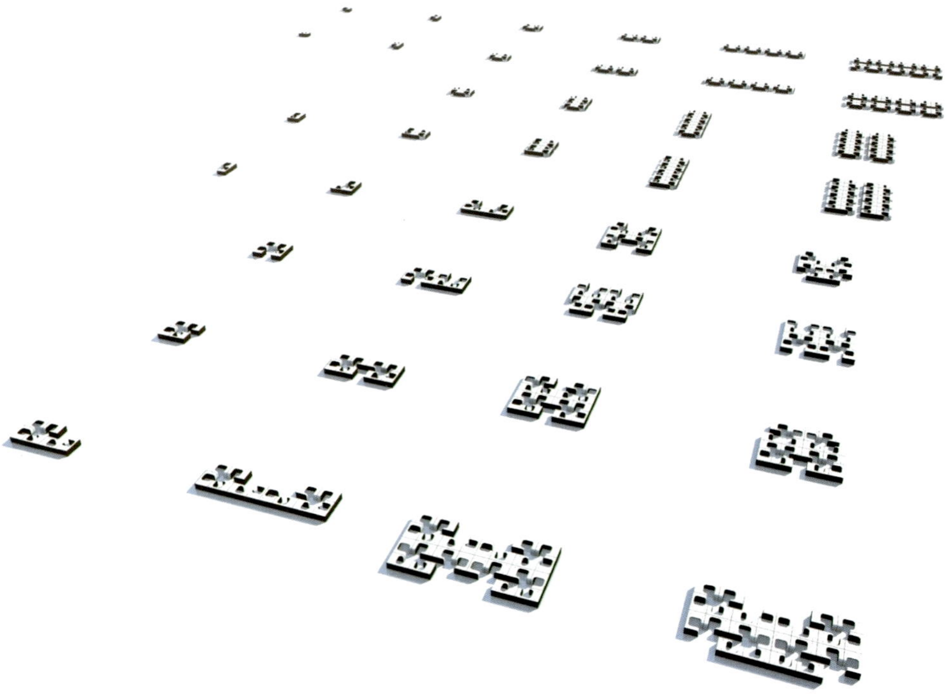

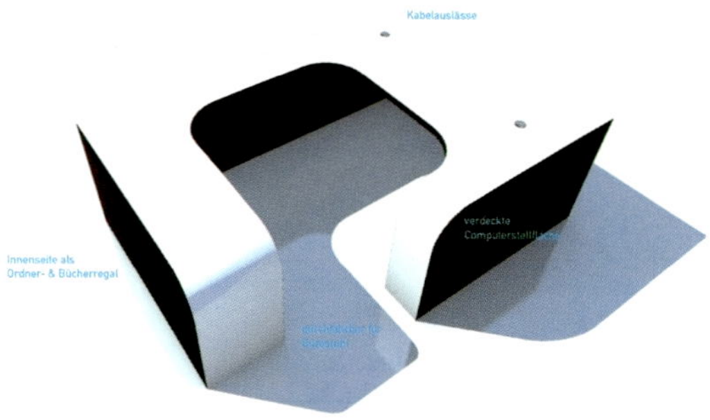

↓ → Ecomplexx • xarchitekten

The entire expanse of the loft's historic window façade can exert its full effect, while the multifunctional Backbone offers all the essentials, such as stacking, archives, coat room, seating areas for relaxation and the bar, as well as the entire technical installation. The Backbone was built in the manner of serial shelf-like furniture, as a mega structure of untreated chipboard to comply with the extremely low budget.

↓ → **Google Zurich** • Camenzind Evolution

Google's offices in Zurich, Switzerland, transmit the message that this is not a conventional company through a design that cultivates an energized and inspiring work environment that is relaxed but focused, and buzzing with activities.
The office areas are organized along a central core and are a mixture of open-plan workspaces for 6-10 people and enclosed offices for 4-6 people. All office enclosures are constructed using a glass partition system, which maintains transparency and optimizes daylight while reducing noise and achieving the required degree of privacy for working teams. There are a large number of small to medium-size meeting rooms situated throughout the office space. Apart from the standard meeting rooms, there are also many informal meeting areas, which have a more relaxed atmosphere for teams to have creative discussions around white-boards. Some of them also incorporate the theme in the floor materials, like the Igloo Satellite Cabins with penguins on the blue floor. Camenzind Evolution also developed themed communal areas associated with sport and leisure, for example, an aquarium water lounge for relaxation and a games room to play billiards, table football and interactive video games. Most spaces contain 'micro kitchens' offering the Zooglers a variety of drinks and snacks throughout the day.

DANGER

→ **Disney Store** • Clive Wilkinson Architects

The original building is wooden-framed and composed of three parts. The front portion is a 16 ft (4.9 m) high space with large timber trusses. The large rear portion is a double height wooden-framed atrium space with a saw-tooth roof that results in dramatic clerestory lighting spanning the width of the space. These two portions are connected by a long interstitial brick walled structure, which inspired the creation of brick-like elements for the interior. These modular elements allude to the playful block building habits of children and remind the staff of their role in creating products for the world of children.
The two major portions of the building are anchored by two main conference rooms. The first, known as the Block Conference Room, is formed on two sides by removable foam block walls. When these foam modules are disassembled for 200 person company-wide meetings, they become the seating system. On most days, they are vertically stacked in a brick pattern to form the walls for a 20 person meeting room.
The second main conference room, formed by a unique modular honeycomb structure, is located in the atrium portion of the building. Originally conceived as a flexible means of managing the Disney sample product display, it became the centerpiece of the space.
Approximately 500 modular honeycombs units, 24" (61 cm) wide by 17" (43 cm) deep and fabricated in rotation-molded plastic, form a dramatic two-story open conference room. The organic configuration of the undulating honeycomb units captures the light from the clerestory windows creating a warm glow in the room as well as in the surrounding space.

← ↓ → **Nije Gritenije** • FLATarchitects

The stairs to the ninth floor end in an entrance space configured by four irregularly shaped objects. Through the gaps and reflective surfaces of the wall, sounds and images are presented to the visitor in fragments. The shifting sightlines of the visitor climbing the stairs were used as a design instrument for these wooden objects. These same objects are used as bookshelves on the side of the workspace. Four of the workstations were to be used by the permanent staff of the foundation while the remaining sixteen were to accomodate a continuously changing group of start-up entrepreneurs and artists. The permanent workstations are positioned next to the entrance, in a fan layout with a shared drawer unit in the center. Their shapes and colors differentiate them from the flexible workstations. Four large tables provide space for the sixteen temporary workstations. The tables consist of a steel frame with a tabletop of steel grid panels. The tabletops can be arranged according to each user's needs by combining various desk elements, such as desktops of several sizes, storage objects, book displays and multiple sockets.

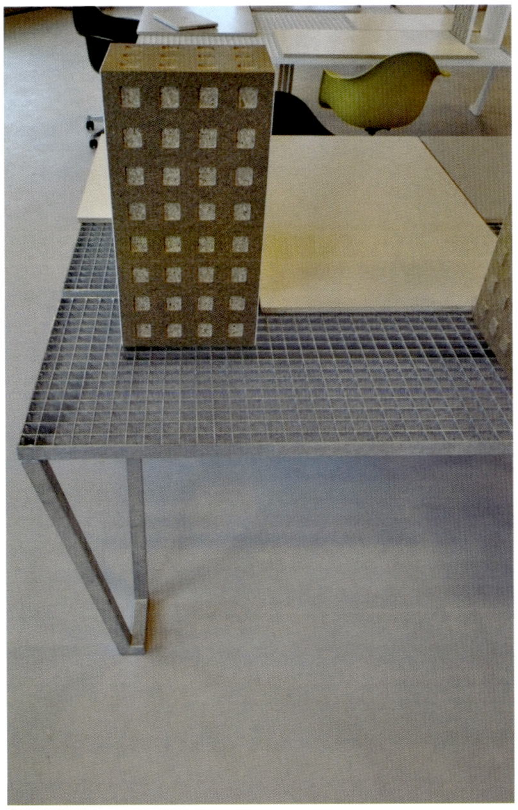

← **Scherpontwerp** • RO&AD architecten

Initial doubts about the practicality and aesthetics of working in this environment made out of honeycomb cardboard were soon resolved as it became clear that it is a sound-absorbent material so reduces noise levels, creating a peaceful working habitat. Furthermore it is a pleasing material which lends a certain warmth to the office and the large-scale repetition of the striped pattern contributes to the peace and uniformity of the space.
There is also a pragmatic element in this scheme which meets the clients' brief. Architects Ad Kil and Ro Koster comment that they could not achieve what the client required with conventional building materials as the budget was 30 % too low. Cardboard is light, relatively cheap, easy to work with and transport and available in different kinds of thickness and finishes. It only took four months to build using nothing but glue. Furthermore the lease for the space will run out after five years so a more permanent material would be wasted and as fashions in office design are bound to change the current fittings can happily be dumped in the recycling bin.
Although the interior may look like a house of cards it is as strong as concrete and can withstand a certain amount of wear and tear. Horizontal joists give the table strength but if it gets damaged it will not be a huge investment to make another.
As a final poetic word it is very fitting that a publisher and design company who work with paper and make a living from it should now be working literally within a paper-based interior.

→ **Uniflair** • Mario Cucinella Architects

The pavilions represent mere circular screens suspended from the ceiling, that air, light and sounds can go through. The material chosen for the walls of these modules is a relatively experimental type of plastic with a particular molecular structure making it outstandingly sound-absorbing. Generally used for backlit double ceilings, it provides the degree of privacy required while transforming each meeting room into a lantern in the full sense of the word.

Surface Finishes

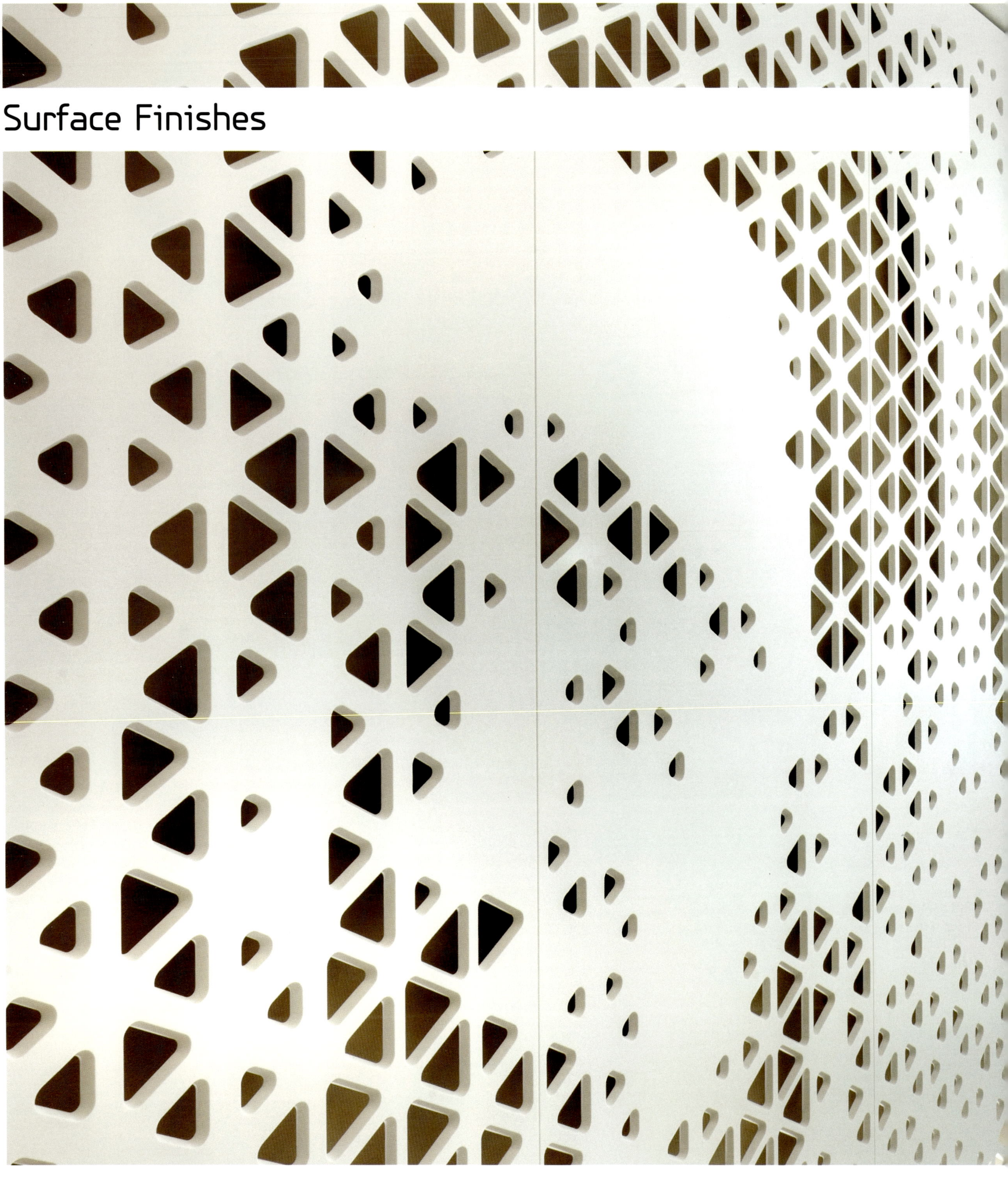

↓ → No Picnic • Elding Oscarson

The client had found a group of 19th century buildings in central Stockholm of which the two principal volumes were listed in the historical buildings register with the highest degree of protection. In the old stable block they were able to strip the room, and added only a custom designed acoustic treatment along the walls, but in the exercise hall, economy and function demanded that a mezzanine constructed in the 1980s was kept. The mezzanine cut the hall lengthwise, destroying the experience of the space. Its edge coincided with the center of the hall, so the architects opted for a method used in industrial design – recreating the illusion of the hall as a whole space by reflecting the half that had been preserved intact, by constructing a delicate aluminum wall along the hall's central axis.

↓ → WongDoody •
Shubin + Donaldson Architects

The building used to be a beer shipping facility with immense refrigerated compartments. The architects retained the large, zinc refrigerator doors, incorporating them into the new design. These original doors were used at various locales, including the main entrance into the facility and at the conference room, where the doors can be opened to bring in natural light that penetrates the room's slotted roll-up aluminum door. The walls of the war rooms are dual functioning. In addition to enclosing the meeting spaces, they are clad in varying materials that can be used to develop ideas. Cork exteriors can be used for pin-up purposes; silver dry erase clad exteriors are ready for ink; chalkboard-painted walls of green and black are set for jotting notes or sketching ideas.

↓ → JWT Headquarters • Clive Wilkinson Architects

JWT, formerly J. Walter Thompson, is one of the oldest and largest advertising agencies in the world. While its credentials and client list were impeccable, the company needed to transform itself to meet the challenges of the new media world. Youthful new leadership at the New York headquarters determined to make that a complete physical, virtual and behavioral transformation. From inception, it was clear that JWT was reframing its core vision about how it engaged with the public. Advertising would no longer focus on projecting messages to the consumer, but creating experiences which rewarded the public's time and attention. Its mission had become 'story telling'.

↓ **Obscura Digital** • IwamotoScott Architecture

IwamotoScott Architecture shares the space with Obscura Digital, and their 1,100 sqft office is located at the eastern end of the main floor, behind the main building façade on Third Street. A digitally-fabricated book shelf and screen wall defines the edge of Obscura Digital's space, while providing a modulated projection surface facing the central space on which they can test out projection mapping techniques. The wall is made of an array of folded laser-cut steel modules following an oblique pixilated pattern that responds to the spherical geometry of Obscura's adjacent geodesic projection dome.

Dentsu London • Essentia Designs

The scheme took inspiration from sources as disparate as Star Trek, Spitfire fighter planes, Buckminster Fuller and Eriko Horiki's paper sculptures. The color pallet of whites and grays is lightened by the vibrant green used in the floor finishes of the building's common areas. The 4th floor studio space has freestanding pods for collaborative brainstorming.

↑ ↓ → **Raiffeisenbank Zürich** • NAU + DGJ

The walls act as a membrane mediating between the open public spaces and intimately scaled conference rooms. Portraits of the quarter's most prominent past residents like Böklin, Semper or Sypri grace the walls, their abstracted images milled into Hi-macs using advanced digital production techniques. While intricately decorative, the design grounds the bank in the area's cultural past, while looking clearly towards the future.

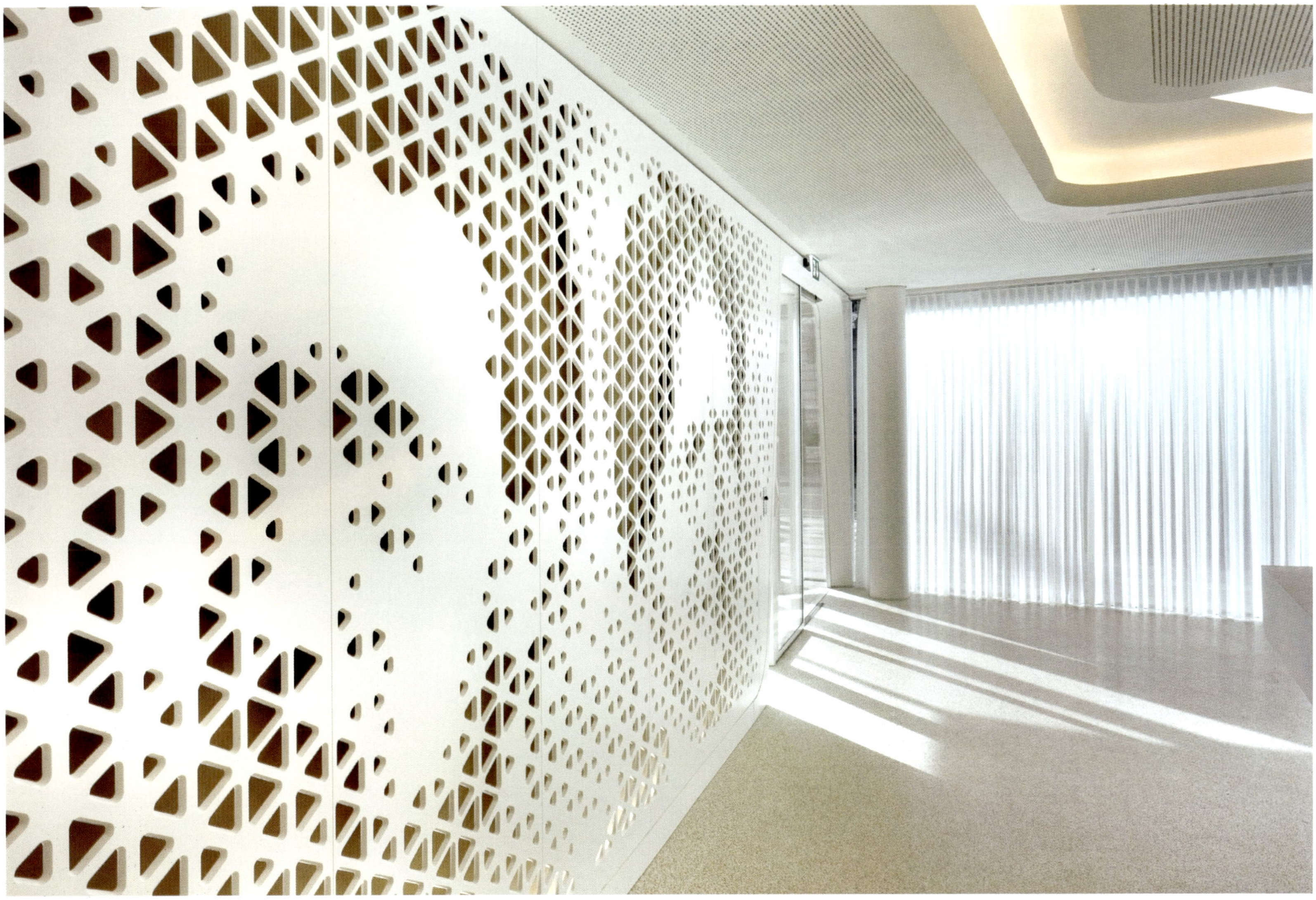

↓ → Forward Media Group Publishing House • za bor architects

In addition to several popular and well-recognized magazines such as 'Hello', Forward Media Group publishes the largest and the most popular magazines on interior design in Russia.
Key communal areas were designed to be transparent and distinctively identifiable. As a result, the elevator lobby, the bright reception areas and the meeting rooms were intentional points of emphasis in the design scheme. A yellow construction hides the entrances to the toilets while the archive room is decorated with a striking black floral pattern. In contrast, operational areas are finished in a neutral gray palette.

↓ → **United Business Media** • Gensler

The primary architectural element of the space is an angular, folding ribbon that moves through the space from floor to wall to ceiling and back to floor. The ribbon represents the quick flow and rapid interchange of information in the new media age. The flowing ribbon contrasts with the rigor of the workstations, ceiling system and lighting, which work with the building's structural grid. UBM wanted to reflect their global nature, while at the same time being respectful and inclusive of the local culture. Three San Francisco street artists and one installation artist were commissioned to work directly on the walls of the folding ribbon.

← Nije Gritenije • FLATarchitects

From the entrance space the stairs lead on to the conference and presentation room on the tenth floor. The carpeting dominates the space, covering parts of the wall as well as the floor. It displays a giant map of Friesland (the Dutch province) designed by graphic artist Martin Draax. The members of the Nije Gritenije foundation gather over this map, around a grand conference table with eleven chairs, one for each Frisian city. By drawing a curtain, part of the space can be dimmed for showing films or presentations. When looking out of the windows the real map of Friesland unfolds.

→ Red Town • Taranta Creations

On the lower floor the individual workstations are placed by the windows. A green sculptural table can be used for communal activities. Informal and contoured, the central staircase is reminiscent of a large droplet of water ready to fall from the ceiling. Inside the stairwell, a highly saturated environment of bright red engulfs and surrounds the individual, dramatically marking the transition between the different office areas. The color is repeated on the second floor as an accent to highlight the recessed work areas.

↓ → **Gummo** • i29 | interior architects

As the space was only going to be rented by Gummo for two years, i29 convinced Gummo to create a stylish office space that would have as small an impact as possible on the environment or on the client's wallet. Everything in the office conforms to the new house style of white and grey. All the furniture was locally sourced via Marktplaats (the Dutch eBay), charity shops and whatever was salvageable from the old office. Everything was then spray-painted with Polyurea Hotspray (an environmentally friendly paint) to conform to the new colour scheme.

↓ → **Cubion** • Jackie-B

The main office houses workstations for eight employees on two groups of green tables. The office is lit by suspended light fittings custom designed for the room by Jackie-B. The office walls are decorated with synthetic grass islands that can be leant on and help to generate a dreamy and calm atmosphere. The glass wall at the entrance to the office has a bubble diagram for brainstorming etched upon it to be used as a whiteboard.

↓ → **MAXAN** • Abeijón-Fernández

The purity of the white space is interrupted through the use of colours representative of the company; these appear in the zones destined for dealing with clients. Work by the advertising company is placed in different spaces throughout the office to form part of the dialogue established between the interior design and the firm's activity.
The office has facades on two streets, thus, in order to ensure a unified reading of the space, black horizontal strips have been placed that control the entrance of light into the interior of the premises while at the same time serving as a support for the company's logotype.

↓ → D&G • Studio Piuarch

The fittings feature polished steel for the supports and unpolished sheet metal for the horizontals. There is a provocative approach to hi-tech, with the most up-to-date plasma screens in the most intimate spaces. The combined use of natural materials such as white Namibian stone together with transparent and reflective materials like glass and polished steel sheet gives the building a luminosity and style that works perfectly with the D&G brand. The design shows off the powerful cross-fertilization between fashion and architecture; and the result is the most seductive tailor-made suit with which to clothe a brand whose very trade mark is sensuality.

Thin walls made from over 23 000 CD\DVD boxes were used to create a space where employees could be by themselves in a "container" of ideas. This space, called "Think Room", alludes to these "digital information containers". When this place is in use, the words "Think Room" lit up. To create a graphic image that would integrate with the surroundings, all the columns of the building were covered, increasing the apparent size of the building and obtaining "light boxes" that transformed into spontaneous images.

↓ → Kapero • N59 architects

This striking fit-out for the Kapero consultants offices in Stockholm is defined by two features: the color scheme – white with canary yellow highlights – and an arrow motif which represents the firm's consulting activities. Heavy sliding glass doors fitted with a canary yellow film separate the meeting room and coffee area from the open-plan working area. The CNC-milled arrows that adorn all areas of the office are more than just aesthetic spice – they also serve as cabinet handles in the furniture pieces and as vents in the heating covers.

↓ → **DATA** • Randy Brown Architects

The design energy and most of the budget was focused on three elements: the green corridor whose sculptural space is the central circulation element of the plan; a glass conference room wall with a design applied with a satin vinyl film that represents the endless data the company sells; galvanized metal shed wall panels which were used to express both the technological side of the business and the rural vernacular of the Midwest where this company was founded.

→ Besturenraad / BKO • COEN!

For the design narrative of the project, COEN! used The Book as a metaphor. Aside from its importance in the Protestant and Catholic faiths, a book also consists of structure, text and images. The decorative elements used in the interior design include stained glass patterns, metal grids with patterns based on the golden section and printed text. The relationship between faith and education is represented by DNA patterns and golden 'office altars'.

← Oktavilla • Elding Oscarson

The magnetic galvanized steel cladding picks up the colors of the surroundings in a hazy reflection and defines the box as an inserted element.

dagenzaal

↓ North • Skylab Architecture

Floral drapery and camouflage Fatboy beanbags allow for reflecting "around a campfire". A series of interspersed glass and metal panels define the editing module, two soundproof rooms without doors. Taking a universal icon for quick creative thought and communication, the media module is Post-it Note yellow. A commercial grade kitchen and adjacent dining area with picnic tables, wall mural, and topographic carpet tiles redefines out-of-doors inside. A visitor module of smoke walls and ice-white lighting is decorated with print, sound, and new media installations fostering an ever changing creative forum and connection with the local community.

→ Facebook Headquarters • Studio O+A

The design takes its inspiration from the patchwork nature of Facebook users and employees, bringing together seemingly disparate elements to form a cohesive pattern and using color and interior spacing to create neighborhoods within the open plan space. The design goal for the new facility was to maintain the history and raw aesthetic of the building and create a fun dynamic appropriate for the company's youthful staff. Many walls and spaces are left unfinished: employees are encouraged to write on the walls, add artwork, and move furniture as needed, allowing the building to evolve continuously.

face book

F3

↓ → Bruce B./Emmy B. • Ippolito Fleitz Group

Antitheses attract the visitor's attention from the very first moment of entering the agency, beginning with the shape of the reception desk. It is crafted in exposed concrete, which displays its materiality in the visible texture of the timber plank shuttering. The concrete form is topped by a white, lacquered surface. Antithetical details are also present in the adjoining conference rooms – usually the second point of call for the agency's clients. The walls of the smaller conference room are panelled with maritime pine boards. Narrow yellow grooves refine their appearance, which would normally invoke simple packing crates, transforming them into attractive wall panelling. The large conference room next door is dominated by a long conference table with randomly spaced table legs breaking up the sober impression it would otherwise have made. Directing your gaze towards the ceiling of the reception area and conference rooms allows you to take in another unusual detail: Stucco elements have been added to the ceiling joists, recalling the cosiness of an old apartment building in the very midst of this industrial landscape.

↓ → Dupon • Studio Ramin Visch

Instead of specific colors identifying specific spaces, color has been used to identify certain objects (such as stairs or walls) that divide, connect or cut across the various spaces. This strategy enhances the sculptural and material presence of the constructive elements of the building and simultaneously allows the space to function as an undivided whole flowing through and around them. Circulation is clear. The red stairs in the hallway cannot be missed, while the main meeting room at the back of the office is visible from the entrance.

← ↓ **Toolbox** • Caterina Tiazzoldi

From the perspective of the design process, the goal was to mediate between the plurality of users' needs and the coherence of the design. The variety of solutions is obtained by use of a unique design rule. A set of initially identical volumes acquires specialisation or differentiation through the use of different materials - cork, rubber or polished paint - according to the programmatic function hosted in the box. The specialisation of a generic volume occurs in accordance with a specialisation generated by acoustic, thermal, and visual requirements. The principle of variation and transformation of a unique element was also pursued in other parts of the project by differentiating the colours of natural rubber floors in the meeting rooms, sound insulation coating alternating with small telephone pods and finally by varying the sizes, colours and levels of transparency of the bubbles that form the external texture of the box-bar.

← ↓ **ANZ** • HASSELL

Access to natural light defines the mood of these rooms, with the wall materials in one of the clusters being translucent to let in filtered light. The partitions of the perimeter learning rooms are angled in plan so that the rooms are asymmetrical. The tree-like branch patterns that appear on the walls and rubber floors are all interconnected to create unexpected pathways: an exploratory itinerary between the learning rooms, meeting rooms and nooks for informal gatherings. On the walls, colors have been applied in large trapezoidal blocks, which dissolve feelings of certainty, enhancing creativity.

← PostPanic • Maurice Mentjens

PostPanic combines a design/animation studio and a production company, producing commercial projects for the international advertising, retail, broadcast and music industries as well as its own internal projects. The starting point was an empty ground floor space over five meters high, with large concrete columns and big windows in the slanted façade overlooking the river. The concrete columns, smooth concrete floors, absent thresholds, fluorescent ceiling lights and unconcealed ductwork emphasize the raw, industrial look. Designer Maurice Mentjens has fitted up PostPanic's Amsterdam studio as a professional playground that emphasizes the company's creative attitude. In accordance with the brief, every department has a distinctive atmosphere, yet the space reads as a whole.

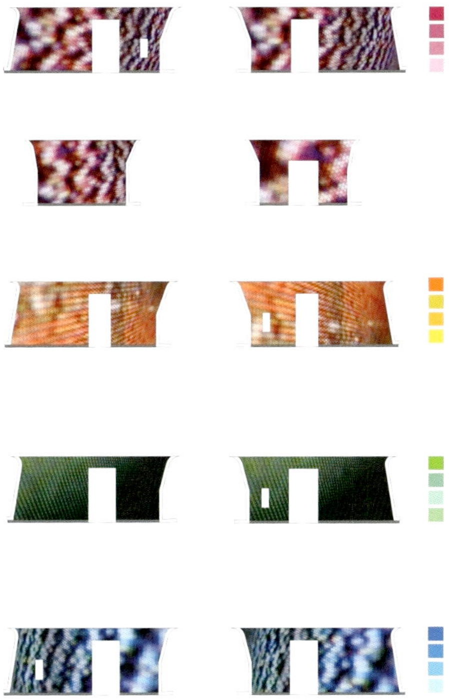

← ↓ Endeavor • Neil M. Denari Architects Inc.

Given the repetitious nature of the office layout, a wayfinding or coding system became a necessary feature. Each of the four zones is given a general color range (Magenta, Cyan, Orange and Green) to orient the agents and their visitors. Walls perpendicular to the length of the building are saturated with these colors, including special wallpaper graphics on the secondary cores. These images were developed in collaboration with 2×4, a New York based graphic design company.

↓ 72andSunny • RA-DA

A limited budget and raw design aesthetic drove the pursuit of simplicity, affecting the warehouse space in a minimal manner: the original concrete floor and wood joist ceiling were appropriate containers for the openness of the client's philosophy and work. In early concept studies, color emerged as an important element and became a key aspect of the design. Striving to combine their goals and the separate functions they needed for an efficient office, it became clear that the square footage was insufficient for their future expansion needs. To solve this, three architectural devices were implemented: The folding 'leaf' to delineate space; the blue solid to enclose space and the white wall to activate space

The 'leaf' starts on the east side of the space at the partners' room, turns up and across to create a small canopy marking the thresholds of the conference rooms, turns down to become a platform at the entry. It wraps up again to create the backdrop for the reception desk, passing over to the west side of the space to create the grand backdrop-wall to the open work area. It then folds under to become the floor plate of an added mezzanine and unfolds in the form of a wide stairway, leading back to the ground floor. Enclosed areas, such as the editing suite and the restrooms, were wrapped in bold 72andsunny blue, supporting the design's strong graphic character.

→ K-Boxing • CL3

K-Boxing is a Chinese fashion brand that relocated its headquarters in 2009 to Shanghai. The sleekly designed offices occupy a brand new seven-storey office building that houses the company's administration, sales and design activities. Sleek, minimalist design, including powerful graphic displays and the use of a visually strong corporate color, further emphasize the identity of this corporation.

K BOXING

→ Simone Micheli Studio • Simone Micheli

The original fifteenth century construction, comprised of ample spaces with stone floors, high wooden ceilings and masonry walls, presented a fascinating starting point for this restoration. The project generated a juxtaposition of the new with the old creating a dialogue which is both harmonious and full of contrasts.
The totemic cylindrical volume of the reception area welcomes the visitor, completely covered in laminate digital print representing the macro-image of a salad. This bizarre feature forms a sharp contrast with the stone floor, white walls and floor to ceiling cupboard finished in gloss black laminate and shiny stainless steel handles.
The black bathroom also serves as a punchy counterpoint to the brightly colored cylinder. The rectangular "Block" toilets are the only hint of white within this small space. A rectangular steel crack in the mirror serves as the source for air, soap and water, all controlled by electronic sensors.
Adjacent to the reception area is the large central space of the archive and waiting room, which conserves the original structure of the walls and large beams of the ceiling. Black rectangular seats alternate with similar volumes in laminated white that serve as tables. The large white metal filing cupboard is also located here. The adjoining project development area consists of two large rooms connected via an arched opening. The plaster walls, wooden ceilings, shelves and tables for the computers are all white with floors of industrial cement.
At the end of the passageway is Micheli's office/-meeting room. The shelves here are surfaced in shiny white laminate with steel supports and there is a central table with wheels laminated with a colorful design. One of the walls has a mirrored surface, behind which is a small bathroom.
The graphics office is decorated with a giant photograph in laminate that covers the entire wall.

Technical Installations and Lighting

↓ → Electric Works • Dive Architects

The architects chose to condense the circulation space by lowering the already low ceiling and use a backdrop of dark grey surfaces contrasted with strong colours, giving the offices a lighter, more spacious feel. All have glazed screens looking onto the corridor with circulation diagrams used as the manifestation.

↓ → GALCIT • John Friedman Alice Kimm Architects

The client wanted the space to reflect the innovative research being performed by the department's teachers and students. The program included a new lobby; new laboratories for teaching and experimental research; new exhibition areas; and new conference, office, and interactive spaces, configured to give GALCIT the strong, dynamic branding they desired to attract the world's best scientists, engineers, and students.

Given the variety of topics that the GALCIT faculty and students research, pinpointing a formal starting point was a challenge. Aerospace engineering includes everything from the way blood cells flow to rocket science, or a new Mars Rover vehicle in collaboration with a group from NASA. How to be inclusive? Ultimately the formal language derived from the notion of Flow. Almost all GALCIT research involves flow – understanding how solids, liquids, and gases behave under differential pressures. As a result, the existing building became a metaphorical wind tunnel a neutral container into which new ceilings and wrappers could be inserted. The resultant flow patterns became the basis of new spatial relationships and definitions.

Autodesk
Autodesk technology helps people who change the world through design. Architecture, engineering, and construction projects around the world are transforming not just the landscape on which they sit, but the hearts and minds of those who see and use them. The Autodesk Gallery reveals the boundless artistry, sustainable design, and technological innovation behind some of today's most inspiring building projects.
That big idea needs to be

← Autodesk AEC • KlingStubbins

The design solution expresses the Autodesk mission and values by exposing and featuring the building systems. A three-story floor opening visually connects the activities between all floors and provides a dramatic demonstration of the energy of the space to Autodesk visitors. Open workspaces and glass conference rooms provide visual connections and encourage collaboration. Open ceilings expose the building's structural and mechanical systems.

← ↓ United Business Media • Gensler

The lighting, building systems, equipment, appliances, furniture, materials and finishes all support the targeted LEED Platinum rating that is essential to UBM's mission of measurably improving their carbon footprint year to year.

↓ → **Facebook Headquarters** • Studio O+A

Reflecting employees' desire for green headquarters, the facility is the first commercial project completed under Palo Alto's 2008 Green Building Ordinance, making extensive use of existing architectural features, recycling millwork from the original lab, and 're-purposing' industrial components for post-industrial use. Other sustainable features include high recycled-content carpet and energy-efficient lighting.

↓ → **CheBanca!** • Crea International

The "Natural Tech" concept designed by Crea International is inspired by "the rules of simplicity" by John Maeda. This influential design idea propounds that the objects that surround us should be simplified to the maximum possible degree. The atmosphere of CheBanca! recalls the warmth and light of sunshine while the layout recalls the logical organization of the solar system with the client at the center. The yellow color that permeates the environment recalls sunshine and the aniline treated wood suggests a straightforward approach, while the metacrylic panels printed with a honeycomb texture create a friendly atmosphere.

↓ → Syzygy • eins:eins architekten

Syzygy moved its central offices into a monumental building located on a prominent corner in the immediate vicinity of Hamburg's town hall. The clients envisaged a working environment in which all employees would be seated together at a single desk. The amorphous textile ceiling is sound-absorbent and features an integrated lighting system. It emphasizes the impression of being seated in one snug enveloping piece of furniture.

→ PostPanic • Maurice Mentjens

The concrete columns, smooth concrete floors, absent thresholds, fluorescent ceiling lights and unconcealed ductwork emphasize the raw, industrial look. Designer Maurice Mentjens has fitted up PostPanic's Amsterdam studio as a professional playground that emphasizes the company's creative attitude.

↓ Kapero • N59 architects

The rawness of the ceiling with its exposed structure and service ducts contrasts with the polished perfection of the shiny white epoxy resin floor.

→ Mother • Clive Wilkinson Architects

On all floors, all surfaces were painted white, with a white epoxy floor, to achieve a neutral art studio space. To mitigate sound in the hard factory space, the architects designed 7-foot long lampshades padded with 3 inches of acoustic foam. The fifty light fixtures were then covered with fifty different patterns of Marimekko fabric, achieving the effect of a large art installation, which is all the more striking in a space where everything else is white. On other floors, customized plastic refrigeration curtains were used to subdivide spaces for different disciplines and subsidiary companies.

The project was expedited in construction and delivered on a tight budget. The reduced density and added meeting spaces have helped the agency to work more smoothly, and voice acoustics in the table area have been effectively controlled through the padded lights.

↓ → **Media House** • Bates Smart Architects

Having eliminated the false ceilings, most services are exposed as is the underside of the structural slab. This creates a "media studio" atmosphere and allows light to penetrate deep into the plan.

↓ → **Raiffeisenbank Zürich** • NAU + DGJ

Advanced technologies make banking infrastructure largely invisible; employees access terminals concealed in furniture elements, while a robotic retrieval system grants 24-hour access to safety deposit boxes. This shifts the bank's role into becoming a light-filled, inviting environment – an open lounge where customers can learn about new products and services. The lounge feels more like a high-end retail environment than a traditional bank interior. Conversations can start spontaneously around a touchscreen-equipped information table and transition to meeting rooms for more private discussions. The information table not only displays figures from world markets in real time, but can be used to discover the history of Hottingen or check the latest sports scores.

← Pack Line Headquarters • Lea Katz architecture

Since the office structure was low and narrow a central service wall was introduced, replacing the existing corridor and increasing the floor ceiling height. This communicates with the open plan office on one side, used for circulation, and with the private offices on the other side. The service wall contains the air conditioning, lighting, and electricity, and organizes the entire space.

← ↓ WWF • RAU

Ceiling strips of felt provide agreeable and satisfying acoustics. The materials applied came from all over the world; for example, the freestanding sanitary blocks are furnished with a colorful African plaster and the banisters consist of bamboo stems. All horizontal elements in the adopted concrete skeleton are covered with mud wrapped up in capillary networks, used for heating and cooling. A solar energy power station on the roof provides energy and all installations run on vegetable oil. This combination of environmentally friendly measures means that the building is energy self-sufficient and is CO_2 neutral.

→ **SAP** • Bucholz McEvoy Architects

SAP Galway is the 'contact centre' of a German software company, located in a business park east of Galway, on an exposed site overlooking the surrounding landscape. The 360-strong international staff deals telephonically with direct technical queries from around the Western hemisphere, according to time zones and languages. The average occupancy is from 7 am to 1 am (18 hours), divided in 3 shifts.
Function and climate were taken to be the defining coordinates of the design process, aiming to create a balanced work environment with minimum non-renewable energy use. Environmentally, this is a high occupancy building with high ventilation demands and a high cooling load, yet the only cooling source utilized is the air outside. A central atrium goes through the building from top to bottom and the various office floors are connected by bridge-like structures.
The floors carry work space; the connecting bridges carry relaxation areas. The atrium is the environmental lung of the building and obviates the need for mechanical extraction systems, functioning as a low-pressure exhaust air space in case of cross ventilation, and supply air in case of one-way ventilation.
Cross ventilation is employed for the natural ventilation of the office and public areas. The building is ventilated from the outer façades, and the atrium is used as a supply and exhaust air volume, single glazed and having, consequently, a fluctuating temperature. The ventilation and heating function is controlled by vertical elements included in the façade.
The SAP Building deals with a range of issues related to sick building syndrome. Vertical brise-soleils of cedar protect the glazed façades of the atrium, but when daylight is insufficient, especially designed up-lights built into the concrete structure project light across the exposed concrete soffit, providing diffuse light to the work-area, reducing eye strain and eliminating glare on VDUs. The natural ventilation system is driven by heat recovery units in the façades, mixing external + internal air to provide a healthy atmosphere.
There is a 'daylight simulation' function to maintain psychometric stimulation for night workers. The atrium is the social heart of the building.

→ Uniflair • Mario Cucinella Architects

The space is lit by a system of indirect lighting positioned in the central part of the table. Next to the long table a series of cylindrical spaces provide meeting rooms, areas for relaxing, and communal areas. They look like circular pavilions and are lit from inside. In clear contrast with the linear layout of the industrial process, these spaces create a new interior landscape, designed with the idea of eliminating all physical barriers between the different activities, yet guaranteeing the necessary degree of privacy for work to proceed in comfort. Thus, a lighting system was devised that would be integrated into that of the main work space.

← SIEEB • Mario Cucinella Architects

The building is closed and well insulated on the northern side, which faces the cold winter winds, and more transparent and open towards the south. The SIEEB maximizes this southern orientation, developing from a symmetrical U-shaped courtyard building stepping downwards towards the south. This allows natural light into the internal spaces and provides the internal garden with light and air. The louvers on this façade are composed of reflective glass panes, tilted at different angles in order to control direct solar radiation and light penetration into the office spaces. Photovoltaic panels that produce energy are integrated into the design as shading elements for the terraces. On the east and west sides, light and direct sun are controlled by a double skin façade that filters sunlight and optimizes daylight in the office spaces. Vertical distribution is granted by two main staircases and lift blocks located in the west and east wings.
The SIEEB design philosophy makes full use of state of the art technologies, such as an automatic light flow adjustment system used in the offices and laboratories. This is controlled by photosensors that detect presence and luminescence and then regulate the required light flux in the rooms.
The overall combination of the building's shape, orientation, materials and high performance façades allows a significant reduction in energy consumption and therefore in CO_2 emissions.

↓ → **Moving Picture Company** • Patrick Tighe Architecture

An appendaged soffit grows from the serpentine walls and serves as an armature for cable trays, mechanical and electrical systems. Light portals equipped with programmable LED lighting pierce the organic forms. Patterns derived from the animated studies are emblazoned onto the laser cut walls and circumscribe the interior. Movement is expressed throughout the space in many ways, one of which is through the lighting scheme. Clusters of LED lights penetrate the serpentine wall and emit color. The custom-made aluminum housings are flush with the outer (public) face of the wall and protrude into the private rooms, adding texture to the walls and creating a more intimate scale within the larger spaces. The intensity and colors of the lighting are programmable enabling the client to fulfill one of the items on their 'wish-list': the creation of an environment in constant flux.

↓ → **WongDoody** • Shubin + Donaldson Architects

The Los Angeles office of WongDoody is the adaptive reuse of a former warehouse. While the shell of the building was mainly left unchanged, the interior construction partitioned the space to accommodate the company's needs. All of the workstations remain open to the soaring, bow-string truss wood ceiling, while a perimeter of original brick surrounds the space. A combination of skylights and vertical recessed fluorescent lighting illuminate the facility.

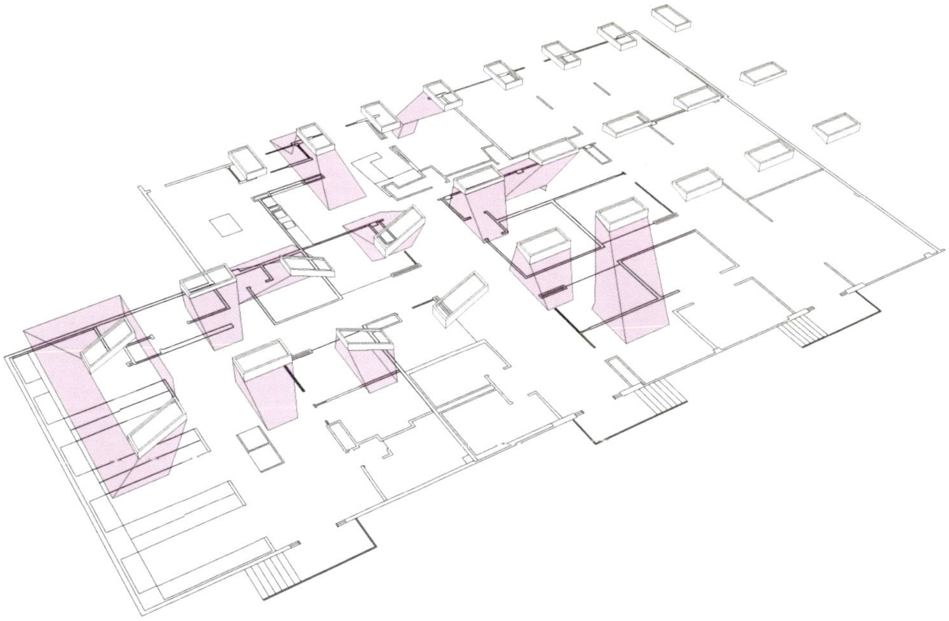

↓ → **Adotta** • Stefano Marinelli, Lucio Massignan + Archingegno

Adotta is a company that processes and builds glazed walls. In their new premises, a renovated 1960's warehouse, the light source becomes architecture. The shell is a large oblong structure with a vaulted roof, a 1200 sqm (12 900 sqft) footprint and some 1000 sqm (10 760 sqft) of offices and exhibition spaces on three levels. Starting from a programmed design, the new inner walls of the workstations were made of glass: behind them, a luminous wall closing the northern end of the building provides a background. Transparency and reflections on the glazed surfaces and the polished concrete floor create a suggestive, homogeneous atmosphere. Every detail contributes to balance the plastic and evocative potential of the light source. From the main ground floor entrance, a luminous trail cut through the ceiling penetrates every space and conducts the visitor towards the great three-floor stairway. The interior looks like a department store or a museum, centered on the long straight stairway, which consists of several flights leading to the highest level. Light is strategically set at the background wall's corners, to interrupt the room's unity, introducing a new spatial logic by means of a plastic relief and a sequence of 160 fluorescent tubes. The staircase, with a black PVC floor, and the constant luminous trail, enliven the vertical or horizontal surfaces. Lines are clear and defined, with gaps and corners that multiply the view points. Under the vaulted roof of the whole building, three air-light ducts distribute the air-conditioning; made of white polyester and containing a double row of fluorescent lamps, these ducts become subtle and effective diffuser lamps.

Products

↓ → Light Frame • SEFAR Architecture

The patented unobtrusive frame makes this an attractive element for use in providing improved quality of artificial and natural lighting and also acoustic properties. New design preferences for using illuminated textile surfaces open up a wide range of innovative applications for architects, lighting and general interior designers.
The thinnest of joint-lines and an elliptically-shaped rigid profile are available for virtually shadow-free, uniform light distribution. The durable wrinkle-free stretched-membrane modules and 2-ply foil are dustproof and also act as sound absorbers.
Special finishing techniques and coating materials produce a high UV resistance; the product never changes color or fades. All fabrics of SEFAR® Architecture products are almost non-flammable B1 according to DIN 4102, producing nearly no smoke and no burning droplets.

↓ → HoloPro • Pronova

HoloPro™ enables projection onto glass in daylight while maintaining transparency. This is made possible by the patented HoloPro™ technology: holographic optical elements are beamed onto a highly transparent film by laser. This is then embedded in glass. The lightguiding effect enables rear projection onto the glass screen. The angle-selective effect of the HOEs means that only the projected picture is directed at the viewer. The result is a sharp, high-contrast picture – even in broad daylight.
HoloPro™ screens become a component of the light and room concept. Individual sizes and shapes create lively information areas that structure the room without disturbing its transparency and effect. The transparency of the projection surfaces will lead to creative ways of presenting information. Interactive elements with touch or gesture control extend the possible areas of use.
HoloPro™ is suitable for a multitude of different presentation applications. For example: as an information system for visitors in reception areas in combination with touch or gesture control; in room-high multimedia glass walls; as a rear-projection screen in shop windows and a screen in broad daylight.
The production of HoloPro™ in 4:3 format (up to 100") and 16:9 format (up to 128") and the manufacture to customer-specified sizes and shapes are both possible. HoloPro™ films can also be embedded in larger glass panes or special glass (e.g. hardened glass). They cannot, however, be embedded in existing glass panes. Instead, the HoloPro™ projection foil can be used in such cases.

↓ → **Architextile** • Aleksandra Gaca

Architextile is the latest collection of three dimensional weave structures by textile designer Aleksandra Gaca. Her research into the technical possibilities and applications of dimensional textile resulted this time in surprising combinations of contrasts. High tech in combination with natural materials, technical next to more traditional solutions, and a cool, detached character versus warm and inviting.

The Architextile collection consists of a number of fixed patterns: Tero, Ŝelo, Floro, Ondo and Ovalo. Most fabrics are two-sided and perfectly applicable as exclusive, autonomous interior objects, like a dividing wall or screen.

The collection also has acoustic qualities. Those, in combination with a robust firmness, make these fabrics particularly qualified to be used as wall screens or wall coverings in an architectural environment.

Aleksandra Gaca has always been fascinated by three dimensional weave structures and through the years this fascination has become more and more prominent in her work. She experiments with weaves she develops herself as well as with unusual materials. She combines technical qualities with a highly developed touch for material, dimension and beauty. Her inspiration she draws from abstract architectural concepts such as structure and repetition as well as from more dynamic concepts as dance, drama and movement.

↓ → **LifeLine** • Upfloor

LifeLine™ tile is made for heavy duty commercial floors. It is the first collection made of a new flooring material, Enomer™, which consists of 80 % natural minerals and 20 % PVC-free thermoplastic polymers. LifeLine is ideal for heavy wear public premises, such as department stores, schools, offices, hospitals, day care centres, etc.

Enomer is a heterogeneous flooring material with a compact, ionomer impregnated wear layer. The product structure gives LifeLine flooring superior wear, scratch and maintenance properties along with an excellent dimensional stability and easy installation. Because of its low flame spread and low smoke and heat production, LifeLine has attained high fire ratings, and it complies with the IMO regulations for use in ships. LineLine's resistance to fire outperforms traditional vinyl, linoleum and rubber floorings.

Throughout its life cycle, LifeLine flooring material is ecologically safe. Because it is primarily composed of natural minerals, it is recyclable during production, can be disposed of by burning, and can be used as energy producing waste. It contains no PVC, halogens, chlorine, plasticizers, or heavy metals, and emissions in indoor environments are minimal.

The LifeLine tile size is 500 × 500 mm and thickness 2 mm. Because of the tile form LifeLine is easy to handle, and the large tile size makes for quick installation.

The first LifeLine collection features a timeless, non-directional chip design in 20 attractive colors. The range of colors is varied and versatile, with modern bright colors as well as more subdued alternatives and several stylish shades of gray. The product line also includes a range of PVC-free welding rods and skirtings in matching colors.

↓ → longlife • longlife Carpeting Systems

With more than 80% sound absorption in speech relevant frequency ranges and a footfall reduction of up to 32 dB, the innovative acoustic floor covering from longlife can make an important contribution towards improving room acoustics, particularly in large, open-plan working areas.
Its special, fully textile structure with integrated comfort, heavy-felt secondary backing – which therefore offers above-average absorption characteristics – is available as loose-lay SL IQ carpeting and SL tiles, and offers both an efficient and economical alternative to conventional construction measures for improving acoustics. The ergonomic benefits are highly impressive. It offers excellent tread comfort, is particularly kind to the back and joints, and its elasticity offers exceptional impact absorption. It is ideal for standing work areas, as well as for tasks which require a large amount of standing and walking around.
In terms of aesthetics, longlife offers a great variety of contemporary designs. Following the relaunch of the Uni Basic Collection, the classic designs have also received a complete make-over in terms of coloring and the range has been extended with the addition of a variety of designs. At the same time, the range of color options has been streamlined and reduced. As longlife offers the option of delivering small quantities of special colors and bespoke designs specially created to suit the individual requirements of the customer, there is no need to offer an endless array of options in the standard range. Clarity and simplicity make it much easier for architects, planner and builders to reach the right decision.

↓ → Spinnaker • OFFECCT - Beat Karrer

Spinnaker is a free standing room divider designed by Beat Karrer that offers unlimited connection possibilities. With a minimum of two elements to provide stability many different shapes can be created.
The frame is a zincked pipe construction with chromed fittings and feet in black ABS.
The fabric is available in three varieties: black transparent polyester net, white sound absorbing 3D Mesh polyester fabric or furniture fabric.

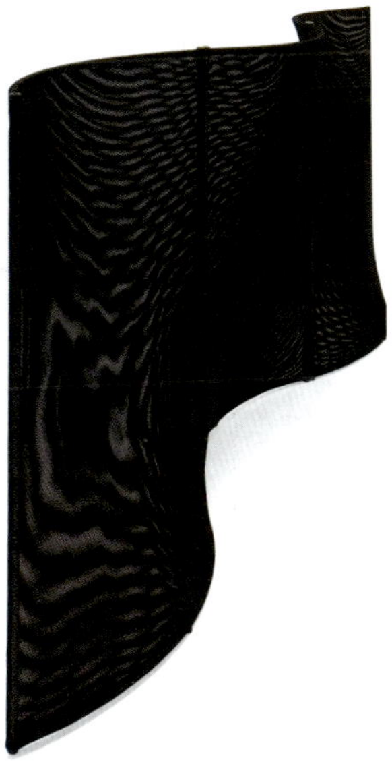

↓ → **Pannello** • Matteo Thun / Ruckstuhl

With people looking for more quiet and comfort in connection with modern interior design, architects and project developers of representative public buildings are now increasingly exploring possible ways of making sound absorption a feature in the design of interiors. More sound absorption means reduced dissemination of sound, and so lower noise levels.

In collaboration with the internationally recognised architect and designer, Matteo Thun of Milan, and the acoustics expert Dr Christian Nocke of the Institut für Akustik (Acoustics Institute) of Oldenburg, Ruckstuhl has been looking into possible solutions that will be in keeping both with product design requirements and with state-of-the-art spatial acoustic research. The designers were concerned not just to develop a solution to the problem in technical and acoustic terms, but also to create an attractive and functional new element as part of an ambitious interior design.

This was how the highly varied Pannello collection came into being: as an option for interior design and spatial separation, for the solution of acoustic problems and as a working resource (with the optional functions of a projection surface or pin board). Pannello gives the room a pleasant and restrained atmosphere. The size, materials and detailed design of Pannello support a wide variety of use situations for the shaping of interior spaces and the design of workstations.

When it comes to sound absorption, the properties of Pannello are outstanding: on practically the entire range of frequencies, more than 80% of the sound is absorbed. The design and the materials have been developed in such a way that both low (150 to 400 Hz) and high (400 bis 4000 Hz) tones will be absorbed in the most effective way. Made of pure virgin wool felt in subdued colors, the surface texture creates a warm and harmonious atmosphere.

↓ → **Stereo** • Texaa

The acoustic comfort of a room can normally be improved by fitting sound-absorbing materials to the surfaces (floor, walls and ceiling). However, sometimes this is not possible – either because of the layout or because of the amount of work involved – In this cases, the solution is to include objetcs within the volume.

The Stereo range of acoustic objetcs produced by Texaa® control the reverberation of sound. (Supple or rigid panels, rigid screens or room dividers, fractus tiles, totems, cubes, cones, or bricks.)

The variety of Stereo objects and the various fastening methods mean that the products can always be fitted optimally to suit the layout of a room and how it is used. Stereo products complement any environment, whether traditional or distinctly contempoary.

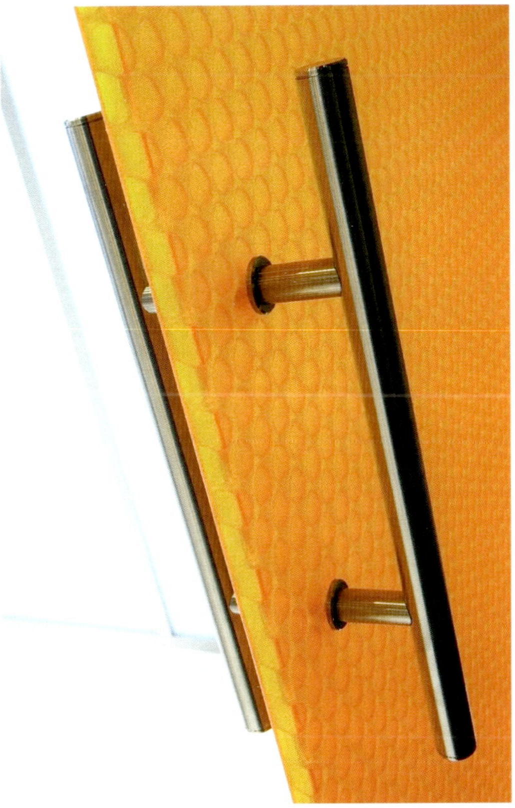

← ↓ clear-PEP® & AIR-board® •
Design Composite GmbH

Based on a unique core production process and a highly developed bonding technology Design Composite GmbH manufactures a broad variety of three-layer plastic panels. Among the best technical product characteristics the excellent translucency opens a wide range of applications for modern design. Natural as well as artificial light sources create the perfect frame for the panels.
The clear-PEP® and AIR-board® lines are for interior use (partitions, wall cladding, floors, ceilings) shop design, booth and design furniture constructions. Due to the excellent stiffness, the high impact resistance, the low weight, the UV resistance and the outstanding light refraction effects, the clear-PEP® panels are perfect materials for innovative design in architecture.

↓ → **Soundwave** • OFFECCT

Each panel in the Soundwave® series is designed for a specific acoustic purpose. The wall panels can be combined in different ways to meet the needs of almost any room or environment.

Flo, designed by Karim Rashid, is designed to be used as lightweight sound absorbers in the upper frequency range (500 Hz and above). These panels help reduce disturbing reflections of environmental sounds such as voices, telephones etc.

Luna, by Teppo Asikainen, is a heavyweight broadband absorber with extended efficiency in the low frequency range [150 - 500 Hz]. This panel efficiently reduces the reverberation time (sound "bouncing around") in a room.

The Mesh panel, by Teppo Asikainen, is designed to absorb lighter sounds in the higher frequencies. It is ideal for eliminating disturbing sound reflection from voices in office environments and restaurants.

Scrunch, by Teppo Asikainen, is designed to be used as a lightweight sound absorber in the upper frequency range.

Skyline, by Marre Moerel, is designed to be used as a lightweight sound absorber in the upper frequency range.

Swell, by Teppo Asikainen, is designed to be used as a lightweight sound absorber in the upper frequency range. The panel provides sound diffusion rather than absorption. Correctly positioned, the diffuser panels will improve speech intelligibility and even improve privacy in open spaces as the speaker does not need to talk loudly in order to be heard. This product is available with all components approved by the Swan eco-label.

↓ → **Microsorber** • KAEFER

Microsorber® is a system of transparent, translucent and printed foils and acrylic glass panels which reduce reflected sound and reverberation time in buildings. It is easy to install and versatile. It allows visions of transparency and open space to come true while meeting demands of acoustics.
The high-performance sound insulation effected by Microsorber® results from its micro-perforation. The foil and acrylic glass elements have holes measuring anywhere between 0.2 mm and 0.8 mm in diameter. As soon as sound waves strike the Microsorber®, a physical reaction takes place; the sound energy is converted into heat through the friction arising at the hole edges. Reverberation times and sound levels are reduced significantly. Whether in open-plan offices, canteens, swimming pools, production sites or entrance halls – the Microsorber® principle of transparent sound absorption allows for creativity in the design of buildings where room acoustics play a crucial role. It is also ideal as a means of optimizing the room acoustics of already existing buildings.
Microsorber® can be installed in front of walls and glass façades and below ceilings. Various systems for fastening the foil make it possible to attach and detach individual elements with ease.

← ↓ **Vision** • SEFAR Architecture

SEFAR® Architecture Vision is a new woven textile made of special black monofilaments. The product range includes six basic fabrics with different mesh apertures from 25% up to 70%. All fabrics are coated on one side with a metal. Possible metals aare aluminum, chrome, copper, titanium, gold as well as an aluminum/copper combination that looks like brass. The metallic side is also printable with digital printing systems.

The fabric is normally laminated inside glass and can be used for several interior or exterior applications. Architects and designers are free to design on the front side with six different fabrics, six different metals and digital prints while the backside stays neutrally black and offers a lightly smoked view through.

Next to the design opportunities SEFAR® Architecture Vision also reduces solar heat gain and glare when it is used as a façade or roof element.

↓ → **Narima** • Schott

Narima® dichroic color effects glass from Schott has been developed to meet the increasing demand from architects and building owners for a glass that changes colors in different environments. Narima® colors vary depending on reflections, light conditions, the angle of view and the background. Variable iridescent color effects are achieved by applying ultra-thin metal-oxide coatings to a range of base glasses. Each layer is applied in a thickness of less than 100 nanometers, and the resulting coating is hard, scratch resistant and extremely resistant to chemical attack. The combination of layers with high and low refractive indices results in a perceived color change.
Due to its unique and striking appearance, Narima® color effects glass opens up many new interior and exterior design possibilities and applications.

↓ → TIMax GL® • Wacotech

TIMax enables a translucent glass façade to have excellent thermal insulation. It is made of very thin yarned glass fibers united with a light-stable binder. The air caught between the glass fibers acts as a very effective insulator. The light that comes through the material, although without some of its original intensity, preserves its color and creates a homogeneous illumination. Besides providing thermal insulation in winter, TIMax also controls solar radiation in summer and reduces heat gain.

↓ → **cellscreen** • korban/flaubert

Cellscreen is a cellular structure exploring rhythm, repetition and sequence that can be used as a free-standing screen. It is a simple, strong and elegant mathematical honeycomb in crisp lightweight aluminum.

There were various sources of inspiration for the creation of cell screen; tiling geometric patterns, natural patterns of packing and cracking as well as the decorative economy of patterns in Islamic architecture.

The aim of the designers was to produce a dense evocative structure from the simplest geometry, using a single line length and a repeated 5-way joint. This has generated a sequence of triangles and squares that optically form larger interlocking ovals and star shapes.

The final effect is transparent and simple from the front view but opaque, deep and complex from the angled approach.

A simple pattern generates an unfolding sequence of larger effects, suggesting motion and transformation while the interaction with light and shadow creates added complexity.

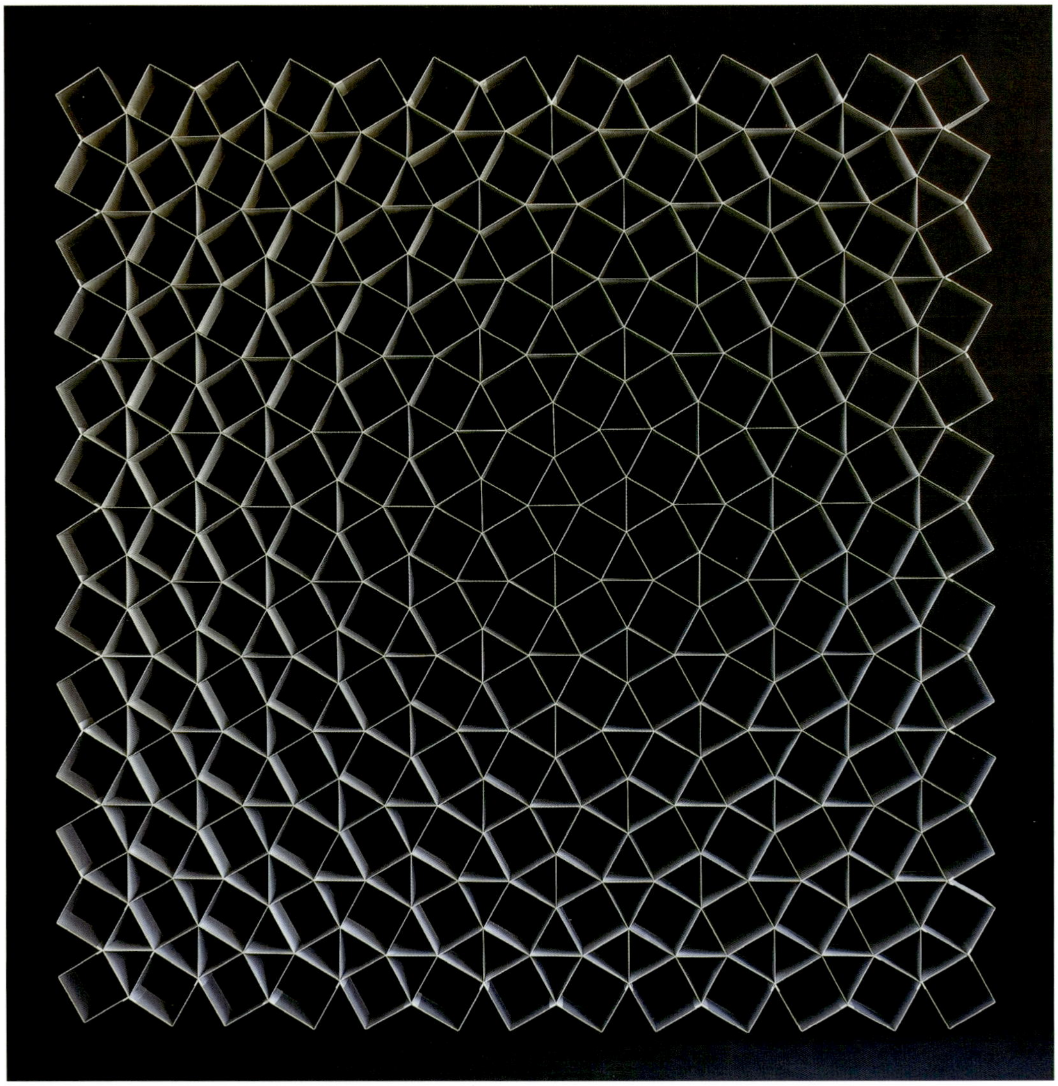

↓ → **Panel Omega Zeta** • CIRCA S.A.

Omega Zeta panels are produced on an industrial scale and can be customized in size, texture, color and mechanic perforations. Because of its versatility regarding its design and the properties that it presents as an effecitve thermal and acoustic insulator this is the ideal solution for modern architecture. It can be assembled three times faster thatn conventional systems, is ecological and recylcable as well as being highly resistant to weather conditions and earthquakes.

The panels for façades are composed of high resistance mortar and metal covering bidirectionally pretensed. They are highly versatile since they can be produced in size, color and finish according to the customer's wishes. The panels allow for perforations also customized in shape and size. This panel is waterproof and fire resistant.

The modular dry construction system implies the industrialization of the construction process, reducing costs and injecting flexibility into assembly. The panels are very light-weight and are 3 cm thick. The panels and the industrialized fabrication system represent a new solution, paving the way towards sustainable and innovative architecture, since they provide 50 to 80 % energy savings, are ecological and recyclable.

The industrial process, which is 95% automatic, allows the panels to be customized to suit the needs of each project regarding size and finish. This modular wall element, assemble from the exterior, comes in different sizes up to 220 × 300 cm.

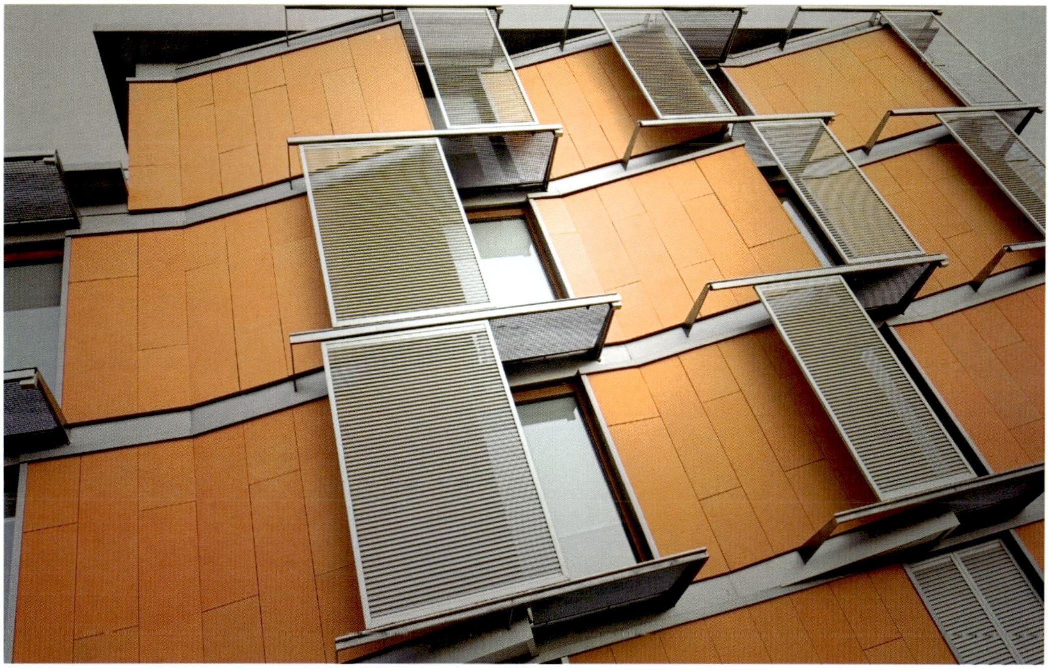

↓ → **Graphic Concrete** • Graphic Concrete Ltd

Graphic ConcreteTM includes patented technology and products that enable the prefabrication concrete industry to produce stylish new concrete surfaces cost effectively and safely.

The technology is based on applying a surface retarder to a special membrane that is spread over the mould table. The designed pattern is created by the contrast between the fairface and the exposed fine aggregate finish. This is a cost-effective, tested and safe method because traditional exposed fine aggregate materials and processes are used in the manufacture of the concrete elements.

Graphic ConcreteTM is a patented technology invented by interior architect Samuli Naamanka.

The membrane's high level of rigidity makes it ideal for the production of large concrete surfaces. The membrane can also be used without the surface retarder for the production of fairface surfaces. The membrane is 3.1 metres wide, which means that it can be used in the production of regular height façade elements without the need for joints. The length of the membrane is mainly limited by the maximum allowable weight of a roll, so it can be hundreds of meters long if necessary.

The surface retarder applied to the membrane slows the setting (hardening) of the concrete to the desired depth in specific areas. The unset surface part is usually washed away from the cast the next day, revealing the aggregate contained in the concrete. The washed surface stands out from the surrounding unwashed concrete surface due to its roughness and the contrasting color of the exposed aggregate. Altering the application area of the surface retarder makes it possible to create the desired patterns on the concrete.

The normal depth of the pattern is so-called fine exposure, i.e. about 1 mm. The cement can also be pigmented, which provides the color of the fairface surface. The aggregates can be a variety of different colors, which are then highlighted in the exposed areas.

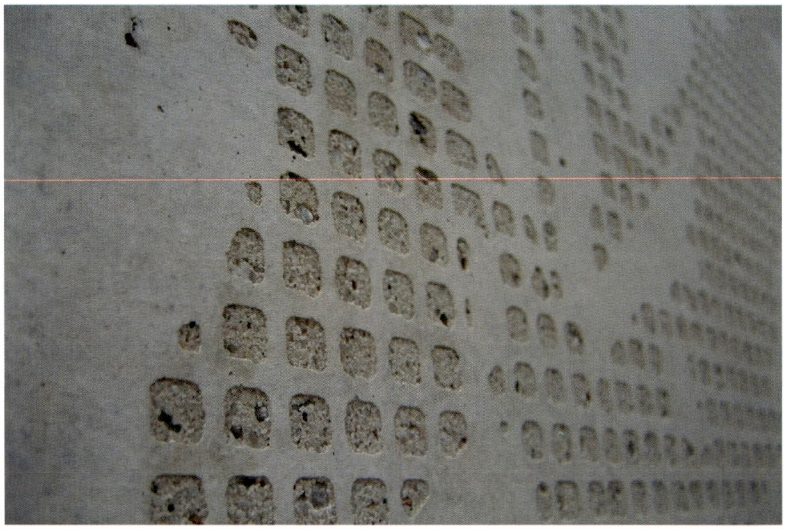

← ↓ **Sculptural** • ArmourCoat

Sculptural™ walls are constructed from a series of pre-cast panels that are bonded to the substrate. The panel joints are then filled and sanded and a final decoration is applied to the surface. Sculptural™ designs are created by combining computer-aided design with traditional hand sculpting to create designs that fit together with total accuracy yet retain the essence of being hand crafted.

Some of the designs are based on a single panel that creates a repeating pattern; others are made from a sequence of different panels that can be integrated together in many different ways to create totally unique sculpted walls. The multiple panel designs make it possible to create non-repetitive seamless sculptural walls where the designs flow and change across the surface just as in nature. As a consequence, no two walls need ever be identical.

Sculptural™ panels are mineral based and incorporate up to 30% post-consumer recycled content (depending on design), are non-toxic and are completely non-combustible. The panels are extremely dense and hard with a smooth ceramic-like surface. Once the panels are installed each design can be finished in a range of decorative surface finishes. Some of the designs have been modeled in such a way as to enable the application of Armourcoat polished plaster finishes whilst other designs are more suited to a sprayed finish.

↓ → Fibre C • Rieder

FibreC is an innovative concrete panel strengthend by glassfibre components. The material provides an ideal solution for modern architecture and interior design.
Concrete is one of the most frequently used building nevertheless still has enormous unutilized innovative potential. Firstly concrete as an authentic building material corresponds to the latest trend for the use of natural, environment-friendly and economic building materials while still being capable of producing modern finishes.
Due to the extreme durability and robust character concrete resists high pressures with maximum panel size at minimum thickness. Available standard measures for fibreC panels are 1.20 × 3.60 m but can be stretched to a length of 5.00 m with a minimum thickness of 13 mm. The material has excellent thermal resistance for absolute safety in terms of temperature stability (standing up to 350°) and therefore provides optimum fire protection for multi-storey buildings up to a height of 100 m. The unique characteristics additionally provide protection against vandalism which is a central decision criterion for material choice especially in the public domain.
FibreC is high-strength, thin, flexible and malleable and can be used in special forms flat as well as rounded. Rough edges as well as roundings and curves can be achieved within a single flowing material without adhesives. It has high durability and breaks the limits for traditional architecture and interior design. Various visual effects can be achieved by using covered or uncovered fixing solutions.
Another dimension for playing with the endless varieties marks the possibilities for color selection and defining of different surface structures. The color palette ranges from any grayscale tone to natural tones such as teracotta, green or brown. Different structures, matt polished or brushed emphasizes the modern face of glass fibre concrete. The characteristics are particlarly evident in interior design. Genuine natural stone mixed with ferric oxide colors creates a perfect color finish and without applying a coating "Technical Marble" evolves over time.

← ↓ **Duralmond** • Duralmond

Duralmond is a composite material that is obtained by mixing synthetic and natural resins, ground almond shell and other additives. After a process of polymerization and subjecting the paste to particular pressures and termperatures within a mold, this is transformed into solid finished objects, adopting from the mold forms and textures that are then applied to decorative soffits, and which sets these apart from most decorative proposals on the market. The organic redisual of the almond shell is thereby converted into a series of biodegradable and recyclable objects which by their mold fabrication can achieve diverse forms and mimick textures giving free reign to the imagination of the more adventurous designers.
Biodegradable, recyclable, light-weight, water resistant (ideal for humid areas), with good acoustic properties, and suitable performance against fire, Duralmond is the ideal material for interior design and decoration.

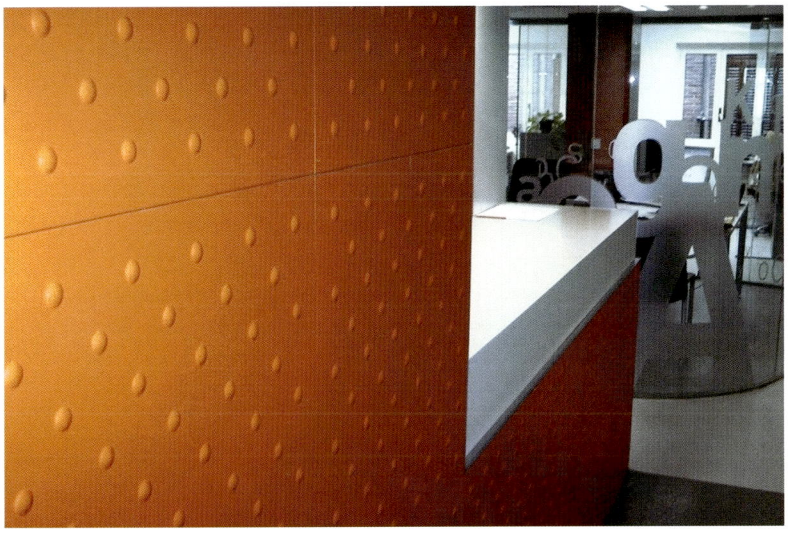

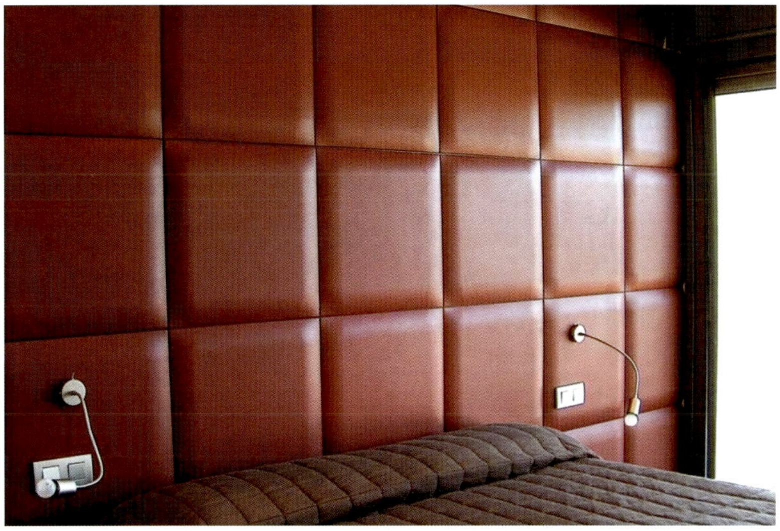

↓ → **Nomos** • Norman Foster / Tecno

The Nomos Desking System is designed for almost unlimited change. Governed by the unchanging needs of the human body, seated or standing, it has metal legs, angled from a central spine, as if poised for flight.

← ↓ CHTH • Richard Meier / Lensvelt

The City hall in The Hague, which was designed by Richard Meier, bears witness to a natural harmony between the exterior and interior. The sculptural geometry of the building with its subtle details appears again in the furniture collection CHTH (City Hall The Hague). This collection is characterised by a dialogue between hard (steel) and soft (wood), as well as open and enclosed elements. The desk is manufactured with enclosed sides that give a feeling of total privacy. It started life as a harmonious product which included the rectangular form of the work top and storage area. The panel and legs are made of steel and cover the mechanism that lifts the table. A manual, mechanical or electronic height adjustment is optional.
The furniture is also available as a side table/bistro table. The height of the sides is the same as the height of the filing cabinet, therefore, painting a rigid picture. Cable ducts, with simple geometric detailing, ensure that computers and other equipment can be connected easily, using the built-in cable grommet. CHTH is made completely out of recyclable material.

↓ → MeterByMeter • Matteo Thun / Belux

Made-to-measure light Meter By Meter is a lighting system and is employed in the field of architecture as light by the meter. Meter By Meter can either be employed as indirect light with a cover shade made of anodised aluminium or satinised art glass. A combination of direct and indirect light sections is also possible.

Meter By Meter can be employed horizontally from wall to wall or vertically from floor to ceiling. Meter By Meter integrates optimally into the most diverse spatial situations such as corridors, reception halls, sales outlets, restaurants and hotels as well as in home areas. Mirrors, doors and passageways too can be framed with this light band. There are hardly any limits to the application possibilities of Meter By Meter.

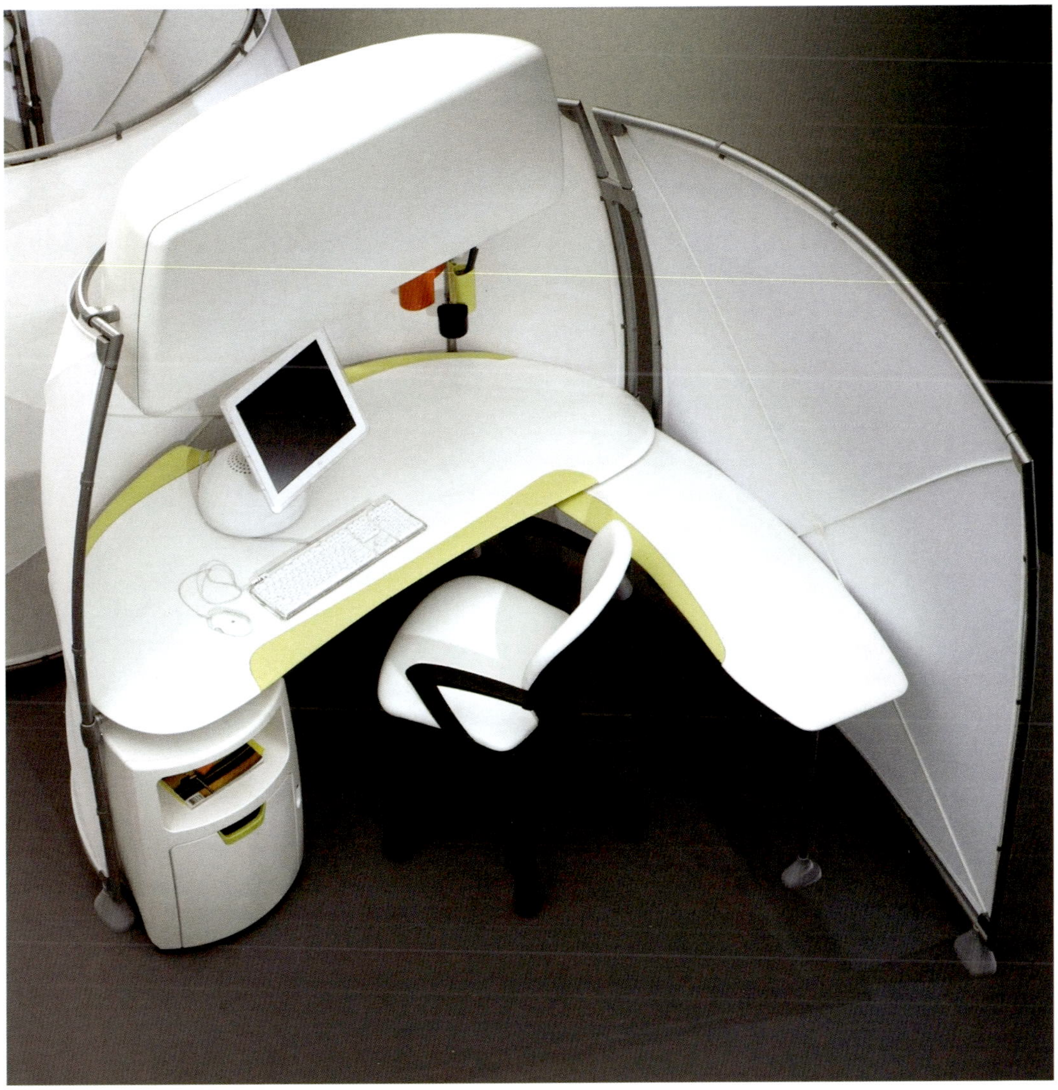

← ↓ **A3 Workstations** • Hani Rashid / Knoll

Independent workstations can be freely reconfigured without affecting other workstations Worksurfaces are adjustable and shaped for comfortable use of computers and portable technology. Accessories attach to frame; Flipp light fixtures transition from task to ambient with a few simple adjustments

The compound curves of individual A3 workstations generate useful, interstitial spaces and lively topography. Translucent mesh screens stretch across elliptical frames, offering privacy while enabling communication.

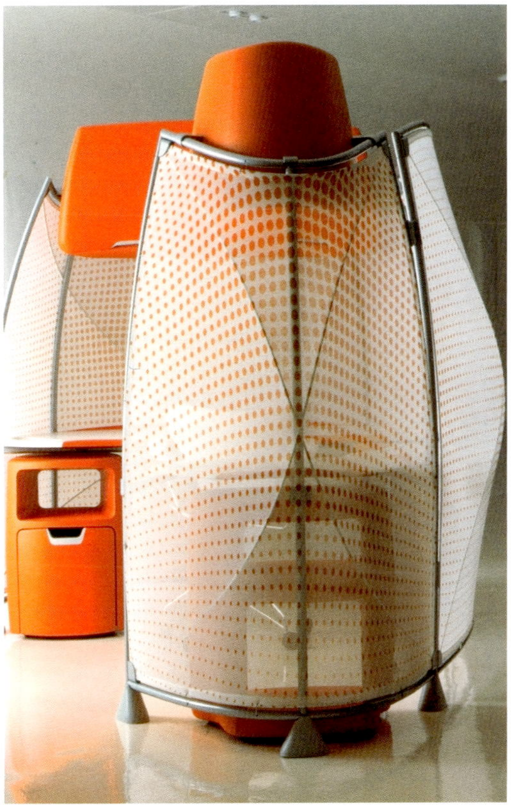

Index of Projects and Photographers